INCULTURATION
AND THE
CHURCH
IN NORTH
AMERICA

The Boston College Church in the 21st Century Series

Patricia De Leeuw and James F. Keenan, S.J.,
General Editors

Titles in this series include:

Handing On the Faith: The Church's Mission and Challenge

Sexuality and the U.S. Catholic Church: Crisis and Renewal

Priests for the 21st Century

Take Heart: Catholic Writers on Hope in Our Time

The Church in the 21st Century Center at Boston College seeks to be a catalyst and resource for the renewal of the Catholic Church in the United States by engaging critical issues facing the Catholic community. Drawing from both the Boston College community and others, its activities currently are focused on four challenges: handing on and sharing the Catholic faith, especially with younger Catholics; fostering relationships built on mutual trust and support among lay men and women, vowed religious, deacons, priests, and bishops; developing an approach to sexuality mindful of human experience and reflective of Catholic tradition; and advancing contemporary reflection on the Catholic intellectual tradition.

INCULTURATION AND THE CHURCH IN NORTH AMERICA

T. FRANK KENNEDY, S.J., EDITOR

A Herder & Herder Book
The Crossroad Publishing Company
New York

The Crossroad Publishing Company
16 Penn Plaza – 481 Eighth Avenue, Suite 1550
New York, NY 10001

Printed in the United States of America

The text of this book is set in 10.5/14 Sabon.

Library of Congress Cataloging-in-Publication Data

Inculturation and the church in North America / edited by T. Frank Kennedy.
   p. cm.
   Proceedings of a conference held in 2005 at Boston College.
   "A Herder & Herder book."
   Includes bibliographical references and index.
   ISBN-13: 978-0-8245-2438-8 (alk. paper)
   ISBN-10: 0-8245-2438-1 (alk. paper)
   1. Christianity and culture – North America – Congresses. 2. Catholic Church – North America – History – 1965- I. Kennedy, Thomas Frank. II. Title.
BR115.C8I455 2006
261.097 – dc22

                                      2006027443

1   2   3   4   5   6   7   8   9   10   12   11   10   09   08   07   06

Contents

Part Two
INCULTURATION AND IDENTITY

Introduction

T. Frank Kennedy, S.J.

❦

THE Jesuit Institute is a research center at Boston College that aims to foster intellectual conversation and investigation on the issues arising at the intersections of faith and culture. In September of 2002, as an institutional response to the problematic issues that arose around the sexual abuse crisis in the Roman Catholic Church, President William P. Leahy, S.J., formed the Church in the 21st Century initiative to act as a catalyst for renewal of the life of the church in North America. This initiative invited the Jesuit Institute to propose an appropriate response to some of these questions, in a manner consonant with the mission of the Institute. One result of that invitation is this volume.

The first stage in this process was a meeting of approximately thirty scholars at Boston College in January of 2003 to brainstorm on a direction that this project might take. In 2005, a smaller group of scholars met again to present papers to each other in order to move toward a monograph that would not only help scholars clarify some of the ecclesiological issues that we face but would also propose some possibilities for the consideration of the larger ecclesial community in North America. These essays are the fruit of the 2005 conference.

Our meetings fairly quickly settled on the topic of inculturation. How does the church in North America appropriate itself within the culture? What is distinctive about the identity of the church in North America that differentiates it from the ecclesial communities of Western Europe, Eastern Europe, or the Third World countries? The discussion was then challenged by Mary Ann Hinsdale, who offered a broader lens to the conversation by proposing a more inclusive possibility with the use of the word "inter-culturation." The deep-rooted sense among Americans that the United States is a melting-pot of cultures can now be seen distinctly in

1

the present composition of Catholic communities that worship together and seek to be faith communities within the borders of North America. The dialectic, if you will, between the notions of inculturation and inter-culturation not only led us actively to consider the various ethnic communities that make up the church in our land but also led us to the realization that there are two questions we need to consider as we go forward.

The first consideration is the *task* question. How do we all participate in the church? What is the history of our participations in the church, and especially, what do we need to remember about ourselves as we continue to strive to be church together? Part 1 of this volume offers a number of important considerations from this perspective of participation. The church teaches, and the process of evangelization is one that looks outward toward the other. From this perspective the church is quite clearly made up of the Catholic community as extrovert.

The second consideration is the *identity* question. Who are we as American Catholics, and are we conveying our identities to each other and to the broader society at large, or are we losing ourselves as we practice? How do we maintain our identities? Part 2 of this volume attempts to address these more reflective questions from various evident identities that are present in the church in North America today. From this perspective, the church is quite clearly made up of different communities. They sometimes appear in competition with one another, but in every human sense one can imagine, they overlap, even though as church we often sense these memberships as separate, yet at the same time also completely participative in the body of Christ.

The volume begins with David Hollenbach's essay on Catholicism and American political culture, which stakes out the common ground between the Christian community and the state by seeking the common good in a way that safeguards the human life and dignity of all Americans. Nancy Dallavalle and Mary Ann Hinsdale both highlight the issues that surround women in the North American church, offering both historical and theological reflections aimed at lifting up the great contribution that women are making as participants in the life of the church. Dallavalle challenges us to consider "what it might mean for institutionally identified Catholics to see Catholic Christianity as a voice not merely *available* within the contours of liberal democracy, but *formative* of its discourse." Similarly, Hinsdale expands the notions of inculturation and its cognate interculturation in the "plurality of feminist discourse" as a first step in listening to the challenge of the multiplicity of voices in the church in North America. Also in part 1, Francis Sullivan offers an enlightening historical example from American Catholic history, revisiting the experience of church governance under Bishop John England (1786–1842), first bishop of Charleston, as a possible model for more open and transparent participation of the laity in decision-making in the church. Finally John Beal writes about the administrative difficulties of church business structures considering the two conflicted models that are presently juxtaposed in the North American ecclesial context. Can designs more similar to plans from the Harvard Business School coexist with regulations from the Pontifical Commission for the Revision of the Code of Canon Law?

Part 2 begins to address some of the identities present in the American church, but by no means all of them. What is offered here are five reflections about cultural identities that presently participate in the Roman Catholic community in the United States. The first essay, by Mark Massa, addresses the problem of division that is an overarching presence in American, if not world, society. Attempting to move beyond the labels of "liberal" and "conservative," however, is difficult precisely because it is a call to move beyond labels that are used in descriptions of almost every aspect of American culture. What are the real theological issues at stake here? Two of the essays take account of the United States as an *omnium gatherum*. Specifically U.S. Catholic considerations come to the fore when Peter Phan explores the Asian American Catholic community, and Natalia Imperatori-Lee, the American Catholic experience within the Latino/a culture. The richness of these essays is their pointing toward a new experience of the transformation happening in the North American church in Christ. Two well-known sociologists of religion, Mary Johnson and Dean Hoge, conclude part 2 with some sobering and yet hopeful statistics. Johnson reminds us that our contemporary generations are all creatures of information technology. They are Internet oriented. If conferences of religious and religious congregations want to make an impact, they need to be Internet-savvy. In fact, she offers a challenging call to the Leadership Conference of Women Religious (LCWR) to consider the Internet possibilities that are already being taken advantage of by some of the more evangelical and traditional Catholic religious groups. Some of these groups have understood that young people come without the issues of the Vatican II generation. Is there common ground here? Finally, Dean Hoge furnishes some stunning figures about the religious commitments of young adult Catholics. He locates for us a threefold task in order to build up Catholic identity: we need to identify the core issues of young adult faith, strengthen the inspirational parts, and tend to the boundaries of what it means to be Catholic in order to avoid a general "anything goes" vagueness about our identity as Catholics in North America.

This volume suggests that inculturation for American Catholics must have two distinct foci. Catholic life in these United States successfully appropriates itself in an extroverted fashion: the doing side of our lives together, especially on the political side of who we are. But Catholic life is also true to itself in its interiority, its introverted side, when it notes the important identity issues that knit us together as a community of brothers and sisters, and especially through our reflections on age, gender, and ethnicity. We hope these reflections move our church in North America to a deeper sense of itself as both local and universal in Christ.

Part One

INCULTURATION AND PARTICIPATION

Chapter 1

Catholicism and American Political Culture

Confrontation, Accommodation, or Transformation?

DAVID HOLLENBACH, S.J.

T HE RELATION BETWEEN religion and politics has always been a controversial topic, and it continues to be controversial today. The crucial role of religion in world politics has been increasingly visible to Americans since personnel of the U.S. embassy in Tehran were captured by militants loyal to the Ayatollah Khomeini in 1979. Embassy staff were held hostage for 444 days, generating public apprehensions that significantly contributed to Jimmy Carter's loss of the U.S. presidency. The role of radical Islam became even more visible to Americans on September 11, 2001, and in the U.S. military engagements in both Afghanistan and Iraq, with no end yet in sight for the latter conflict. In a much noted and controversial article in *Foreign Affairs,* Samuel Huntington conjectured that the conflicts in the world politics of the emerging post–Cold War era will be driven by a clash of civilizations and cultures rather than ideology or economics. Huntington noted that civilizations are communities distinguished from each other by "history, language, culture, tradition, and, most important, religion."[1] Huntington's diagnosis raises the specter of religious conflict on a global scale. In the United States, the visibility of the so-called religious right has been of particular interest. Political involvement a decade ago by conservative Christians such as Jerry Falwell and Pat Robertson raised concern that public activism by religious communities inevitably tends to support right-wing politics. Others saw it as a good thing that religious communities committed to crucial values were confronting secularist relativism in a kind of "culture war." In the 2004 election, these concerns were magnified by the public support given to President George W. Bush by both some Catholic and some evangelical Christian leaders, though the precise degree to which religion actually influenced the outcome of the election remains a debated topic.[2]

In the context of these discussions there has been considerable controversy about the proper role of the Roman Catholic community in the U.S. political process. The recent Catholic debates have focused especially on several practical ethical issues, particularly abortion, but also including embryonic stem cell research, euthanasia, human cloning, and gay marriage.[3] One of the most forceful political positions on these matters was that taken by Bishop Michael Sheridan of Colorado Springs. In a pastoral letter to the Catholics of his diocese on May 1, 2004, Bishop Sheridan noted that the Congregation for the Doctrine of the Faith had declared that "a well-formed Christian conscience does not permit one to vote for a political program or an individual law which contradicts the fundamental contents of faith and morals."[4] Bishop Sheridan affirmed that issues of the protection of life, especially as they relate to abortion, euthanasia, and embryonic stem cell research, have special status among the fundamentals of faith and morals. There is, he wrote, "one right that is 'inalienable,' and that is the RIGHT TO LIFE. This is the FIRST right. This is the right that grounds all other human rights. This is the issue that trumps all other issues."[5] Bishop Sheridan went on to conclude that politicians who support permissive abortion laws and Catholic citizens who vote for such politicians have placed themselves outside the church. For this reason they should not receive Communion, and they should be denied the Eucharist if they present themselves to receive it. In his words,

> Any Catholic politicians who advocate for abortion, for illicit stem cell research or for any form of euthanasia *ipso facto* place themselves outside full communion with the Church and so jeopardize their salvation. Any Catholics who vote for candidates who stand for abortion, illicit stem cell research or euthanasia suffer the same fateful consequences. It is for this reason that these Catholics, whether candidates for office or those who would vote for them, may not receive Holy Communion until they have recanted their

positions and been reconciled with God and the Church in the Sacrament of Penance.[6]

The archbishop of Denver, Charles J. Chaput, agreed with his fellow Colorado bishop that abortion is a foundational issue. Chaput got more specific, however, when in an interview with the *New York Times* he applied this position directly to the Democratic presidential candidate Senator John Kerry and to those who would vote for him. As quoted by the *New York Times*, Chaput asked: "if you vote this way, are you cooperating in evil? . . . And if you know you are cooperating in evil, should you go to confession? The answer is yes."[7]

Here Chaput goes in a notably different direction from the statement *Faithful Citizenship* issued in 2003 by the Administrative Committee of the bishops conference. This document had said: "We do not wish to instruct persons on how they should vote by endorsing or opposing candidates. We hope that voters will examine the position of candidates on the full range of issues, as well as on their personal integrity, philosophy, and performance."[8] By clearly suggesting that a vote for Kerry would be sinful, Archbishop Chaput departed from the consensus shared by most U.S. bishops that taking public positions, pro or con, regarding specific candidates would be unwise. This clearly placed Archbishop Chaput in the thick of the politics of the presidential campaign. Several other bishops became similarly engaged when they declared the policy positions of individual politicians on abortion, stem cell research, or gay marriage to be morally unacceptable.

In the midst of this controversy the bishops conference as a whole considered whether it should adopt a stand like Bishop Sheridan's that abortion "trumps all other issues." In effect such a stand would make a politician's position on abortion legislation into a definitive test of his or her moral worthiness to participate in the life of the church through eucharistic Communion. Though it was not addressed directly by the conference in its June 2004 meeting, this argument also had implications for whether a politician was morally worthy to receive the votes of Catholics, and if not, whether Catholics who nevertheless vote for an unacceptable candidate would be excluding themselves from participation in the life of grace and from the Eucharist. The conference avoided taking a single, unified position on these matters. Because of the "wide range of circumstances involved in arriving at a prudential judgment on a matter of this seriousness," the conference decided not to adopt a practice that would be uniformly applied across the country to all politicians.[9] Rather it decided to leave the determination of whether to exclude certain Catholic politicians from Communion to the pastoral judgment of individual bishops within their own dioceses.

Thus the bishops conference recognized the need to take account of the complexity of circumstances in making prudential pastoral judgments about how to deal with Catholic politicians. But they did not give Catholic politicians similar flexibility to make prudential judgments about how to vote on particular pieces of abortion legislation in light of the circumstances confronting either them as politicians or the women facing decisions about abortion. A very visible minority of the bishops is thus on a collision course with a notable group of Catholic legislators of both parties, even though the bishops conference as a whole was clearly not of one mind about how to deal with politicians who take a permissive approach on abortion legislation.[10] This minority of the bishops is also at odds with lay Catholics who voted for John Kerry and others who support civil laws that permit abortion.[11] Indeed, this developing conflict suggests that some bishops believe that the Catholic community should take a strongly oppositional stance to those trends in American political culture that support civil laws permitting abortion. These bishops seem to be suggesting that the time has come for the Catholic community to become a countercultural force in the United States today on issues having to do with the protection of human life in the domains of abortion, euthanasia, and embryonic stem cell research. To the extent that American political culture contains permissive attitudes toward such practices, these bishops appear to be advocating what H. Richard Niebuhr called a "Christ against culture" posture toward key trends in American life.[12] Such a posture involves drawing a clear distinction between the values entailed by Christian faith and the Catholic tradition on the one hand and the values present in the ambient culture of the United States. This also implies that it is desirable to mark a sharp boundary between those inside and those outside the community of faithful Catholics, with the abortion issue as the principal marker. Some have raised the question of whether distinctions and boundaries of this sort will make it impossible for faithful Catholics to participate successfully in American electoral politics.

The bishops who advocate this counter-cultural position often appeal to Pope John Paul II's condemnation of a "culture of death." For example, Archbishop Sean O'Malley of Boston urged the priests of his diocese to preach in a way that will lead Catholics "to resist the temptation to conform to the culture of death, to consumerism, hedonism, individualism." O'Malley used the same terms in a sermon calling Catholic lawyers in Washington "to counter the culture of death with a culture of life."[13]

John Paul II's encyclical letter *Evangelium Vitae* set forth the pope's vision of a world marked by a dramatic conflict between a "culture of life" and a "culture of death." The phrase "culture of death" appears twelve times in this encyclical. Both through an extensive presentation of a biblical and theological reflection on the value of human life and a detailed discussion of the moral norms that should govern respect for human life, the pope presents a picture of at least some contemporary cultures as caught up in an agonic struggle between forces of life and death. This critique sometimes takes on an apocalyptic tone. For example, the concluding chapter of the encyclical is constructed as a meditation on selected texts from the book of Revelation, invoking the end-time clash between the satanic beast of death and the life that is Christ's gift.[14] This imagery certainly sets the church on an oppositional course over against contemporary cultures that fulfill the pope's description. The bishops who suggest that the United States has become a "culture of death" are surely suggesting that the church must become a force of opposition to such a culture. Conflict and even martyrdom will be the price of such opposition.

What is the source of this starkly oppositional stance? For certain, it is the view that American society has become far too tolerant of practices such as abortion and too ready to consider the possible legitimacy of euthanasia and embryonic stem cell research. At the same time, John Paul's critique also touches what he regards as the cultural roots that make people too ready to tolerate these practices and too reluctant to outlaw them through civil legislation. In the pope's analysis, this excessive openness to practices that threaten human life has a deeper cultural root. This root is the tendency of Western cultures to elevate the freedom of individual choice to the level of the highest, even the only, value. In the United States this philosophy is called libertarian; in Europe it goes by the name of liberalism. The pope argues that this cultural philosophy protects the freedom of action of those who possess power and subjects the weak and the powerless to severe threats to their dignity and even their lives. *Evangelium Vitae* sees abortion and euthanasia as key symptoms of this threat. In addition, the encyclical sharply criticizes inadequate response to global poverty, war, and the plight of refugees and traces the failure to deal with these urgent matters to this philosophy as well. Abortion and euthanasia are particularly symptomatic, however, because of the way that individual freedom of choice is related to an understanding of civil law in the debates about these issues. Abortion and euthanasia are not new phenomena today, but the call for "legal recognition" or "legal approval" is new. Thus the "sign of the times" that so alarms the pope is the fact that these forms of life-taking are increasingly not regarded as crimes but as *"legitimate expressions of individual freedom, to be acknowledged and protected as actual rights."*[15]

At the root of the critique of the "culture of death" by both the pope and by some U.S. bishops, therefore, is a concern that a libertarian/liberal set of values has come to permeate culture and that these values are themselves contrary to the deeper cultural orientations that flow from Catholic faith and the Catholic intellectual tradition. Cardinal Francis George of Chicago presented a version of this analysis in an essay revealingly entitled "How Liberalism Fails the Church." Cardinal George argued that in American liberal culture "freedom is the primary value," and this leads to a "willingness to sacrifice even the gospel truth in order to safeguard personal freedom construed as choice." Thus the deeper crisis that opens the way for abortion and other threats to life is cultural in nature. American culture threatens to smother the gospel with "a pillow of accommodation" to the "relativism and individualism" that have come to prevail in the United States today.[16] From this viewpoint, therefore, it is not accidental that advocates of permissive abortion laws call themselves "pro-choice." For permissive abortion laws follow readily from accommodation to a culture that regards individual choice as the primary value.

Pope John Paul II's experience under totalitarian rule in Poland has, of course, given him a deep appreciation of the importance of freedom in social and political life. He has approvingly affirmed that the "universal longing for freedom is one of the truly distinguishing marks of our time" and called the quest for freedom "one of the great dynamics of human history."[17] *Evangelium Vitae,* however, argues that the quest for freedom is marred by internal contradictions today. The *mentalité* engendered by the experience of pluralism is at the root of problem. The diversity of moral and religious worldviews suggests to many people that judgment of their truth or falsity is unattainable. Thus the freedom to choose one's own understanding of how to live becomes the central or even the only value on which social agreement can be expected. The pope sees this as ethical relativism. It is at the heart of the cultural tendencies that so alarm him. On the political and social level, respect for individual freedom becomes the sole moral criterion for judging public policy and legislation. In practice, however, absolute respect for the moral opinions of every single citizen would give a lone dissenter veto power over every legislative proposal. Thus the best that can be achieved under conditions of pluralism is respect for the opinion of the majority, whatever this opinion may be. What begins as tolerance ends as simple majority rule. Minorities, especially those whose physical weakness, social marginalization, or economic poverty gives them little public influence, become radically vulnerable to the power of the strong.[18] John Paul does not hesitate to call this kind of politics totalitarian.[19] Relativism on the level of culture thus leads to the political denial of the human rights of the weak, including the right to life of the unborn through abortion and those at the end of their lives through euthanasia. The critique, however, extends much wider than this, touching the inadequate acknowledgment of the rights of the poor, of victims of war, and of migrants and refugees, to mention only a few examples. The "culture of death" is the pope's name for the value system that "tolerates" violation of the human life and dignity of the weak whenever their protection demands limitations on the freedom of the strong. Critique of this mentality is shared by U.S. bishops who have presented critiques of abortion, euthanasia, and embryonic stem cell research in the forum of recent U.S. electoral politics.

Evangelium Vitae, therefore, opposes theories of democracy based on libertarian and individualistic presuppositions and proposes an alternative understanding of democracy. The pope would agree with John Courtney Murray's assertion that the democratic experiment rests on the existence of a public philosophy willing to affirm with Jefferson that "there are truths, and we hold them."[20] Among these truths is the affirmation that the human person possesses a dignity that is sacred, and that all those conditions necessary to the realization of human dignity are due persons as human rights.[21] These rights certainly include freedom of conscience and religious liberty. But they also include a wide array of other rights such as the right to life, to at least minimal levels of nutrition, to adequate health care, to political participation and participation in economic life, and to the juridical protection of all these rights through due process of law and adequately designed public policies.[22]

In other words, John Paul II is proposing a theory of human rights based upon truth claims about the human good. He rejects the notion that human rights can be secured or that democratic freedoms can be stable without agreement about at least the most fundamental elements of a good human life. The pope's statements in *Evangelium Vitae* that human freedom has an "essential link with the truth" must be understood in this light.[23] Political democracy depends on the presence of a certain level of cultural consensus about the human good. Skepticism about whether we can know what is genuinely good, even when this is accompanied by tolerance of diverse visions of the good life, is not enough to sustain the democratic experiment. A culture of "pure tolerance" becomes a culture in self-contradiction. It has no standards to which it can appeal to protect the weak against the strong. This, the pope argues, is evident in the appeal to tolerance to legitimate permissive abortion and euthanasia laws. It is also evident in appeals to individual freedom in the marketplace without regard to the impact of the market on the poor. John Paul II thus advances an ethic similar to the late Cardinal Joseph Bernardin's consistent ethic of life, which seeks to defend human life across an array of issues from abortion, to the provision of health care, to overcoming poverty in developing nations, to warfare, to capital punishment, to euthanasia.[24] But the distinctiveness of the pope's approach to such a consistent ethic is his insistence that skepticism and the elevation of free choice to the status of the highest value are serious threats to such an ethic, even in presently democratic nations. Without richer virtues than tolerance these democracies risk undermining themselves.[25] Indeed in the pope's analysis, such self-destruction has already begun in such societies. Legalized abortion and efforts to liberalize legal restrictions on euthanasia are signs of this in the pope's analysis. Such a reading of the dangers of the exaltation of individual choice and of skepticism about the authentic human good is shared by U.S. bishops such as Chaput, O'Malley, and George.

John Paul II's diagnosis of some of the challenges of liberal culture to the Catholic tradition certainly has relevance in the United States today. On the level of moral and political theory, American liberal thinkers such as the late John Rawls make the freedom of individuals to choose their own values the center of their vision of liberal democracy. This is largely because they have abandoned hope of achieving agreement on values other than individual freedom. The primacy granted to individual choice of values is evident not only in sophisticated political and moral theory but, perhaps more importantly, it is widespread among the educated public and in popular culture. Alan Wolfe's survey- and interview-based research makes a very strong case that individual freedom of choice has indeed become the dominant value in U.S. culture today. Unlike the pope and Archbishops Chaput, O'Malley, and George, however, Wolfe thinks this is a good thing in the face of the grim history of conflict and even war in the name of religious beliefs.[26]

The pope's recommended response to the view that pluralism means individual choice should be given social primacy is to set forth his Christian vision of the human good in its theological depth. As I read it, *Evangelium Vitae* is suggesting that the problems present in contemporary culture can be overcome only by the presentation of a capacious vision of the human good. Thus John Paul is quite unabashed in claiming that the sacredness of human life is rooted in God's love for every human being, a love made manifest in the redemptive death and resurrection of Jesus Christ. On this level, the pope seeks to have an effect on the way people use their freedom by influencing the deeper cultural values that shape their decisions. This approach seems grounded in a conviction that high rates of abortion will drop if people's larger cultural vision becomes shaped by a deeper appreciation of the sacredness of human life as understood in the Christian narrative. This implies that influencing the deeper cultural values of society will be a precondition for influence on both the behavior of citizens and their judgments about what civil laws can and should govern this behavior. Thus at times the pope seems to suggest an approach to issues like abortion and euthanasia that would call the church to work first at influencing the deeper cultural values and only later expect to see these values carried out in social practice and embodied in civil law. This approach seems to be suggested by his extensive discussion of the need for a "new culture of life" informed and shaped by the Christian "gospel of life."[27] This is the type of ethic that H. Richard Niebuhr called "Christ transforming culture."[28] John Paul II's theological vision aims to challenge and transform what present-day culture regards as acceptable and to influence behavior and law through this cultural route.

At the same time, however, John Paul II also holds firm to traditional Catholic convictions about the role of reason and natural law in both ethics and in the domain of civil legislation. He maintains that the truth about the value of human life is reasonable and can be grasped by all persons, whether they are Christian or not. This truth should shape the behavior of all people, and all people can be held responsible to respect and protect human life. Thus it is entirely reasonable to pass civil laws that require such respect for human life. John Paul II, therefore, advocates civil laws banning abortion, euthanasia, and other practices that he sees as direct attacks on the sacredness of human life. He also affirms that it is never legitimate to support or vote for laws permitting these practices.[29] Looked at this way, civil laws prohibiting abortion and euthanasia appear as reasonable restrictions on individual freedom. Just as civil legislation outlawing assault, robbery, and murder do not place undue limits on personal freedom but are rather protections of such freedom, restrictions on abortion do not illegitimately restrict religious freedom.

I think this analysis of the papal arguments in *Evangelium Vitae* brings the controversies over the relation between Catholicism and American politics today into sharp focus. In some parts of his argument, John Paul challenges *cultural* presuppositions operative today that he sees as threats to human life and dignity. John Paul has been followed in this approach by those American bishops whose primary approach to the issues of abortion and euthanasia is via their critique of American political culture, a critique that goes so far as to call it a culture of death. On the other hand, John Paul also advocates specific forms of legislation that touch the protection of human life, and he calls for legislative bans on abortion and euthanasia. We have seen that a number of U.S. bishops follow this legislative route. They denounce laws permitting abortion and have declared legislators and voters who support these laws to be guilty of objectively grave sin.

Thus there are two different kinds of discourse and analysis involved in the current controversies. One approach is cultural and the other is legal or legislative. How the two levels are related is a crucially important consideration in determining whether the approach taken by the bishops who would deny Communion to some legislators is advisable. The unresolved problem can be put this way: Does culture shape law or does law shape culture? The way one answers this question will have significant impact on how one thinks the church should respond to the issues we are considering. If culture shapes law, then the necessarily coercive power of the civil law should not be invoked unless the culture will support such legislation. This means there needs to be a sufficiently strong cultural consensus that such law supports the values and freedoms that people hold. On the other hand, if law shapes culture, it may be reasonable to invoke the coercive power of the civil law as one of the forces that help shape the values that are held by the citizens in the society involved.

It is doubtless true that the relation between culture and law is, de facto, a two-way street. The values embedded in the *mentalité* or culture of a people will set the direction and limits for what they think law can accomplish. At the same time, the juridical norms that are operative in a society surely play an important role in educating its people about what that society regards as valuable. There is a significant practical difference, however, between an understanding of the law/culture relation that sees culture as playing the primary formative role and one that sees law in this role. In the former understanding, law cannot run too far ahead of the culture without violating the will of the people. Thus in this approach there can be no legitimate legislation that does not reflect a significant degree of consensus on values held by the people. In the latter view, law has an educative role. It can take the lead in forming the values of the culture and the people. *Evangelium Vitae* seems to hold both views.

The Second Vatican Council's Declaration on Religious Freedom, *Dignitatis Humanae,* suggested that the church's influence on social life should normally be through a form of persuasion that shapes values and culture in a context of full respect for freedom. In the council's theology, religion is certainly not a purely private affair relegated to the sacristy or confined to Sunday morning. In the council's words, "it comes within the meaning of religious freedom that religious communities should not be prohibited from freely undertaking to show the special value of their doctrine in what concerns the organization of society and the inspiration of the whole of human activity."[30] But this influence will normally be through the persuasive power of witness and efforts at persuasion through reasonable discussion, rather than through the coercive power of law backed up by the police. Again as the council put it, "the usages of society are to be the usages of freedom in their full range: that is, the freedom of persons is to be respected as far as possible and is not to be curtailed except when and insofar as necessary."[31]

The last phrase in this quotation, of course, suggests that limits on freedom are sometimes socially necessary. The council recognized that even religious freedom itself might have to be limited. It must be restricted if the exercise of this freedom comes into conflict with other fundamental moral values. Thus all freedom, including religious freedom, "is subject to certain regulatory norms."[32] In the first instance, the limits on freedom of religion are matters of civility and are personal moral responsibilities. They become legal obligations enforceable by the use of coercion only when the exercise of freedom violates the rights of other citizens, seriously disrupts the public peace that is based on true justice, or transgresses those standards of public morality on which consensus exists in society. These norms spell out what the council means by public order.[33] Public order, so understood, is not the fullness of morality but it is nevertheless a moral concept. It includes the protection of human rights, justice, and peace. These are the most basic requisites of social life and are what is minimally required if a society that is civil is to exist at all. When such requirements of public order are endangered, the use of the coercive power of the state is justified. This is what the bishops we have cited believe to be true in the cases of abortion and euthanasia.

The question that emerges, therefore, is whether the case has been or can be made that abortion, euthanasia, embryonic stem cell research, and other issues some bishops claim are "trumps" in fact threaten the most basic requirements of morality that the council calls "public order," i.e., basic human rights, the minimal requirements of justice, and fundamental elements of public morality. It seems that this case has not been made in a way that has persuaded most Americans that all abortions should be simply banned and that this ban should be enforced by the coercive power of criminal law and the police. The cultural background that would support criminalization of all abortions does not presently exist in the United States. Of course, it would be possible to argue that putting such a criminal law in place would itself gradually lead to the formation of a cultural consensus that supports the rejection of all abortion.

In my judgment, however, the status of the embryo within the first fourteen days, i.e., before implantation, is sufficiently ambiguous to make it necessary to present a persuasive argument that all abortions "from the moment of conception" violate human rights, and should therefore be outlawed by the criminal law as the equivalent of murder. Indeed, it is difficult to know what counts as "the moment of conception," since, in current embryology, conception appears more of a process than a moment. In addition, the possibility of the development of identical twins from one conceptus, and the fact that the spontaneous loss of early embryos may be as high as between 50 percent and 80 percent of all those conceived, raise questions about whether a full human person is present from the earliest stage. These scientific data do not, of course, settle the theological question of the moral status of the embryo. Nor do they tell us how to judge the morality of abortions at stages of pregnancy after the first fourteen days. Nevertheless, as Margaret Farley has pointed out, the Roman Catholic moral tradition's grounding in natural law theory claims that moral norms and obligations are rooted in a reality that is ultimately intelligible. This means that we can discover our moral obligations through discernment, deliberation, and careful attention to the concrete reality of our world.[34] Revelation in the Bible and church moral teaching can contribute to our understanding of the reality of human beings and the world around us, and thus of the moral demands reality makes upon us. But the Catholic tradition's belief that the world created by God is intelligible to us, at least partially, means that determination of our moral obligations in areas such as abortion and stem cell research must pay serious attention to insights into the status of the fetus provided by contemporary science. Thus, attempting to settle the issue of the morality of abortion apart from serious moral argument shaped by consideration of all relevant scientific understanding would be to abandon the central commitment of the Catholic tradition to the role of reason in determining our moral obligations.

John Paul II in fact acknowledges that the scientific data does not definitively settle the question of whether the early embryo is fully a person. But he argues that because the stakes are so high the "mere probability" that the embryo is human justifies a clear ban on taking its life.[35] On the other hand, others interpret the scientific uncertainty in a permissive way in light of the weight that they grant to values that may conflict with the life of the early embryo. Similar considerations come into play at later stages of pregnancy. If probabilities are involved, and if a developmental understanding of the humanity of the fetus can be supported by reasoned arguments, it would appear that the only legitimate way to challenge and change such understanding is by presenting countervailing, persuasive arguments. This means that when bishops address the issues of abortion and embryonic stem cell research in the United States today, they should move forward in the first instance by presenting the most persuasive arguments they can in the domain of cultural interchange. It would be precipitous to appeal to the coerciveness of law when these substantive moral arguments are as unresolved in our culture as they are. Indeed I fear the appeal to law may have the opposite effect from the one desired by the bishops who make this appeal. Americans, including American Catholics, value the freedom of the individual so deeply today that many are likely to reject the bishops' positions on abortion and euthanasia simply because they appear to call for the use of coercion by the power of the state. This is even more true when the values at stake are matters of intense debate in the culture.

Far better and more likely to succeed would be a church strategy of persuasion that operates on the cultural rather than the legal level. My own judgment on this question is that the appeal to law should generally follow the cultural consensus rather than preceding and seeking to form it. This is so whether the matter at issue is abortion, euthanasia, embryonic stem cell research, same-sex marriage, or some of the other matters declared to be "trumps" by several bishops. This certainly does not mean that I simply accept abortion or euthanasia. In fact, I believe that a strategy of persuasion can lead to a significant reduction in the number of abortions if it is pursued by making intelligent appeals to the insight and experience of American women, almost none of whom think abortion is a good thing. Politicians, too, can be persuaded that recognition of the complexity of the tragic circumstances that lead some women to abortion does not mean that all abortions should be regarded in the same way or discussed in the same way in political discourse. A more persuasive case can be made than we have yet heard from the Catholic bishops for why some abortions are much more serious moral failures than are others. Drawing such distinctions in persuasive discussion would be a significant step toward reducing the number of abortions. So would advocacy of policies that seek directly to alleviate the poverty that leads some women to see abortion as their only way out of desperate economic circumstances.[36] Similarly, I also believe that intelligently developed arguments on care for the seriously ill and dying can show that legalization of direct euthanasia is socially and medically undesirable. But making such arguments in persuasive ways in our context today calls for setting aside suggestions that the coercive power of the law is the first resort in dealing with these matters.

Threats directed against Catholic politicians or voters who do not advocate coercive laws in these areas are likely to be counterproductive, perhaps very counterproductive. The wariness of many toward the public role of the Catholic Church today is likely to be intensified if church leaders appeal to the arm of the state to settle matters about which a significant number of Americans experience uncertainty. It would be salutary to remember that the pastoral strategy adopted by Catholic leaders toward their relationship with the state before and during the French revolution was a key source of the marginalization of Catholicism from both politics and culture in France. Pastoral errors of this sort also played a role in the extraordinarily rapid secularization that took place in French Canada in the mid-twentieth century and that is under way in Ireland today. I fear that the approach being adopted by some U.S. bishops today could well lead to such secularization in the United States. It could lead to a further loss of influence by both the leadership and the lay members of the church. Were that to happen, the transcendent importance of church engagement in shaping our social life would be undermined.

In conclusion, I propose that the interaction of the Catholic community with political life in the United States today should be neither confrontational nor accommodationist. There is a deep need for both laity and clergy to work effectively to secure human rights, justice, and peace in American public life today. They need to do this by working hard to protect the human life and dignity of all Americans. But the effectiveness of this mission will be compromised by misdirected appeals to the coercive power of the state and by failure to make carefully reasoned and persuasive contributions on these matters in the cultural debates of the United States today. Transformation of a culture is a demanding project that requires courage, patience, and wisdom. All three of these virtues are very much needed in the U.S. Catholic community today, both among its clergy and especially among all its lay members. I hope this essay makes some contribution to discerning the path ahead.

Chapter 2

Resilient Citizens

The Public (and Gendered) Face

of American Catholicism

NANCY A. DALLAVALLE

C ATHOLICS IN THE UNITED STATES have undergone several paradigm shifts as they have negotiated and renegotiated their identity in the public "church-state" story in the United States. While the election of John F. Kennedy in 1960 was certainly a high-water mark, that success only highlighted the difficulty of inculturating Catholicism in the United States. The visible symbol of the Kennedy election, with his clear statement of the distance he would keep between his Catholic faith and his exercise of political office, did not reflect the daily, complex, and subtle negotiation of identity that continued to go on at the local level, in the relationships between public and parochial school systems, in the administration of hospitals, and, most importantly, in the day-to-day lives of American Catholics in the 1960s, who lived in a network of parishes, workplaces, schools, and town halls. Forty years later, even as the day-to-day lives of American Catholics are no longer bound by parish affiliation, the progressive distinction of church and state, marked by the Kennedy presidency and articulated by prominent Catholics such as Mario Cuomo, the former governor of New York, has come under fire for a variety of sociological, political, and economic reasons. In addition to — and probably intertwined with — these reasons, the hierarchy of the Roman Catholic Church has, in recent years, raised its voice against this progressive understanding of church and state, taking a more active role in naming the ways in which Catholics should bring their voices into the public square. This study asks about the rationale for and ramifications of this new effort, explores the unarticulated presuppositions about gender and sexuality that undergird some aspects of this effort, and suggests an alternative direction.

This effort is timely, as the "American Catholic" paradigm, already the site of contestation and development, is undergoing yet another re-working, and the direction of this paradigm shift is still not settled. Thus I will, first of all, agree with the many who generally reject the adequacy of the "Kennedy/Cuomo compact," but I will also note some problematic assumptions found in the work of some who propose a more vigorous "Catholic" presence in the public square, using the public discussion of abortion as an example. Second, I will detail what I think is at least part of the theological impetus afoot in much of this discussion, which is a drive to reinscribe more traditional gender roles for women. Third, I will suggest a different understanding of the "American Catholic" paradigm, making flexible use of the term "resilient citizens" as a term that could tap some of the wisdom of the Catholic sacramental sensibility in order to reframe Catholic ecclesial and civic self-understanding.

Throughout, my lens is that of a Catholic feminist, one who under-stands that the power of gender and sexuality to shape our world — as part of the story of creation, made in the image of God — is both in-escapable and continually in need of theological criticism. Luke Timothy Johnson cuts to the heart of the issue:

> In short, the women's movement, the most controversial and threat-ening element in the cultural revolution, forced all Americans to recognize that sex is also always about gender, and that gender always involves social construction, and that social construction always involves somebody's interest.[1]

Indeed, I would argue (with the Catholic tradition and against those who would argue that questions of sexuality are "private" questions) that not only does our understanding of gender "always involve some-body's interest"; our public story about gender and sexuality always involves everybody's interest.

"Life Issues": Gender Questions in the Public Square

As it became clear that John Kerry would be the Democratic nominee in the 2004 presidential race, the conversation about the place of religious faith in public life in the United States was launched anew, and with a new resonance for Catholics. Coming in the wake of the resurgence of the evangelical voice in political discussion, the notion that Kerry could simply reiterate the privatized understanding of religious faith put forward by the "Kennedy/Cuomo compact" quickly proved unrealistic. It was no longer possible for a Catholic politician to claim that her or his religious faith was completely "separate" from civic life. At the same time, the already well-established distinction would continue to be made with regard to which religious issues could be reasonably debated in public: moral questions that Catholic theology understood to be matters of the "natural law" were appropriate for public discussion, but doctrinal questions based on divine revelation were not. Catholics, for example, hold that the entire range of "life" issues represent values pertinent to all human beings, values that can be discussed based on publicly available criteria (drawn from biological sciences, philosophy, etc.). Other matters of doctrine, such as a belief in the afterlife, or the doctrine on the Trinity, are clearly matters of faith, drawn from Scripture or the tradition of the church, and thus not appropriate for public discussion.

This kind of clarification is typically "Catholic" in that it recognizes a distinction between the faculties of faith and reason without abandoning their necessary relationship. One problem with the use of this distinction in the election season, however, was that the use of careful distinctions did not adequately signal the passion of religious allegiance. On the contrary, in the national election of 2004, the popular understanding of the role of "religion in public life" was primarily framed in *anti*-intellectual terms; the turn to religious faith was seen, in that milieu, as the triumph of feeling over reason. A politician who professed "religious faith" was understood to be boasting that, with regard to certain matters, she or he would be bound by the virtue of faith, not the calculus of reason; indeed, in this scenario, employing reason is seen as diluting the intensity of the faith expressed. Thus, instead of foregrounding the moral or religious rationale for various positions or policies relating to public life and the social order, the Democratic nominee was reduced to signaling his Catholic faith by reminiscing about his years as an altar boy.

Contributing to the anti-intellectual tone, perhaps unwittingly, were the handful of bishops who chose that moment to speak publicly about the need for Catholics in public life to legislate in a manner consistent with Catholic faith. While the issues in question, particularly abortion and euthanasia, are questions that Catholics can and should debate in the public court of reason, the framing of these issues as a one-dimensional litmus test for Catholic orthodoxy (on the pain of having oneself publicly turned away from the reception of the Eucharist) shifted the terms of the debate from rationality to obedience. The discussion was further muddied by the association of some Catholic voices with standard media fixtures such as James Dobson's "Focus on the Family," and the clumsy machinations of "Catholic outreach" by political organizations. While a few bishops publicly counseled a more moderate approach, they were not organized around a strong counterargument, which left them to argue for "moderation."

A typical bishop's response to the situation was that of Archbishop William Levada, commenting on a statement by forty-eight Democratic Catholic members of Congress that argued against the actions of some bishops who warned pro-choice legislators not to present themselves for Communion in their diocese. Levada's response to the politicians' argument that the church was "legislating in public" with the threatened refusal of Communion reiterated that these issues were not matters of Catholic faith, but rather had to do with "the application of just moral principles in the arena of American political life, constitutional issues, and party politics."[2] Levada echoed the bishops' general sense that the withholding of Communion was therefore not a problematic intrusion of Catholicism into the public square but rather a reasonable question as to whether a politician should be held accountable, in church, for her or his actions in the public square.

But accountable for which actions? Levada's response then turned to the question of whether abortion — Levada adds euthanasia — should be seen as a foundational issue, in a way that other aspects of the "seamless garment" of life issues are not, resulting in a "single issue" approach to politics. It is not a "single issue" approach that drives the current efforts, according to Levada, but rather the gravity of the act of abortion. In the same month, the U.S. Conference of Catholic Bishops agreed, releasing the text *Catholics in Political Life*.[3] The language of this statement is absolute in its insistence that the killing of an unborn child is "intrinsically evil," and it strongly condemns those who would make such an evil act legal. Yet when it comes to whether a bishop should refuse

Communion for those who have given "their public support for abortion on demand," the language of the text changes tone to a significant degree, turning to phrases such as "prudential judgment," "wide range of circumstances," and a recognition that "bishops can legitimately make different judgments on the most prudent course of pastoral action."

Yet the bishops then return to absolutist language as they insist, without nuance, that Catholic institutions should not honor those who allow for the legality of abortion. Is it possible that the Catholic decision-makers at these institutions — executives charged with running universities, hospitals, and large charitable organizations — might be able to make similar prudential judgments about the "wide range of circumstances" that would lead to such an honor? Apparently not. Is it possible that a variety of Catholic institutions might, in fact, *inform* the debate about abortion's status as a foundational issue by their careful discussion of institutional identity and the question of honoring thinkers and artists and those who work for the public good? Again, no; wise, prudential, and pastoral judgments are possible for bishops alone.

A Test Case: The Exception for Rape in Abortion Policy

To raise the question of the shape of this dialogue in the public mind, and to bring forward some questions that should be more commonly asked, the always-difficult issue of abortion will be useful. While the Catholic prohibition on abortion does not make an exception for rape, an examination of the presuppositions of this commonly evoked exception reveals the need for much broader discussions of gender with regard to the "life issues." Indeed, at the level of practical implementation, some of the real issues at stake in the rather disembodied debate over abortion reveal abortion to be a complex, as well as contentious, issue. "Moral positions," as Dennis O'Brien observes in a recent issue of *America,* "do not automatically create public policies." The "pro-life" banner has been used as a "posture," O'Brien claims, one that ignores the pragmatic policy questions that a direct repeal of *Roe v. Wade* would raise.[4] To illustrate the need for a gender analysis in the public discussion of "life issues," I suggest further that one version of a "pro-life" posture, the exception for rape, exemplifies the elevation of posture over policy.

In the weeks and months before the 2004 election, as some bishops took it upon themselves to chastise Catholic Democratic politicians for their pro-choice voting records, a strong impression was created that Catholics should support the "pro-life" candidacy of President Bush. President Bush's position is not unreservedly "pro-life," however. In company with 23 percent of Americans (according to an April 2004 Zogby poll), he holds that abortion should be allowed in cases of rape or incest, or if the mother's life is at stake. Using these poll results, the folks at Zogby added that number to their finding that 18 percent of Americans reject all abortion and a further 15 percent would allow abortion only if the mother's life is threatened, and concluded that a "majority of Americans," a hefty 56 percent, were "pro-life." The United States Conference of Catholic Bishops immediately trumpeted that "pro-life majority" conclusion, claiming that the hundreds of thousands of activists who rallied for abortion rights in Washington in mid-April 2004 were "out of step with the American people." President Bush was reelected the following November.

Yet if 23 percent of all "pro-life" Americans would allow abortion in certain cases, almost half of this so-called "pro-life" majority, while finding abortion to be wrong, somehow also find it to be permissible in specific situations. Perhaps these Americans call themselves "compassionate conservatives," conservative in their assertion that abortion is morally wrong, yet compassionate in their sense that the claim of this nascent life may be too much to bear, physically or emotionally, by women in specific circumstances. We value life, they may think, but we cannot reasonably require heroism. One can understand the appeal of such reasoning to the average person, but a closer look raises serious questions about the use of this position by (presumably) policy-wise politicians. Indeed, this position, particularly as it makes a specific exception for rape (or incest, if this means rape by a biological relation), is deeply flawed in two ways.

First of all, while it is certainly true that carrying to term a child that resulted from a rape would be emotionally impossible for many women (though perhaps possible for others), the fact of being conceived as a result of rape does not, in any way, lessen the value of the unborn human life in question. (There is, I realize, a knee-jerk reaction here, as I find when I raise this issue in my undergraduate classes: several students are usually resistant to the notion that a child conceived as a result of rape is not "damaged goods," the product of a "bad seed.") Further, in singling out all raped women as a class, this "pro-life" position indicates that the extraordinary burden of the pregnancy in question is *not* the basis for the exception; rather the exception is based on the victimized woman's moral status: "innocent." (And, along with the "damaged goods" notion above, I often hear lurking beneath this blanket exception almost an *expectation* that a raped woman should want to have an abortion — at least, the discussion reveals, any woman who was "really" raped.) In short, the unspoken framework that drives this exception effectively shifts the emotional engine of the question from the value of unborn human life to the moral status of the pregnant woman; in other words, the "commonsense" exception for rape reveals "pro-life," in this case, to be mere "posture," as we are no longer in the realm of protecting nascent life, we are in the business of judging women.

Which leads to the second flaw in this position: the only way to enact this exception is for a public determination of the moral status of the woman in question. (Notice the shift here: the focus of this legal proceeding would be on the innocence or guilt of the victim, even though this is not what our legal system is designed to adjudicate.) Which legal mechanism will determine that a woman has been raped and is thus "eligible" for an abortion? What about the prosecution nightmare of "date-rape"? Will we require that the entire legal process runs its (months-long) course before we authorize the abortion? What if there is an appeal?

The policy implications are obviously problematic, and for a serious public official to hold a position so obviously unworkable in practice makes no sense unless, of course, this position is precisely the kind of "posture" that O'Brien decries. The official Catholic position (held by at most 18 percent of the population) opposes all abortion as a grave moral wrong. Yet the intent and effect of the bishops' statement in 2004 was clearly to support the position of President Bush, as it was produced at a critical time in a particular context (and did not clearly repudiate his position). In addition, the problematic implications of "pro-life, except for rape" went unchallenged and were allowed to reverberate in the subtext of the debate. "Pro-life, except for rape" is not a "policy on abortion." It is a political sleight-of-hand that pretends to assert both opposition to abortion and compassion for women, but in fact exchanges an appropriate focus on the value of human life for a deeply problematic manipulation of rather crass notions of what women "deserve." Catholic voters are not immune to the cultural tug of these subtexts, narratives that are both unacknowledged and powerfully resonant. And effective.

Women in Public, Women in Private

Feminist ethicist Christine Gudorf has observed that the nineteenth-century Roman Catholic Church, finding itself marginalized in the post-Enlightenment secular milieu, reserved its social teaching for the politically powerful elites of society and directed its teaching on marriage and family to the average Catholic in the pew. By focusing its broad message to the pews on the themes of marriage and family, the church often cast itself as the protector of the rights of the family against the modern, secularized state. But the result of this response to modernity, Gudorf argues, was that "many persons came to understand their faith *solely* in terms of contracting marriages according to canon law, attending Sunday Mass, abstaining from adultery, contraception, and abortion, and raising children who received a Catholic education."[5] It is not surprising, then, that these domestic issues, insofar as they intersected with public policy issues, came to dominate not only the private realm, but also the self-understanding of a "Catholic" public order.

Supporting this perspective was a variety of papal texts in which women were portrayed as both guardians and objects of this domestic-centric church. In the early twentieth century, Gudorf reports, Pope Benedict XV (and the following papacies of Pius XI and Pius XII) emphasized that women were protected in the private world of a home guarded by the feminine values of the gospel, but vulnerable in the public world precisely because its secularity was inherently masculine.[6] Even Pius XII's wartime recognition of women's increasing role in the workforce did not change his judgment that women's "sensibility and delicacy," while an asset in the private realm, represented a liability in the public realm. The same qualities that made women particularly attuned to the rhythms of the hearth, notably "discerning [with regard to]...domestic life, public assistance, and religion," rendered them, he claimed, dangerously vulnerable in the world of commerce and politics.[7] The public world was seen as harmful to women, a place in which their nature was in danger of becoming misshapen; a place in which they would become enslaved to idolatry, that is, a place in which "our women" would be easily corrupted.

Counter-voices did emerge. Writing on the role of women in church and society, in 1964, Karl Rahner refers to "feminine qualities" but, wisely, refrains from parsing these too closely. Women themselves, he claims, will need to seek out their own "concrete pattern[s] of life," patterns which will be manifold: "a whole range . . . and these must be of various kinds." And the finding of such a pattern "is for the Christian woman herself to decide . . . as her primary, proper, and inalienable task."[8] Those familiar with Rahner's work will recognize the existential urgency of the language of a "primary, proper, and inalienable task"; in using this language it is clear that Rahner finds the project of self-definition, for contemporary women, to be a moral imperative. Indeed, this challenge was taken up by women, particularly by women who, in the decades following the Second Vatican Council, joined the ranks of theological scholars as systematicians, moral theologians, scripture scholars, and historians. Yet the contributions of these women have yet to make their way into the magisterial narrative of Catholic thought in any substantive manner, just as the growing ranks of women in administrative positions in the church have little to do with shaping the practice or content of the Catholic faith.

Moreover, the magisterial narrative is now moving in the opposite direction. Twenty years after Rahner, with similar urgency but seemingly less restraint, Pope John Paul II also addressed the theme of the "special nature of woman," but his treatment of the theme has given rise to a detailed anthropological program, one which professes to "treat" both genders, but which is finally an extended treatise on "the female." Drawing on his early meditations on Genesis, John Paul II emphasized the role of motherhood as central to female self-understanding, particularly in his 1988 apostolic letter *Mulieris Dignitatem* and his 1995 "Letter to Women."[9]

In the "Letter to Women," he invokes what he calls a "new feminism," a term he had also used earlier in 1995, in the encyclical *Evangelium Vitae* (99). This "new feminism" embraces biological sexuality as the ground for women's self-understanding, a ground which therefore finds heterosexual complementarity and the possibility of motherhood (perhaps "spiritual") to be fundamental to "the female." John Paul argues further that this perspective is "new," drawing upon postmodern "differ-ence" feminism, in contrast to "old" — secular, liberal, individualistic — feminism. Setting aside the question of whether this can be seen as a gen-uinely "postmodern" account, the stated contrast of the "new feminism" with a cartoonish rendering of liberal/radical feminism conveniently overlooks the fact that much of the recent championing of women in the documents of John Paul II is "new" in a theological tradition that is replete with negative stereotypes. While this new story is laudable in that it does not reinscribe explicitly misogynistic views of women (curiously, these texts have few parallels in their extravagant praise for the gifts of women), it is hard to see the rationale behind the argument that this "new feminism" is visionary for its repudiation of the worst excesses of the feminist thought of thirty years ago. It would be more accurate to claim that the "new feminism" is most charitably viewed as a modest updating of the church's own problematic record on women.

But this is not the entire story, as in this new magisterial narrative there is more than simply a corrective at work. In these texts, the story about "woman" is not merely fulsome; it is *novel* in that "woman" is now put forward as the model for a theological understanding of all humanity. The qualities that are peculiar to women are the qualities that are central to an understanding of the role of the human person before God; *humanity is now best understood as "feminine."* The exemplar for this is, not surprisingly, Mary of Nazareth's lived *fiat* as a profound acceptance of the will of God. Most explicitly, given the contours of the "new feminism," I think it important to highlight that the Marian *fiat* is not only a profound acceptance of God's will — a model for the disciple's wholehearted yes — but a profound acceptance of maternity *in particular.*

This understanding of humanity as theologically "female"[10] is re-inforced when read alongside other claims. For example, in the 2004 statement from the Congregation for the Doctrine of the Faith, "On the Collaboration of Men and Women in the Church and in the World," a claim is made that a problematic "tendency" in contemporary and fem-inist scholarship downplays important aspects of tradition, for example, "this tendency would consider as lacking in importance and relevance the fact that the Son of God assumed human nature in its male form."[11] Little is said about precisely what relevance the alliance of "male" and

God might have, though a careful reading of the text leads one to assume, by default, that this assertion's "relevance" has much to do with the complementary understanding of the alliance of "female" and human. This alliance of "male" and God might also have relevance for the continued refusal to ordain women to the Roman Catholic priesthood. Though recent texts that attempt to close this subject argue on the basis of the "will" of Christ as revealed in the choice of men as apostles, finding this, and the subsequent "constant practice of the Church" to be the "fundamental reasons" for the exclusion of women from the ordained priesthood,[12] there is no attempt, in these texts, to reject the *in persona Christi* argument of the 1976 text *Inter Insigniores*. Not surprisingly, some recent scholarship has, following these magisterial initiatives, put forward the nuptial metaphor as a fundamental model for theology, even a theological "truth" in itself.[13]

These concurrent developments cannot be received apart from the current complicated social terrain that is the context for a public discussion of abortion, particularly in the United States. When the U.S. bishops assert that abortion is the most fundamental of the "life" issues, not part of a "seamless garment" but somehow its foundation, consideration must be given to the presuppositions of this assertion, specifically the fact that this fundamental life issue is a women's issue. Coupled with the growing movement within the magisterium to emphasize the role of biological sexuality in theological anthropology, abortion seems now to be not merely a sinful denial of life but, more fundamentally, a sinful denial, *by women*, of their capacity for maternity, a capacity, it is now suggested, that is central to their humanity. Even further, if the true face of humanity is understood to be that of the Marian *fiat*, insofar as this *fiat* is not an acceptance of God's will in general but maternity in particular, a logic develops that finds abortion to be a singular crime by humans (*qua* female) against humanity. The most fundamental sin of Adam, hubris, is now transformed, essentialized, and assigned, exclusively, to the daughters of Eve.

A similar recognition of the extent to which the theological story of gender complementarity is shaping the current narrative about the human person might also call for a reconsideration of the aforementioned standard "Catholics in public life" distinction. Is this narrative about the human person, particularly as it is a narrative about the human person created as male and female, drawn from the natural law, or does it in fact rest on a truth that has been "revealed"? For example, in the discussion of euthanasia, the notion of the value of human life, including the dying process, seems to be a discussion that can take place in a public context. The question of abortion, if it focuses on the value of human life, and the claims that one life can make on another, seems to be a similar question, treated on the basis of publicly available criteria. Yet, as the discussion of rape as an exception to abortion policy reveals, the distinction between Catholic teaching based on the natural law and Catholic teaching based on revealed truths may not always be clear — or may not always be clearly delineated, particularly when unarticulated assumptions about gender are operative.

Catholic Christianity and the Development of "Resilient Citizens"

Thus far, this essay has argued that an analysis of the more energetic role of religion in American public discourse, particularly by those who speak as Christians or Catholic Christians, must include an analysis of the role played by gender and sexuality in shaping that discourse. Also, I have suggested that the understanding of gender and sexuality in Roman Catholicism is undergoing an important and problematic shift. Taken together, these movements highlight some positive directions insofar as they take seriously the role of religion in public life and the de facto role of biological sexuality in shaping our sense of self-in-community. Examined more carefully, however, the Roman Catholic reflection on what it means to be female, most problematically the suggestion that humanity is best understood as female before God, presents a variety of theological problems (not treated here) that reverberate, unacknowledged, in a variety of public discussions.

Consider the issue of national security, now recast as "Homeland Security." In an essay in the September 2004 issue of the journal *Foreign Affairs*, Stephen Flynn argues that, in response to the 9/11 attacks, the United States has devoted too many resources to a strategy of fighting terrorism abroad and too few resources to preparing the "homefront" for everyday life in a world of risk. In the words of President George W. Bush, the current strategy is to "engage these enemies in these countries and around the world so we do not have to face them here at home."[14] This is a misguided, and wasteful, approach, Flynn argues. The more important task, he suggests, is to develop stronger internal strategies for responding, confidently and comprehensively, to an attack on our own soil. Such a strategy would have as its goal the minimizing of damage to essential structures and the recovery of those things vital to civic and social functioning. Most importantly, such an approach would have as its goal the creation of a scenario that does not rest on a promise of "never again," but rather on an affirmation of the ability of the country to move forward after a disruptive event. The greatest danger posed by a terrorist attack of the most likely types — a simple truck bomb, the limited release of a biological or chemical agent — would not be the attack's immediate effects but rather the possibility of panic, overreaction, or paralysis.

Flynn's analysis is based on a pragmatic discussion that weighs the risks of one strategy against those of another, with regard to national security. Setting aside an evaluation of the merits of his argument on those grounds, what I find compelling about the scenario he paints is his realization that a border-focused, top-down approach to threats is not merely ineffective, it also leaves most people poorly prepared to live in a (permanently) unpredictable world. "What is required" in such a world, according to Flynn, "is that everyday citizens develop both the maturity to live with the risk of future attacks and the willingness to invest in reasonable measures to mitigate that risk."[15] As an example, Flynn cites the way in which Americans deal with airline safety in general: even though planes occasionally crash, most people continue to assume that the airlines are operating in a reasonable manner. This works, he says, because of three attitudes, attitudes that are generalizable to other risk situations. First, there is, with regard to the issue in question, a public mind-set that recognizes both the fact of risk, and the possibility of managing risk. Second, the issue is understood to represent a risk that is best managed in a responsive system at the local level. Third, there is widespread public confidence in government agencies committed to the enforcement of risk-management protocols.

This scenario for security relies not on the swagger of a hyper-militarized border to protect a naïve and vulnerable populace from the ravages of a hostile external world, but rather on a publicly accountable system of institutionalized checks and balances put in place by a citizenry that is informed, mature, and — as Flynn says — "resilient." This scenario integrates the risk and responsibility of living in a dangerous world with a lived and local sensibility for negotiating that world. In contrast, the current approach to national security relies on an appeal to a story that splits "public" and "private," with gendered overtones that are hard to ignore. Put more directly, the current "harden the borders" security scenario presupposes that security depends on a (masculine) program of public aggression "out there" so as not to breach the private (feminine/infantilized) homeland. Besides the morally problematic and culturally isolationist lens with which this response views those outside of our borders (the other, our neighbor), this split perspective renders inflexible the institutional culture of those charged with border protection as well as enfeebling those left behind on the "homefront" of the "homeland." A mature understanding of risk coupled with a realistic commitment to developing structures to promote personal, social, and structural resilience would be a far better response, not only for managing the risk of terrorism but also, I suggest, for developing the kind of personal maturity and resilience that Americans will need on a variety of "fronts," from Social Security reform to the development of a competitive workforce in a global economy. And, I suggest, this sense of "resilience" offers much for the development of a similarly resilient ecclesial citizenry.

For it is precisely such resilience that seems lacking in the pews of American parishes. Flynn's analysis, as it insists on the development of internal responsive structures for managing risk, offers an interesting frame for the reconceptualization of church/state issues, particularly in a time when Roman Catholics in the United States find themselves "adrift" in a sea of internal failures and external challenges.[16] For Catholics, this analogy of risk management is fruitful, in that this situation calls for a critical assessment that requires an engagement with real problems that is finally an engagement with institutional self-identity. This frame provides not only the outlines of a pragmatic response to a time of challenge; even more, *its call for the development of resilient citizens is a moral mandate that Catholics should recognize and welcome as a fruitful model for both civic and ecclesial life that is already deeply Catholic.* Indeed, Catholic social thought provides ample theological resources for precisely this kind of communal involvement that is based on principled individual actions by adult actors. With regard to the issue raised earlier in this essay, for example, we should not assume — and Catholic moral teaching has not assumed — that a raped woman is incapable of making moral decisions, nor would we regard rape as a breaching of borders that can never be integrated (thus, abortion as the only response). Yet it is my guess that many Catholics fall into the mistaken reasoning that undergirds "no abortion except in cases of rape..." precisely because they continue to regard the demands of moral theology as an exercise in the "border patrol" model above, rather than as a body of wisdom about the development of virtuous adult Christians. This kind of moral formation, a formation that has obedience as its refrain and a "border patrol" mentality as its subtext, is hardly likely to produce the kind of virtuous adult actor who can respond with resilience in a situation of extremity.

To be sure, Catholics can also point, with some pride, to counter-evidence, in their proven record of producing responsive intermediate institutions — hospitals, religious orders, schools, and social service agencies — institutions that have, more often than not, provided a formative context for the development of principled adult actors. Voluntary organizations, such as the Knights of Columbus, have also brought skills and support to those in need in the social order. All of these institutions and organizations self-consciously evoke the Catholic social tradition as well as Catholic belief and practice to ground their investment in the common good. Yet, curiously, these same skills and habits of mature citizens are often left in the parking lot as these citizens take their place in the ecclesial body, one that increasingly emphasizes the difference between "active" clergy and "receptive" laity.

Further bifurcating Catholics' civic and ecclesial lives is a failure to nurture a full-bodied Catholic aesthetic sense. Just as economists have lamented the fact that rationality rarely gives full accounting of consumers' behavior and choices, so too would this model be shortsighted if it imagined that abstract lessons in ethics and disembodied notions of the common good would in fact produce the resilient citizens our social fabric so clearly needs. The cultivation of these skills and habits requires more than technical training and catechetical formation. As Ignatian educational models realize, growth happens only when education is directed at the whole person. Jesuit David Hollenbach, for example, notes the importance of a lively engagement with the arts as a formative part of the liberalizing change that happened in Czechoslovakia.[17]

These important aesthetic resources are readily retrievable for Catholics. If seen as more than an exercise in obedience, the public sacramental character of Catholic Christianity could both articulate and cultivate a deeply resilient understanding of the person in the social order. Properly viewed, the ordered sacramental action of Catholic Christianity is not an exercise in conformity and obedience; rather, such ordered sacramental action allows Catholic Christians to live the reality of God-with-us. For Catholics, institutional structures — and not only ecclesial ones — are not incidental to the life of faith. On the contrary, the mechanism of human culture, the social order in all its relational complexity, and the tangible, living world mediate the saving presence of God. The primary mode for the cultivation of the habits proper to Catholic "resilient citizens" cannot be reduced to the exigencies of a quasi-patriotic exercise in "preparedness" (bottled water, batteries, duct tape), or a catechetical immersion in duties and obligations (weekly Mass, observance of holy days, regular confession). It is, I suggest, an active engagement in the movement of grace in history.

Unfortunately, such schooling is not a common practice in the current ecclesial climate, which too often resorts to a "harden the borders" response to perceived external threats to a Catholic narrative of obedience and control. One example is the adoption of a policy of "zero tolerance" for sexually abusive clergy, as put in place by the United States Conference of Catholic Bishops (USCCB) at a meeting in Dallas in 2002. The public outrage over the revelation of a widespread practice, among the bishops of this country, of ignoring, covering up, denying, or simply rejecting reports of sexual abuse by priests led to a demand by a shocked Catholic populace that any priest who had ever committed such an offense be removed from ministry. While the notion that sexual abuse of any kind, to any degree, is incompatible with service in the church is an important and obvious claim, the movement toward such an absolutist policy seemed to be fueled more by a widespread distrust of the insular clerical structure than a call for a purified clergy.

As the Dallas norms were being reconsidered in 2005,[18] Cardinal Avery Dulles spoke out against the notion of "zero tolerance." His argument was that such a policy violates the rights of priests as it denies them "due process of law." For example, this policy does not allow for the possibility of a response that is proportionate to the wide variety of offenses in question and it seems, in practice, not to fully honor the presumption of innocence that is integral to accepted legal practice. He observes that "having been so severely criticized for exercising poor judgment in the past, the bishops apparently wanted to avoid having to make any judgments in these cases."[19] Dulles is right to suggest that avoiding judgment is not an option for a bishop. What is missing in Dulles's analysis, however, is a general sense that *all* Catholics are called to make careful — even "prudential" — judgments in a complex world of relationship and risk. The cultivation of the ability of the laity to make good judgments would certainly seem to be part of the teaching office of the bishop. But, as the current crisis demonstrates, no such sensibility has ever been nurtured in the laity, and thus there was no common practice of lay resilience in the face of a threatening situation. Thus, the rush to "zero tolerance" by concerned laypeople represented, I suggest, not simply outrage at the horrific accounts of abuse, but a complete lack of confidence in the bishops' ability to function as bishops. As the revelations of the bishops' failures seemed to be the norm rather than the exception, the call for "zero tolerance" (zero judgment) seemed to be the only option. And the bishops agreed.

A further problematic aspect of the clerical response to the crisis in their ranks in the eyes of many lay people was the quick shift from a scattered acknowledgment of the wrongdoing of others ("mistakes were made") to a strong clergy chorus exhorting the laity to greater faith. "This is a crisis of faith" was often the message that came from the pulpit, a message that seemed, from the pew, designed to deflect attention from the wrongdoing by priests and bishops (whose crisis? whose faith?). Similarly, the vigorous implementation of background checks and training in sexual abuse awareness for all church employees and volunteers, while understandable from a legal perspective, seemed, to many in the pews, merely punitive. Bewildered, many questioned why the laity was the focus of such a vigorous "reeducation" effort, when the fault was that of the clergy. Lay volunteers of several decades' standing — some of whom previously had raised questions about clergy behavior, only to be ignored or silenced — protested the sudden intrusion of background checks. Those who refused were banned from service. Small home-based catechetical groups could no longer meet outside of the "scrubbed" premises of the parish (now, curiously, the official site of the domestic church).

In the wider picture, the overall response to the crisis in the U.S. church not only replicated the "harden the borders" strategy; it also promoted the overly privatized, domestic approach to the Catholic social order found in the mid-twentieth century, as discussed above. Three aspects describe the general sense of the response to this crisis. First, there has been a reassertion of the need for "faith," which reduces, in practice, to the "orthodoxy of obedience," a reaffirmation of magisterial positions on bioethics, sexual morality, and the refusal to ordain women. Second, there has been an ongoing emphasis of the need for further immersion in this "faith" by a revitalization of the parochial school system (a valuable resource, but not the primary school system for most Catholics). Third, there has been a call for a renewed and purified (quasi-donatist) priesthood, a call in which the laity's participation is limited to praying for vocations (often linked to eucharistic adoration). These efforts all have some worth in themselves. Taken together, however, they do little to bring about a resilient Catholic laity. On the contrary, this program is likely to produce just the opposite: a passive laity whose subservience in ecclesial matters guarantees that their faith will never be integrated with their adult development. (Indeed, the laity's shock that they should be part of the response to the crisis, engaged in sexual abuse education, and affected financially by the cost of the settlements with the victims, indicates the extent to which they equated their passivity with innocence.) Given that adult development means the confrontation with the issues of religion in the public square, how shall these Catholics respond?

One response would be to echo the firm separation of church and state, with the legacy of Kennedy and Cuomo. In a thoughtful updated version of this, Michael and Kenneth Himes have attempted to articulate a theological understanding of "the Catholic in the Public Square" by delineating a "public theology" not unlike that of Martin Marty's "public church."[20] In this version, religious affiliation is one of a number of competing voices in the square, accountable, insofar as it is publicly exercised, to the worldview of liberal democracy. A contrasting response is offered by Michael Baxter, who rejects the Himeses' analysis as overly accommodating to the liberal state:

> In view of the church's mission as *lumen gentium,* the very notions of "public church" and "public theology" rest on what can only be regarded as a category mistake. They identify the church as a subset of the nation-state. Theologically, it is the reverse that is true. The nation-state is the narrower social formation. The broader, more universal, genuinely catholic, and truly public social formation is the church — as is obvious to the vast majority of Christians in the world who live outside the territorial borders of the United States of America.[21]

The impasse between these two views — both of which take a "top-down" approach that too readily consigns "the Catholic" to a fixed institutional model — could be broken, I suggest, by a reframing of the discussion to more broadly consider what it might mean for institutionally identified Catholics to see Catholic Christianity as a voice not merely *available* within the contours of liberal democracy, but *formative* of its discourse. In this sense, the Himeses's approach is more helpful, as it incorporates inner-critical elements that allow for development within the narrative of liberal democracy. In turn, of course, such a "public" Catholic vision will exhibit resilience precisely to the extent that it is genuinely and formatively engaged with the broad culture. Such an engagement does not abandon the worldwide sweep of Christianity's catholicity but, rather, recognizes its real incarnation in history.

One healthy sign of the ability of Catholic Christianity to root the gospel in the contemporary world has been the birth and flourishing of prayerful lay groups, from the ecumenism-and-justice orientation of the Community of Sant' Egidio to the more traditionalist orientation of Communion and Liberation. But even more important for the concerns here would be projects that propose a specific "site" for institutional self-criticism, such as Cardinal Joseph Bernardin's Common Ground Initiative. In the articulation of that vision, the use of the term "accountability" functions in a similar manner to this essay's sense of "resilience":

Accountability to the Catholic tradition does not mean reversion to a chain-of-command, highly institutional understanding of the church, a model resembling a modern corporation, with headquarters and branch offices, rather than Vatican II's vision of a communion and a people.... Authentic accountability rules out a fundamentalism that narrows the richness of the tradition to a text or a decree, and it rules out a narrow appeal to individual or contemporary experience that ignores the cloud of witnesses over the centuries or the living magisterium of the church exercised by the bishops and the Chair of Peter.[22]

In other words, public statements of identity and orthodoxy should not be reduced to an exercise in "brand management," as if the teaching office of the bishop were best understood as an extended exercise in staying "on message" (often accompanied by claims of pastoral concern for the "simple faithful"). Part of the strength of the Common Ground Initiative is precisely the way in which it counters "simple faith" of all kinds (even those with complex epistemologies!), cultivating a "resilience" of intellect and heart in those who participate in its discussions. It is not easy to revert to "public" caricatures of "left" and "right" about those with whom you have shared "private" space, in careful conversation, liturgy, and table fellowship. Moreover, these activities happen only because of the "intermediate institution" of the Initiative. Another example, of much longer standing, would be the well-respected network of Catholic Relief Services. After the December 2004 tsunami in South Asia, CRS exemplified the kind of efficient, "already on the ground" social and institutional resilience such a disaster required. Many more intermediary structures, of all varieties, are needed, structures that would foster a flexible "catholic resilience" in individuals, in family-centered households, and in strong local and regional social and civic networks.

These structures would nurture the "catholic" essence of the Catholic vocation — the call to think clearly, in public, about our common humanity and the common good. Such a vocation requires the support of resilient selves and social contexts and should resist at all costs the efforts to reduce "Catholic" to a tribal affiliation, club membership, or voting bloc. And, as I argue above, one critical lens for the examination of the story of Catholics in the public square is a lens that takes seriously the unarticulated, but powerful, presuppositions about gender, sexuality, and personhood that undergird our social narratives, whether drawn from popular culture or from magisterial decrees. Examinations of the numerous and elusive presuppositions that attend terms like male, female, public, private, family, church, state — terms that drive the dominant narrative of Catholic faith "in the public square" — are important not only for critical insight but also for their constructive value as they inform and enrich the kind of faith resilient adult actors need for a genuine and credible evangelization of culture.

Chapter 3

Women Theologians as Gift of an Inculturated U.S. American Church

Mary Ann Hinsdale, I.H.M.

Introduction

"INCULTURATION" MAY BE a modern term, but the idea has pervaded Christian missionary activity since the time the first disciples were enjoined to "go forth and spread the Good News to all nations" (see Matt. 28). However, the history of the church's missionary activity has been mixed concerning to what extent it has acknowledged that the Holy Spirit was already at work in a culture before the Good News arrived. And yet both Paul and Luke recall for us that the disciples of Jesus employed concepts and customs derived from the local culture in their work of evangelization.[1]

Vatican II did not use the word "inculturation," but spoke rather of the need for "a profound adaptation" of the gospel message in different cultures.[2] Unfortunately, the missiological approach of "adaptation" often assumed that both the gospel and its transmitters were cultureless. The Western church's long legacy of colonialism attests to the fact that this approach, more often than not, brought along a blatant cultural imperialism.[3]

In an extended footnote to his article "Inculturation and Cultural Systems, Part I" Carl Starkloff attributes the first use of the word "inculturation" to Pedro Arrupe, S.J. In his "Letter to the Whole Society on Inculturation,"[4] Arrupe defined inculturation using the symbol of incarnation:

[Inculturation is] the incarnation of Christian life and of the Christian message in a particular local cultural context, in such a way that the experience not only finds expression through elements proper to the culture in question (this alone would be no more than a superficial adaptation), but becomes a principle that animates, directs, and unifies a culture, transforming and remaking it so as to bring about "a new creation."[5]

The incarnational understanding of inculturation would eventually be supplanted, however. For, while it acknowledges that Jesus himself was subject to inculturation (i.e., the human Jesus must be understood in terms of the intercultural dynamics of the Jewish and Greco-Roman worlds of the first century), the incarnational understanding does not emphasize enough the challenge that Jesus brings to these cultures, a challenge that ultimately leads to his crucifixion.[6] Thus, Aylward Shorter recommends a "paschal mystery" approach to inculturation that stresses a dialectical and hermeneutical approach to the relationship of revelation and culture. In this refinement, inculturation becomes "a term that denotes the presentation and re-expression of the Gospel in forms and terms proper to a culture, processes which result in the reinterpretation of both."[7]

Today many missiologists prefer the term "*inter*culturation," pointing to the realization that the gospel, itself a product of particular cultures, must be brought into dialogue with another culture in order to effect *mutual* transformation. Coined by Bishop Joseph Blomjous in 1980, "interculturation" refers to the reciprocal character of the church's evangelizing mission.[8] It emphasizes that the handing on of the faith is not simply a "one-way street." Given both an incarnational and trinitarian understanding of revelation, Christians believe that the Holy Spirit has always been at work in the world and thus is already at work in a culture. Furthermore, the belief that the Incarnation takes place in history implies that faith can be expressed only by means of and *within* human cultural realities.

Despite the rhetoric concerning the need of a dialogue between faith and culture and the positive consideration given to the understanding of "interculturation" in contemporary missiology, there has been a noticeable reluctance on the part of the church's *magisterium* to acknowledge that aspects of particular cultures might be "transformative" of the broader (universal) ecclesial reality of the church. Whether this is due to ignorance or conscious resistance is difficult to say. Certainly, since "cultures" are the creation of human beings, they do not always live up to the ideals of Christian faith.

Ten years after *Gaudium et Spes,* Vatican II's Pastoral Constitution on the Church in the Modern World, Pope Paul VI was describing the split between faith and culture as "the drama of our time." Thus, in *Evangelii Nuntiandi* (1975) he called for an "evangelization of cultures." Pope John Paul established the Pontifical Council for Culture in 1982 precisely in order to address a matter that he, too, believed concerned the very survival of the faith. In 1985 the Extraordinary Synod of bishops, called to assess the accomplishments of Vatican II, also stressed the need to transform culture:

> Because the Church is a communion which joins diversity and unity in being present throughout the world, it takes from every culture all that it encounters of positive value. Yet inculturation is different from a simple external adaptation because it means the intimate transformation of authentic cultural values through their integration in Christianity in the various human cultures.[9]

John Paul II's 1990 encyclical, *Redemptoris Missio,* represents a further articulation of how the church benefits from inculturation; yet there is still little awareness of *inter*culturation, with respect to how the gifts of particular cultures might transform the whole church:

> Through inculturation the Church makes the Gospel incarnate in different cultures and at the same time introduces peoples, together with their cultures, into her own community. She transmits to them her own values, at the same time taking the good elements that already exist in them and renewing them from within (cf. EN, no. 20). Through inculturation the Church, for her part, becomes a more intelligible sign of what she is, and a more effective instrument of mission.[10]

The encyclicals of Pope John Paul II during the 1990s continued to stress the need of a "new evangelization" of culture,[11] calling into question many elements of postmodern U.S. culture and of the West in general as being in dire need of transformation. Even if one disagrees with some of the elements that John Paul locates in "the culture of death,"[12] it is difficult to ignore his fundamental criticism. He holds the cultures of "the North" responsible for its "soulless development model" and the "culture of consumerism," which has fueled the globalization of the economy.[13] Certainly, in failing to embrace an ethic of right relationship, based upon the gospel values of human dignity, justice, peace, and the integrity of creation, the United States in particular deserves such indictment.

How the papacy of Benedict XVI will respond to the challenge of interculturation remains to be seen. One might expect a certain wariness toward interculturation, given the characterization of contemporary culture as a "dictatorship of relativism" in his pre-conclave homily of April 2005. The pope's desire for a "clear faith" is indeed important; however, it is equally important to engage contemporary cultures in a discerning manner. How (and with whom!) will such discernment take place, so that what truly is the will of God for the church of the third millennium can be determined? There are many structures already in place for such discernment to take place. What remains to be seen is whether an intercultural discernment process can be implemented.

Inter/inculturation from the U.S. American Experience

The 1899 censure of "Americanism" in Leo XIII's *Testem Benevolentiae* produced a negative legacy regarding the possibility of an inculturated U.S. Catholicism — which seems to have had a lasting effect on the American Catholic ecclesial psyche.[14] A notable exception was the American influence exercised at Vatican II in its teaching on religious liberty. The Declaration on Religious Freedom, in fact, serves as an excellent historical example of how an inculturated U.S. Catholicism provided a gift to the universal church. Issued in 1965, *Dignitatis Humanae* was largely the work of the American Jesuit John Courtney Murray, a theologian who, ironically, had been silenced by the Vatican in the 1950s for promoting the very position espoused by the declaration.[15] There are other notable contributions to the wider church that might serve as indicators for how the inculturated Catholicism of the United States has contributed to the mission of the church. Several of them are chronicled in this book. They include events that were unsuccessful, yet will remain "dangerous memories" for later generations to unearth.[16] The particular example of interculturation that this essay wishes to lift up as a gift from the American church is one that has yet to be recognized sufficiently — either by the Vatican or by many U.S. Catholics themselves: namely, the ever increasing number of academically trained American Catholic women who serve the church as theologians.

Since Vatican II the number of Catholic women entering the fields of systematic and practical theology, church history, ethics, and biblical studies has grown enormously. Today there are more Catholic women theologians from the United States than from any other country in the world. In keeping with the understanding of *"inter*culturation" articulated above, I want to argue that this unrecognized gift needs to be acknowledged for its potential to transform and enrich the universal church. Indeed, such a transformation is already under way, particularly in the theologies that have been developed by women. It is especially urgent to foster this recognition today, since women's wisdom and experiences are not represented within the Catholic hierarchy due to the prohibition concerning the ordination of women. Given the many difficulties and obstacles Catholic women theologians have endured in following their vocations as theologians, it is important to increase awareness of this underutilized ecclesial resource.[17]

The Emergence of North American Women as Professional Theologians[18]

American Catholics growing up after the Second Vatican Council are often surprised to learn that there was a time when Catholic women did not teach or write theology. Before the council, even in Catholic women's colleges, the theology professor was often a priest, usually the college chaplain. Today, there is scarcely a Catholic college or university where women are not teaching theology or religious studies. How did such a dramatic change come about?[19]

There are at least four significant catalysts that can be cited as responsible for the emergence of the growing contingent of Catholic women theologians in the United States: (1) the Sister Formation Movement;

(2) the establishment of Catholic higher educational institutions for women; (3) the lay-led Catholic Action and volunteer service movements which, in newer incarnations, continue to foster the theological and ministerial formation of the U.S. laity; and (4) the Second Vatican Council itself. Certainly other important formative influences were also operative in the lives of American women who have become Catholic theologians, such as the civil rights, anti-war, and the secular women's liberation movements.[20]

The Sister Formation Movement

The history of U.S. Catholic women as professional theologians cannot be told without giving testimony to the women who shaped so many of the first women theologians in North America, Catholic sisters. The Sister Formation Movement, which celebrated its fiftieth anniversary in 2004, has been acknowledged only rarely for the role it played in providing the fertile soil from which would spring an educated cadre of American Catholics.[21] Thus, it is important to acknowledge the debt the U.S. Catholic Church owes to the visionary, systematic plan that revolutionized the professional training of women religious and the impact this endeavor had on the education of later generations of North American Catholic women — whether they became theologians or not.[22] As a transformative process, "it converted American sisters into the most highly educated group of nuns in the church and placed them among the most highly educated women in the United States."[23]

The beginnings of the Sister Formation Conference as a "movement" can be traced back to the 1940s, to Sister Bertrande Meyers's 1941 doctoral dissertation on "The Education of Sisters"[24] and the presentations made by Sister Madeleva Wolff, C.S.C., and Sister Mary Patrick Riley, I.H.M., to the National Catholic Education Association in 1949. The majority of teaching congregations of women religious at that time were on "the twenty-year plan" with respect to how sister-teachers who entered religious life without bachelor's degrees (which was the majority) received a college education. Meyers had urged that a plan for the updating and professionalization of sister-teachers be undertaken, and Wolfe's path-breaking lecture, "The Education of Sister Lucy," galvanized the process.[25]

Normally, during the novitiate, the one- or two-year period of spiritual formation required by most orders, young sisters traditionally received little formal education. Nevertheless, immediately after (and sometimes, even before) pronouncing her first vows, a sister was put into a classroom and charged with teaching anywhere from fifty to seventy children. She would then attend summer school for as many as fifteen summers to complete her bachelor's degree. Young women in these situations must have been desperate simply to control their charges. The postwar baby boom also put an enormous strain on the teaching orders as pastors started parochial schools in order to respond to the edict of "every child in a Catholic school."[26] The detrimental repercussions of such decisions — all made without any consultation with the teaching orders — can be seen, for example, in the predicament that faced the California Immaculate Heart Community, whose poignant story is told by Anita Caspary in *Witness to Integrity: The Crisis of the Immaculate Heart Community of California.*[27]

One of the upheavals following Vatican II was a dramatic decline in the numbers of active orders of women religious.[28] Despite the decline in membership, a number of orders that adopted the Sister Formation plan — the Adrian Dominicans, the Immaculate Heart of Mary sisters of Monroe, Michigan, the Sisters of Notre Dame de Namur, the Sisters of the Holy Name, and the Sisters of St. Joseph to name a few — began to educate their members in theology. Margaret Brennan, for example, herself a graduate of the School of Sacred Theology founded by Sister Madeleva,[29] dreamed of having a pool of sisters with doctorates from the leading faculties in Europe and North America:

> [Margaret] saw clearly that if women were to have any influence in shaping the future of the church they had to be able to speak with an educated theological voice. Those first ten voices were joined by the voices of other IHM theologians who followed their lead, prompted by Margaret's inspiration and encouragement.[30]

During the 1980s the majority of Catholic women who received doctorates in theology were members of women's religious congregations. This demographic would begin to change in the 1990s. At the present time, the majority of American Catholic women theologians are laywomen.[31]

U.S. Educational Institutions Founded by and for Women

A second important influence on many American women who have become Catholic theologians is the role played by the educational institutions for women that were established by women's religious orders, both high schools and colleges. For the most part, these single-sex institutions aimed to be "places apart, but open to the world." In the nineteenth century, several American orders of women religious established "academies," secondary boarding schools for girls, many of which later evolved into Catholic colleges for women. Although the guiding ideal for women's education right up through the 1960s was preparation for the role of wife, mother, and educator of children, by the first decades of the twentieth century, several of the schools run by nuns were noted for their highly educated women faculty.[32] Because few U.S. Catholic universities offered first-rate doctoral programs, sister-educators sought advanced degrees at Johns Hopkins, the University of California at Berkeley, the University of Chicago, the University of Michigan, Harvard, and MIT. When bishops balked at the idea of nuns studying at secular institutions, the women in charge found ingenious solutions, such as having a sister remain a postulant until she completed her degree. As a result, some sisters remained postulants for as long as five years instead of the usual six months!

Jane Redmont points out that Catholic women's colleges, despite their traditional understandings concerning women's roles in society and church, nevertheless produce "strong women, live minds, yearning spirits and enduring ties."[33] This impression is underlined in Tracy Schier and Cynthia Russett's *Catholic Women's Colleges in America,* a book that fills what, until a few years ago, was a large gap in the history of American Catholic higher education.[34] It is difficult to determine exactly how many of today's U.S. Catholic women theologians graduated from schools sponsored by women religious. Jill Ker Conway, however, affirms the abundant anecdotal testimony — that of my own and other women theologians — that suggests that students in schools sponsored by nuns were provided with role models of women who "represented a Catholic tradition of powerful intellect and religious force":

> Protestant or nondenominational women's colleges could not call
> up the tradition of Saint Catherine of Siena or Saint Teresa of

Avila, advisors to popes and respected theologians, or the magisterial rule of some of the leaders of powerful abbeys, like Hilda
of Whitby or Hildegard of Bingen. These historical figures meant
something to students who could observe Sister President or Sister
Dean daily at work running an all-female institution. So, although
Catholic women's colleges faced the same contradictions as the
rest of America about the purposes of women's education, they offered a counter social model to the standard male-headed women's
college.[35]

Among these role models, there was probably no other woman in
Catholic higher education during the 1940s equal to Sister M. Madeleva Wolff, C.S.C., the president of St. Mary's College in Notre Dame,
Indiana. In 1943, nine years into her presidency of this women's college,
Wolff discovered that there was nowhere in the United States where a
Catholic woman could obtain a doctorate in theology. Undaunted, she
decided to start one of her own.[36] Beginning with eighteen sisters in the
summer of 1943, the St. Mary's Graduate School of Sacred Theology
became the first Catholic institution in the United States (and most probably, in the entire world) to offer advanced degrees in Catholic theology
to women. In the twenty-six years of its operation the school awarded
76 doctoral degrees and 354 master's degrees, not only to Catholic
sisters, but to laywomen and laymen as well.[37] The first two U.S. Catholic women theologians admitted to the Catholic Theological Society of
America in 1965, a year after the society opened membership to "all who
were professionally competent in Sacred Theology," were graduates from
Sister Madeleva's School of Sacred Theology.[38] Other graduates from the
school assumed leadership roles in their religious communities, became
personal theologians to bishops, and served as directors of retreat centers. It is a little-known fact that the post-Christian feminist theologian
Mary Daly received her first Ph.D. from the Graduate School of Sacred
Theology.[39]

Pre–Vatican II Catholic Action Lay Movements

A third catalyst that influences many American Catholic women today to
pursue further theological studies is participation in one of the many service corps sponsored by religious orders, by non-profit, government, or

charitable agencies, or by faith-based movements. The Jesuit Volunteers (JVC), Holy Cross Volunteers, Mercy Corps, Vincentian Volunteers, Teach for America, the Peace Corps, and the Catholic Worker are just some of the organizations that offer today's youth formative experiences of living in community and working among the poor. Interestingly, many younger Catholics who participate in these programs go on to seek further education in theology.

Although the surge in lay theological education began in earnest only after Vatican II, even before the council opportunities for laity existed in the various "Catholic Action" and "lay apostolate" movements of the day, many of which provided a spiritual and apostolic formation in the lives of many young Catholics that is similar to the experience of young people in today's volunteer corps.[40] "Grailville," located in Loveland, Ohio, is one example of such a movement. The Grail, a secular institute of laywomen, hosted week-long, live-in programs for high school girls in the mid-1960s, which stressed prayer, community, manual labor on the farm, and participative liturgy. The goal of these weeks was to train women leaders who would join in the Grail's project to "Christianize" society. Group dynamics inspired by humanistic psychologist Carl Rogers, combined with the liberating pedagogy of Paulo Freire, became powerful influences on these programs. After Vatican II, Grail members developed the "Semester at Grailville" (1968–75) and the "Seminary Quarter at Grailville" (1974–78),[41] initiatives that might be regarded as precursors of today's volunteer corps. In *Women Breaking Boundaries: A Grail Journey, 1940–1995,* Janet Kalven recounts how these Grail programs were intended to be "a post-audit of [women's] educational experience." She describes how the U.S. Grail movement began as a vision to provide "a novitiate for the laity" in the early 1940s.[42] Her account of the growth and transformation of the Grail is an important bellwether in the history of U.S. Catholic women and offers many lessons to ponder as Catholic theology today becomes increasingly lay-centered.[43]

The Catholic Worker is another example of a formative, lay-led movement that has been influential in the lives of many Catholic theologians, both women and men. Peter Maurin and Dorothy Day's practice of Christian personalism and nonviolence aimed at creating a harmonious balance of urban living with agrarian spirituality through the establishment of houses of hospitality and Catholic Worker farms. An interesting experiment located in South Bend, Indiana, is a Catholic Worker community founded by two theologians, one of them a woman professor at the University of Notre Dame.[44]

The Second Vatican Council

Probably more than any other formative factor, Vatican II was the catalyst that promoted enthusiasm for the study of theology among the laity, particularly women. The shifts in theology that the council ushered in demanded educational updating. With theological education no longer looked upon as only the province of the ordained, many women took advantage of the new opportunities that were open to the laity.[45] Even though women were not invited to the council until its third session,[46] Vatican II opened a door for women to become more involved in the U.S. Catholic Church beyond serving as nurses in Catholic hospitals or teachers in Catholic schools. It would not be long before the influx of women seeking credentials for the new ministries and teaching opportunities that began to open up would start to flood seminaries and theological schools. By their very presence women would usher in changes to the questions and subject matter of Catholic theology.[47]

The Development of Feminist Theologies:
A U.S. Gift to the Universal Church

Robert Schreiter, in *The New Catholicity: Theology between the Global and the Local,* uses the concept of global theological "flows" to explain how cultural and ritual movements are able to "move across geographical and cultural boundaries, and, like a river, define a route, change the landscape and leave behind sediment and silt that enrich the local ecology."[48] While religion may not qualify as a "global system" in the same way as politics or economics, global theological discourses, or "flows," play an "antisystemic" role by offering the *telos* that global systems lack: a vision of coherence and order. According to Schreiter, they represent theological discourses that comprise

> ...a series of linked, mutually intelligible discourses that address
> the contradictions or failures of global systems.... They speak out

of the realm of religious beliefs and practices. They are not uniform or systemic.... Yet they are intelligible to discourses in other cultural and social settings that are experiencing the same failure of global systems and who are raising the same kind of protest.[49]

Of the four global theological flows[50] that Schreiter regards as playing a significant role in today's world, feminism, especially feminist theologies, stands out as the key contribution of U.S. women theologians. As a global theological flow, "feminist theologies point to the failure of global systems to live up to the values of equality and inclusion."[51] They work on several levels to address failures in the realms of education, politics, and social advancement, "by analyzing the situations and systems of oppression, by reconstructing theological histories to foreground women and lift the silence, by constructing theologies as resources for women's identity."[52]

As mentioned above, the 1970s saw increasing numbers of Catholic women entering higher education, assuming positions of ministerial leadership, and attending seminaries and theological schools. The result of this influx was that the traditional theological disciplines began to be reshaped by the questions and concerns of these women. Feminist theologies began in the United States "out of and alongside of the women's emancipation movement of the 1960s," as Schreiter notes, and have now spread to all continents.[53] While some have considered the feminist theological perspective an "unwanted export" of globalization, Susan Frank Parsons's evaluation underscores Schreiter's observation that it now constitutes a significant global theological flow:

As knowledge of and interaction with peoples of diverse cultural and religious backgrounds was expanding in the late twentieth century, so opportunities for the development of intercultural and interfaith relationships became available. Ordinary women from all parts of the world began to know one another, to discover common problems, to be challenged by unfamiliar ways of life, of speaking, and of understanding and to be returned to their own traditions with new questions. This has led to a scholarly interest in the place of women in religious practices, institutions, and beliefs, and in the impact of these things upon women's lives and welfare.[54]

It is beyond the scope of this essay to recount the history of the development of feminist theologies; what is important is to point out that U.S. Catholic women pioneered this significant theological movement.[55] And if anything is certain after more than thirty-five years of academic theological writing produced by these women, it is that so-called "feminist theology" is pluralistic. Thus, any attempt to convey the impact of this perspective must attend to, in the words of Kwok Pui-lan, "the multicultural, multivocal and multireligious character of women's expressions of faith that bear witness to the inclusive and compassionate God."[56]

No matter how the story is told, however, three U.S. Catholic laywomen, Mary Daly, Rosemary Radford Ruether, and Elisabeth Schüssler Fiorenza, can be considered as having charted the course of feminist theologies. Although Daly has long since repudiated Catholicism, her 1968 book, *The Church and the Second Sex,* still is widely regarded by many as inaugurating the ferment that would become known as "feminist theology."[57] Ruether's early work, *New Woman, New Earth: Sexist Ideologies and Human Liberation,* first published in 1975, pointed to dualistic thinking as the common denominator linking racism, sexism, anti-Semitism, and ecological destruction.[58] As a critical principle to be used in evaluating feminist constructive or reconstructive theological work, Ruether proposed the criterion of "that which promoted the full humanity of women" in her foundational work *Sexism and God-Talk.*[59] Elisabeth Schüssler Fiorenza, though not a U.S. citizen, has spent most of her professional life as a theologian in the United States. For her, feminist theology is a "critical theology of liberation."[60] According to this conceptualization, "doing" feminist theology means that one (1) starts from the experiences of women's suffering and oppression, caused by the structures of patriarchy in church and society; (2) utilizes a "hermeneutics of suspicion," as well as a "hermeneutics of retrieval," in order to bring a critical lens to the traditional beliefs and practices which justify women's oppression, to unmask "*his* story" and, where possible, recover the lost traditions concerning women (*her* story); (3) takes an upfront, "advocacy" stance for women and the goal of women's liberation (as opposed to so-called "academic neutrality") and works to effect the transformation of patriarchal structures and patterns that justify male dominance; and (4) seeks to reconstruct the symbols of "the tradition" in an inclusive and liberating way, by restoring and re-imagining women's contribution to faith communities.

Catholic feminist theologians who have succeeded these pioneers comprise a veritable litany that bears witness to the intercultural character of U.S. feminist theologies today. Thus, in addition to white, Anglo, feminist theologians such as Anne Carr, Lisa Sowle Cahill, Elizabeth Johnson, Catherine LaCugna, Mary Catherine Hilkert, Mary E. Hines, Susan Ross, Sandra Schneiders, Mary Jo Weaver, and many others, since the mid-1980s, U.S. women theologians have included Latina/Mujerista theologians such as Ada María Isasi-Díaz, Yolanda Tarango, María Pilar Aquino, Jeannette Rodríguez, Michelle González and Nancy Pineda-Madrid. The Catholic contingent of African American/Womanist theologians includes Toinette Eugene, Diana L. Hayes, M. Shawn Copeland, Jamie T. Phelps, and Stephanie Mitchem. Although Asian feminist theologians have long contributed in the global arena of feminist theological discourse, Asian American Catholic women have just begun to enter the intercultural discourse that characterizes U.S. Catholic feminist theology today.[61]

A Missed Opportunity in Interculturation

Given its status as a "global theological flow," one would think that the important contribution of feminist theologians would have had greater influence on the official teaching of the Catholic Church. However, until recently the Vatican mostly has taken a critical view of feminism and rarely, if ever, has seriously addressed feminist theologies or the work of Catholic women theologians.[62] The statements dealing with women that were issued by Pope John Paul II during his pontificate, while acknowledging roles for women in the church, tended to ignore the major contributions of feminist theologians and depended upon the anthropological view of sex complementarity held by such theologians as Hans Urs von Balthasar.[63] The mention of a "new feminism" in John Paul II's 1995 encyclical *Evangelium Vitae* is rather remarkable and, at first glance, would appear to indicate that the pope was listening to the global theological flow of feminism.[64] Specifically urging women "to transform culture so that it supports life" — not in itself an objectionable call — singles out women for bearing exceptional responsibility to promote life. Thus the "new feminism" canonizes the theological anthropology of sex complementarity, a position that the majority of U.S. feminist theologians reject. The fact that little or no interaction with the global theological flow of feminism took place in the pontificate of John Paul II was made evident in a document from the Congregation for the Doctrine of the Faith, "Letter to Bishops of the Catholic Church on the Collaboration of Men and Women in the Church and the World," which was issued with the pope's approval in 2004.[65]

The secular press greeted the document predictably, with an outcry regarding Vatican intransigence, noting its romantic view of women, its castigation of "radical feminism" (something which few Catholic feminist theologians actually endorse), its continued denial of priestly ordination to women (the document insists that such exclusion "does not hamper in any way women's access to the heart of Christian life"). As in previous papal documents, the Congregation for Doctrine of the Faith (CDF) continues to stress sexual difference ("a fundamental component of personality"), women's vocation to love and nurture life, and her primary responsibility for human relationships (seen in her "capacity for the other"). Most disturbing is that the 2004 document caricatures contemporary feminism as giving rise to antagonism, making women adversaries of men, and adamantly resists the notion that sexual difference might be socially constructed.

Needless to say, many Catholic women theologians who responded to the document assumed there was no consultation with women, let alone women theologians. Thus Tina Beattie asked,

> What other institution today would produce a document about women, written by one group of men (the Congregation for the Doctrine of the Faith, under the signature of Cardinal Ratzinger), addressed to another (the bishops), without quoting or referring to any women's ideas? Given that the letter is titled "On the Collaboration of Men and Women in the Church and in the World," its lack of collaboration with women is slightly ludicrous.[66]

Sidney Callahan, writing in *Commonweal,* also saw "no evidence of women's theological collaboration," despite its stated goal to serve as "a starting point" and "an impetus for dialogue."[67]

Ironically, there *was* consultation with women on the "Collaboration of Men and Women" document. But this fact was known only to the bishops who received this summary statement accompanying Cardinal Ratzinger's transmittal letter:

> This document, *prepared with the help of women especially competent in this field*, focuses first on some questionable theories of the human person currently in discussion. The document then gives the Church's perspective, in light of the biblical understanding of the human person, elucidating the concepts which underpin a correct understanding of active collaboration, in the recognition of their difference, between men and women. A reflection follows on the importance today of feminine values in the life of society and in the Church, as a starting point for further reflection on these issues in conversation with all men and women of good will.[68]

Since no names of the "women especially competent in this field" are mentioned, one can only speculate who they might be. A number of names come to mind, such as Mary Shivanandan, Monica Migliorino Miller, Janet Smith, Barbara Hallensleben, or Michele Schumacher. Schumacher had just edited a collection of essays espousing the pope's "new feminism."[69] Shivanandan, a professor at the John Paul II Institute in Washington, D.C., is author of *Crossing the Threshold of Love: A New Vision of Marriage in the Light of John Paul II's Anthropology.*[70] Smith is a philosopher and editor of *Why Humanae Vitae Was Right: A Reader*[71] and Hallensleben, whose German commentary on the CDF document can be found online, is one of the first two women John Paul II appointed to the International Theological Commission.[72]

Meeting the Challenge of Interculturation:
A First Step

While it is laudable that women theologians finally have been admitted to the International Theological Commission and even more laudable that the Vatican consulted women in this most recent document (though in a very clandestine way), all the other magisterial documents dealing with women have failed to attend to what Robert Schreiter calls "intercultural hermeneutics."[73] If truly appropriate and effective intercultural communication is going to take place in the church concerning such a major theological issue as what it means to be human as male and female, then ought there not be much wider theological consultation? It is my contention that with respect to this issue the church has missed an important opportunity in ignoring the "gift" that U.S. Catholic women theologians are offering to the universal church.

A first step in recognizing the gift that American women theologians might bring involves listening to the plurality of feminist theological discourses that are present within an inculturated U.S. Catholicism and in other Catholic cultures throughout the world. The very emphasis on relationality which characterizes Pope John Paul II's personalist anthropology argues for such dialogue. When a multiplicity of voices are heard and listened to, there is the possibility of both mutual critique and enrichment. This can occur, however, only if there is a genuine commitment to interculturation, including an understanding that God's revelation in Christ (in this case, concerning the meaning of being human as male and female) is not the possession or a commodity of any one particular culture. Rather, interculturation regards revelation as a dynamic, Spirit-filled reality that is always being constructed in relation to others' experience of the same Spirit. Only with this kind of engagement will there be any hope of what Robert Schreiter has called "a new catholicity" in our postmodern, globalized culture. In these still beginning days of the third millennium, it would be a shame to keep on ignoring the theological wisdom that American Catholic women might contribute to an intercultural theology.

Chapter 4

The Participation of the Laity in Decision-Making in the Church

An Example from American History and Present Possibilities

FRANCIS A. SULLIVAN, S.J.

MY CONTRIBUTION to the study of the inculturation of the Catholic Church in the United States is based on the premise that a good way to measure the degree to which our church has adapted itself to the positive aspects of the democratic culture of our nation is by the opportunities that the church provides for the participation of the laity in its decision-making.

One can distinguish four periods in the history of the American Catholic Church on the basis of the participation of the laity in decision-making. During the colonial period and that of the early Republic, i.e., until the 1830s, laymen played a decisive role through the trustee system, which gave to laymen legal control of the parish property, and in some cases led to their claiming the right to hire and fire the parish priest. The following half-century was the unique conciliar period in the history of the American Catholic Church, during which the bishops held no less than ten national councils, seven provincial and three plenary. Through the laws enacted by these councils, the bishops gradually gained control of all church property, with the consequent concentration of decision-making in the hierarchy. During the century from the Third Council of Baltimore in 1884 to the promulgation of the new Code of Canon Law in 1983, the laity played no significant role in decision-making in our church. As we shall see in the second part of this essay, the new Code has opened up a number of possibilities for such lay participation which, if fully implemented, could bring about some welcome changes in the life of the American Catholic Church.

An Example from American Church History

What I shall do in the first part of this essay is describe how one bishop eliminated the abuses to which the trustee system was prone and at the same time gave to the laymen who had formed the congregations and built the churches a significant role in deciding how they should be governed. The bishop I have in mind is John England, who became the first bishop of the newly created diocese of Charleston in 1820 and governed that diocese until his death in 1842. Although he was largely responsible for the inauguration of the series of councils through which the bishops gained control of all church property, John England proposed a different solution to the problem of trusteeism. One can only speculate how different the history of the American Catholic Church might have been if the other bishops had recognized the soundness of John England's ideas and followed his lead. Instead, they judged his proposal too democratic and rejected it.

Fortunately, he spelled out his ideas in a written constitution, which is published in his *Works*.[1] I think it can be instructive to know what provisions he made in this constitution for the participation of the laity in decision-making. But first I must say something about John England and about the situation that he faced when he became the bishop of Charleston.

John England was born in Cork, Ireland, in 1786, entered the seminary at the age of sixteen, and was ordained to the priesthood in 1808. While serving as a priest in Cork, he was also editor of a newspaper and rector of a seminary, and he took an active part in promoting public opposition to a proposed concordat between the Vatican and the British government that would have given that government a veto over the appointment of bishops for Ireland. When the Vatican Congregation for the Propagation of the Faith established the diocese of Charleston, it named John England as its first bishop. He was ordained to the episcopate in Cork and arrived in Charleston on December 30, 1820, to assume the leadership of a diocese consisting of three states: North and

South Carolina and Georgia. When he arrived, the Catholics in that region were being served by a total of five priests. The largest Catholic churches were in Charleston, Savannah, Augusta, and Columbia, and there were small congregations of Catholics in a number of other places. The building of churches was at the initiative of laymen, who pooled their resources, bought a piece of land, built a church, obtained legal status for the congregation as a corporation, and elected some of their members as trustees. The trustee system was accepted by the first bishop of the church in America, John Carroll, as a practical necessity for the legal protection of the congregations and their property. However, problems arose when the articles of incorporation gave the trustees unlimited control over the local church, which led them to claim the right to name the pastor and to dismiss him if they found him unsatisfactory.

During the five years prior to John England's arrival, such a claim on the part of the trustees of the church in Charleston had brought them into open rebellion against John Carroll's successors as archbishops of Baltimore: Leonard Neale (1815–17) and Ambrose Maréchal (1817–28). They had both attempted to remove two Irish-born priests whom the trustees wanted to retain and to appoint a French-born priest whom the trustees rejected. The problem was compounded by the fact that the two Irish-born priests sided with the trustees in their rebellion. Fr. Benedict Fenwick (later to be bishop of Boston), whom Archbishop Maréchal sent to Charleston in 1819 as his vicar, managed to defuse the schism so that John England found his episcopal see in a state of relative peace when he arrived. But he was well aware of the trouble he could have with his board of trustees, especially when he found that their statutes excluded the parish priest from membership in their board and gave them absolute control of the administration of the local church.

England spent his first year as bishop traveling, first on a visitation of his own vast diocese and then visiting the other episcopal sees, getting to know their bishops and the state of their churches. He returned to Charleston convinced of the necessity of particular legislation for the church in the United States that would remedy the abuses of trusteeism but would also be appropriately adapted to the American style of government and the character of the American people. He was convinced that such legislation should be enacted by a council of the American bishops, but finding Archbishop Maréchal unwilling to convoke a council, he decided to draw up a constitution for his own diocese. During the next two years he studied the Constitution of the United States and the laws of the states of his diocese and consulted a number of legal experts. He also studied the constitutions of several American Protestant churches, in particular the one that the Protestant Episcopal Church had adopted in 1789. On September 25, 1823, he wrote in his diary:

> Having paid great attention to the state of several Churches in America, and studied as deeply as I could the character of the government and the people, and the circumstances of my own flock, as well as the Canons and usages of the Holy Roman Catholic Church, and having advised with religious men and Clergymen, and lawyers, I this day, after consultation and prayer in the Church of St. Finnbar, published the Constitution by which the Roman Catholic Church under my charge is to be regulated, and I trust with the blessing of Heaven much disputation and Infidelity restrained. It was subscribed by the Clergy and by many well-disposed Laymen.[2]

What is most distinctive of his constitution is summed up in a statement that England made in a letter he wrote ten years later to the cardinal-prefect of Propaganda. Referring to his constitution, he said, "By these rules . . . the laity are empowered to cooperate but not to dominate."[3] The same letter makes it clear that the acceptance of these rules was not achieved without difficulty. He wrote, "I had to induce the various congregations to accept this Code; since in America the congregations cannot be legally held without their voluntary acceptance. In this endeavour I encountered many difficulties. . . . Now, however, thanks be to God, that code has been generally accepted by my flock."[4]

John England's Constitution of the Diocese of Charleston

England's constitution is based on a distinction between the church as a spiritual body, consisting of all the Catholic men, women, and children in his diocese, and the diocese as a corporation, consisting only of the clergy and the adult male lay Catholics resident in the diocese who have subscribed their assent to this constitution.[5] Only members of the corporation could vote and be elected to office. The preface explains that the system of government of the Roman Catholic Church is divided into two parts, the one of divine institution and the other of human regulation, and that it has always been the rule that in making those regulations the principal, *if not the exclusive power of legislation*, should be vested in the bishops.[6] The part of the system that is the result of human regulation is further divided. It comprises both ecclesiastical discipline and the regulation of temporalities. The first of these is necessarily under the exclusive regulation of the bishops. Various arrangements have been made in the course of history for the role of lay persons in the regulation of temporalities. "One great principle, however, was kept sacred and inviolable throughout, viz.: that the management of ecclesiastical affairs was solely in the prelates, and that they had *at least a negative* upon the management of church property."[7] It was this "great principle" that England proceeded to follow in his constitution, which grants to laymen a positive role in the management of church property but limits it by the possibility of the bishop's veto of their decision in a number of major areas.

The preface is followed by a profession of faith in the doctrines of the Roman Catholic Church and a profession of belief with regard to the principles by which the church is governed. Members of the corporation must subscribe to these doctrines and beliefs, the latter of which includes the following: "We do not believe that our Lord Jesus Christ gave to the faithful at large the government of the Church, nor any power to regulate spiritual or ecclesiastical concerns."[8] "We therefore disavow and disclaim any right or power, under any pretext, in the laity to subject the ministry of the church to their control, or to interfere in the regulation of their sacred duties."[9] It is obvious that such a profession was aimed at the elimination of the abuses of the trustee system, which had caused a schism in Charleston and would continue to plague the churches of Philadelphia and New York for some time.

The Management of the Temporalities of the Local Churches

The diocese was divided into districts, only some of which had been canonically erected as parishes. The constitution prescribed that "in each district there shall be, for the management of the temporalities, a vestry, consisting of the clergyman or clergymen of that district, and of a number of laymen to be chosen by the members of that district."[10] The members of the district would decide how many lay members their vestry was to have, and they would meet each year on the first Sunday of January to elect the members of the vestry for that year. "The churches, cemeteries, lands, houses, funds, or other property belonging to any particular district, shall be made the property of the vestry of that district, in trust for the same." However, the vestry's power to make decisions concerning that property was not unlimited. "The vestry shall not have power to sell, nor to alienate, nor to let for any term, any part of the real estate or property without the consent of the bishop or vicar. No church shall be built, or taken down, or removed, or materially altered...without the consent of the bishop or vicar."[11]

> For the validity of an act of vestry there will be required the assent of a majority of the lay members who may be present, and of the proper clergyman, — or in case of the refusal of the clergyman, the assent of the bishop or of the vicar.... But in making contracts or agreements for the performance of any work or duty which shall have been directed by an act of vestry, and in all elections and appointments to be made by the vestry, no clergyman shall have a negative power, but shall only possess his right of precedence and his right of vote.... The vestry shall have the right of electing the organist, the clerk, the sexton, and the other lay-officers or servants of the church; also they have the appointment of their own secretary and treasurer, and of the church wardens of their district.... The vestry shall every year lay a fair and correct statement of their accounts and of the situation of the church before the congregation, and another before the bishop. Should the vestry of the district be displeased with the conduct of the clergyman of the same, they shall have power...to assemble without the clergyman, for the sole purpose of conferring together upon their cause of complaint and of embodying the same in writing; to be immediately transmitted to the bishop or his vicar for his judgment thereupon.[12]

The vestry could appeal against the bishop's decision to a higher ecclesiastical tribunal, but they must abide by his decision until it is set aside by the higher tribunal.

The Annual Convention

It is probable that in his legislation concerning the annual convention Bishop England was influenced by the constitution that the Protestant Episcopal Church had adopted in 1789. Members of the convention were to be the bishop or his vicar, the clergy having spiritual jurisdiction in the diocese, and lay delegates from each district of the diocese. The lay delegates were to be chosen by the voters of their district, the number from each district being in proportion to its Catholic population. The convention began with the celebration of Mass, at which Bishop England regularly gave an address. Then the house of the clergy and the house of lay delegates met separately for business and each elected its own president. The constitution listed the matters on which the convention had no authority: the doctrine and discipline of the church, the administration of sacraments and ceremonies of the church, spiritual jurisdiction, ecclesiastical appointments, ordinations, and the superintendence of the clergy. The convention was not to be considered as a portion of the ecclesiastical government of the church, but "rather as a body of sage, prudent and religious counselors to aid the proper ecclesiastical governor of the church in the discharge of his duty." It had authority to dispose of the general fund of the church, to examine into and to control expenditures made from that fund, to regulate and control, with the exception of their spiritual concerns, all establishments of its own creation, and to appoint the lay-officers and servants of such establishments. For an act of convention to be valid, it had to be passed by a majority of both houses and assented to by the bishop or his vicar. In a matter where the convention had no authority to act, either house could submit advice or present a request to the bishop, on which "he will bestow his best consideration at the earliest opportunity, and, as far as his conscientious obligations will permit, and the welfare of the church will allow, and the honour and glory of Almighty God, in his judgment require, he will endeavour to follow such advice or to agree to such request."[13]

The General Fund of the Diocese and the General Trustees

Every layman of the diocese was required to contribute a sum of two dollars each year toward the general fund of the diocese. The main purposes of this fund were the erection and maintenance of the cathedral, the erection and support of the diocesan seminary, and giving aid to missionaries for ministry in the poor and neglected parts of the diocese. The property for the general purposes of the church, whether real or of other kind, was vested in a board called "The General Trustees of the Roman Catholic Church of the Diocese of Charleston." This board consisted of the bishop, his vicar, five other clergymen chosen by the clergy at the annual convention, and twelve laymen, to be chosen by the house of lay delegates at the annual convention. The treasurer of the general fund was to be chosen every year at the convention, by the joint vote of both houses voting together, and approved by the bishop. The board of general trustees had no power to expend any part of the general fund, except in conformity to an order or act of the general convention of the church, unless where some unusual and unforeseen occurrence would clearly render the expenditure of a small sum prudent and beneficial to the church.[14]

Implementation of the Constitution

Since the Catholic Church was at different levels of organization in the three states that constituted his diocese, Bishop England decided to begin with the church in South Carolina. He invited the clergy and a number of laymen of that state to meet on September 25, 1823, at the cathedral in Charleston and presented the constitution to them. Finding them well disposed to it, he convoked the first convention of the Catholic Church in South Carolina, which assembled two months later. He explained the terms of the constitution, which was still in manuscript, to the gathered members. They voted to approve it and passed a motion to have copies printed. At the next Convention, in 1824, when printed copies were not yet available, England explained the delay as due to the fact that some amendments were still to be decided on and further said, "We have also sent an abstract of the constitution, in the Latin language, to Rome, for inspection, and to be informed whether it was in any part in opposition to the general discipline of the church, and we thought it right to delay the execution of the order [for printing] until the decision and the judgment of Rome should be known."[15] In the preface to the constitution England says, "The outline of the entire, together with some of the most important of its special provisions, was laid before the Holy See.... No objection having been received from that quarter, and its provisions having been maturely examined and tested by some experience, it is now published for the use of the members."[16] Guilday says, "Whether the Holy See ever gave its formal approval of the constitution is not clear from the fragmentary documents at our disposal."[17] What does seem clear to me is that England did not think it necessary to get formal approval of his constitution from Rome. It sufficed that within at least a year, "no objection had been received from that quarter."

On the other hand, he did receive plenty of objection from some of his fellow bishops in America. One who was particularly vehement in his criticism of the constitution was Bishop Conwell of Philadelphia, who said, in a letter to the cardinal prefect of Propaganda Fide, "If this Constitution or *democratic* method of ruling the church be approved by the Holy See, it might become necessary to extend it to all the dioceses here, and it would mean the quick collapse of the American church.... It is to be hoped that the sanction of the Sacred Congregation will be withheld from this, or at least supreme caution be used, for if it were once sanctioned, ecclesiastical liberty would end in this country."[18] (I suspect that by "ecclesiastical liberty" he meant the freedom of the bishops to exercise absolute control over their churches.)

In any case, despite the opposition from his fellow bishops, England went ahead with the gradual implementation of the constitution. Annual conventions of the church in South Carolina were held every year beginning in 1823, in Georgia every year beginning in 1826, and in North Carolina every year beginning in 1829. In 1839, delegates from the three states met in the first convention of the church of the diocese, held in the cathedral of St. Finnbar, in Charleston. Annual diocesan conventions were then held each year until 1842, when John England died. None was held by his successor, Ignatius Reynolds, who admired England enough to publish his works but shared the opposition of the other bishops to his constitution. None of them chose to follow it in the government of his diocese. In my opinion, if they had seen the wisdom of his constitution that "empowered the laity to cooperate but not to dominate," they could have brought the Catholic Church in the United States to a level of inculturation it has not yet achieved.

The Participation of the Laity in Decision-Making in the Catholic Church Today

Having looked at this example of lay participation in the early history of the American church, we shall now consider the possibilities for such participation that have been opened up by the Second Vatican Council and the new Code of Canon Law.

Participation of the Laity Encouraged by Vatican II

Vatican II's Dogmatic Constitution on the Church laid the groundwork for a new era of participation of the laity in decision-making with its teaching on the church as "people of God," in which "all the faithful enjoy a true equality with regard to the dignity and the activity which they share in the building up of the body of Christ."[19] "To the extent of their knowledge, competence or authority the laity are entitled, and indeed sometimes duty-bound, to express their opinion on matters which concern the good of the church. Should the occasion arise, this should be done through the institutions established by the church for that purpose."[20] In its Decree on the Pastoral Ministry of Bishops, the council went on to say: "In exercising their ministry, bishops should ensure that the faithful are duly involved in church affairs; they should recognize their right and duty to play their part in building up the mystical body of Christ."[21] In the same document the council proposed and highly recommended a new structure for such involvement of the laity in church affairs, saying, "It is highly desirable that in every diocese a special pastoral council be established, presided over by the diocesan bishop himself, in which clergy, religious, and laity specially chosen for the purpose will participate. It will be the function of this council to investigate and consider matters relating to pastoral activity and to formulate practical conclusions concerning them."[22]

The council also decreed that after the close of the council, the Holy See should prepare a *Directory on the Pastoral Ministry of Bishops,* which would offer to the bishops guidelines for the implementation of the conciliar decree. This *Directory,* issued by the authority of Pope Paul VI in 1973, has the following to say about the diocesan pastoral council:

The pastoral council is a body set up to investigate and carefully consider whatever pertains to diocesan pastoral activities and to arrive at practical conclusions to help the People of God pattern their lives and actions more closely on the Gospel. By its study and reflection, the council furnishes the judgments necessary to enable the diocesan community to plan its pastoral program systematically and fulfill it effectively. Although the pastoral council is not mandatory, it is highly recommended. It is made up of clergy (deacons, therefore, being in no wise excepted), religious and laity, specially chosen by the bishop. The council has only a consultative voice; nevertheless, the bishop has great respect for its recommendations, for they offer his apostolic office the serious and settled cooperation of the ecclesiastical community. To make the council's work more effective, the bishop can order, if the good of the faithful requires it, that in every parish, among the other offices of the apostolate, parish pastoral councils be set up and that these be aligned with the diocesan council. These councils, grouped together according to areas, could choose their representatives to serve on the diocesan council, so that the whole diocesan community may feel that it is offering its cooperation to its bishop through the diocesan council.[23]

Participation of the Laity Encouraged by Pope John Paul II

After the Synod of Bishops on the Laity, Pope John Paul issued his apostolic exhortation *Christifideles Laici,* in which we find the following statements encouraging the use of structures in which the laity are enabled to participate in the process of decision-making in the church:

> The participation of the lay faithful in *Diocesan synods* and in *local councils,* whether provincial or plenary, is envisioned by the Code of Canon Law. These structures could contribute to Church communion and the mission of the particular Church, both in its own surroundings and in relation to the other particular Churches of the ecclesiastical province or Episcopal Conference. Episcopal Conferences are called upon to evaluate the most opportune way of developing the consultation and the collaboration of the lay faithful, women and men, at a national or regional level, so that

they may consider well the problems they share and manifest better the communion of the whole Church. The recent Synod [on the Laity] has favored the creation of *Diocesan Pastoral Councils* as a recourse at opportune times. In fact, on a diocesan level this structure could be the principal form of collaboration, dialogue, and discernment as well. The participation of the lay faithful in these Councils can broaden resources in consultation and the principle of collaboration—and in certain instances also in decision-making—if applied in a broad and determined manner.[24]

The council's mention of examining and solving pastoral problems "by general discussion" ought to find its adequate and structured development through a more convinced, extensive, and decided appreciation for "Parish Pastoral Councils," on which the Synod Fathers have rightly insisted.[25]

More recently, in *Pastores Gregis*, his exhortation on the ministry of bishops, John Paul II said:

Ecclesial communion in its organic structure calls for personal responsibility on the part of the Bishop, but it also presupposes the participation of every category of the faithful, inasmuch as they share responsibility for the good of the particular church which they themselves form.... A lived ecclesial communion will lead the Bishop to a pastoral style which is ever more open to collaboration with all. There is a type of reciprocal interplay between what a Bishop is called to decide with personal responsibility for the good of the Church entrusted to his care and the contribution that the faithful can offer him through consultative bodies such as the Diocesan Synod, the Presbyteral Council, the Episcopal Council and the Pastoral Council. The particular Church involves not only the threefold episcopal ministry but also the threefold prophetic, priestly and kingly function of the entire People of God.[26]

John Paul II stressed this same theme in the address that he gave to the bishops of Pennsylvania and New Jersey on the occasion of their *ad limina* visit in 2004. Speaking of the church's need of "a purifying reevaluation of her institutions in the light of the Gospel," the pope said:

In the present circumstances of the Church in America, this will entail a spiritual discernment and critique of certain styles of governance which, even in the name of a legitimate concern for good "administration" and responsible oversight, can run the risk of distancing the pastor from the members of his flock, and obscuring his image as their father and brother in Christ. In this regard, the Synod of Bishops acknowledged the need today for each Bishop to develop a "pastoral style which is ever more open to collaboration with all" (*Pastores gregis* 44), grounded in a clear understanding of the relationship between the ministerial priesthood and the common priesthood of the faithful (cf. *Lumen gentium* 10). While the Bishop himself remains responsible for the authoritative decisions which he is called to make in the exercise of his pastoral governance, ecclesial communion also "presupposes the participation of every category of the faithful, inasmuch as they share responsibility for the good of the particular Church which they themselves form" (*Pastores gregis* loc. cit.). Within a sound ecclesiology of communion, a commitment to creating better structures of participation, consultation and shared responsibility should not be misunderstood as a concession to a secular "democratic" model of governance, but as an intrinsic requirement of the exercise of episcopal authority and a necessary means of strengthening that authority.[27]

Structures of Participation in the 1983 Code of Canon Law

Plenary Council

An episcopal conference can take the initiative to convoke a plenary council of the church of its nation or region. The plenary council has much more extensive power to make laws for the church in its region than the episcopal conference does. Another difference from the meetings of the conference is that there only the bishops take part, whereas in a plenary council many others besides the bishops either must or may be invited to participate and thus are entitled to express their opinion on whatever is being discussed, with consultative voice. Those who must be invited are a number of superiors of religious orders, both men and women; the presidents of Catholic universities in the region, the deans

of faculties of theology and canon law, and a number of rectors of seminaries. Other priests and lay persons may be invited to participate; their
number must not exceed one-third of the total. Others, who may be from
other churches, may be invited as observers.[28]

Provincial Council

The provincial council has authority to make particular laws for its own
ecclesiastical province, which is a group of neighboring dioceses, one
of which is the archdiocese, whose bishop is the metropolitan. Rules of
membership correspond to those for the plenary council, which means
that here also members of the clergy and laity may be invited to participate, making up one-third of the whole assembly.[29] In addition, there is a
special provision for provincial councils: that the presbyteral council and
the pastoral council of each diocese of the province is to send two of its
members, chosen in a collegial manner, to participate with consultative
vote.[30]

Diocesan Synod

We know from the letters of St. Cyprian, bishop of Carthage in the third
century, that lay people took part in diocesan synods in the early church.
However, for many centuries a diocesan synod has simply been a meeting
of the bishop with his clergy. It is therefore an innovation when the 1983
Code describes a diocesan synod as "a group of selected priests and other
Christian faithful of a particular church which offers assistance to the
diocesan bishop for the good of the diocesan community." Its members
must include representatives of the religious and laity of the diocese,
who are to be chosen by the diocesan pastoral council. The diocesan
bishop makes the final decisions, but first he must listen to what the other
participants have to say, since, according to the law, "all the proposed
questions are subject to the free discussion of the members during the
sessions of the synod."[31]

Diocesan Pastoral Council

While a diocesan synod takes place only when convoked by the bishop,
the pastoral council has a continuing existence. Its establishment was
termed "highly desirable" by Vatican II, as we have seen above. The
Code of Canon Law falls short of the council on this point, saying only

that a diocesan pastoral council is to be established in each diocese to the extent that pastoral circumstances recommend it. It describes it as consisting of clergy, religious, and especially of lay persons, to be designated in a manner determined by the diocesan bishop. The pastoral council has the responsibility to examine matters relating to the pastoral works of the diocese and to propose practical conclusions about them. It serves as a consultative organ for the bishop, who must convoke it at least once a year.[32]

Diocesan Finance Council

In each diocese a finance council is to be established, composed of at least three of the faithful, expert in financial affairs and civil law. The bishop must consult this council on more important acts of financial administration and, to make extraordinary expenditures, he needs its consent.[33]

Parish Pastoral Council

If the bishop considers it opportune, a pastoral council is to be established in each parish. In this council, members of the laity, together with those who by virtue of their office are engaged in pastoral care in the parish, give their advice to the parish priest in fostering pastoral action.[34]

Parish Finance Council

Each parish must have a finance council, in which the Christian faithful aid the pastor in the administration of parish goods.[35]

Conclusion

It is striking how many of the provisions of the 1983 Code of Canon Law, which have opened up new opportunities for the participation of the laity in decision-making in the church, were anticipated in the constitution that Bishop England drew up for the diocese of Charleston almost two hundred years ago. It seems a fitting conclusion to this essay to recall the many points of similarity between his constitution and the new Code on the role of the laity in the church.

In 1820, and still in 1917, a diocesan synod was simply a meeting of a local bishop with his clergy. The laity had no part in it. When Bishop

England saw the urgent need of legislation that would solve the problem of trusteeism in his church, he recognized that if such legislation were to succeed in its purpose, it could not be enacted by a diocesan synod in which the laity would have no part. He could not change canon law regarding the diocesan synod. His solution was to draw up a constitution and present it to a representative body of the laymen of his diocese, making it clear to them that it would be enacted into law only if they accepted it. This constitution further involved the holding of an annual convention of the diocese, in which the clergy and lay representatives elected from each district would play an active part in the governance of the diocese. In effect, one might say that what England introduced was a kind of non-canonical diocesan synod, held annually and involving the active participation of the laity. The 1983 Code has done what England could not do; it has changed the canonical diocesan synod into "a group of selected priests *and other Christian faithful* of a particular church which offers assistance to the diocesan bishop for the good of the diocesan community."

Canon law in England's day, and in 1917 as well, made no mention of such a thing as a diocesan pastoral council consisting of clergy and laity that would serve as a consultative organ for the bishop with regard to the pastoral work of the diocese. While England's annual convention primarily dealt with financial matters, it would not seem unreasonable to see it as also fulfilling the role of a diocesan pastoral council, since he encouraged it to offer the bishop its advice on other matters regarding the life of the church.

When he received such advice, Bishop England assured the convention that he would give it his best consideration at the earliest opportunity, and, as far as his conscientious obligations would permit, seek to follow it. On this point there is also a parallel in the new Code, although only with regard to a consensus of those whom the bishop is obliged to consult before taking a certain decision. The Code says that he should not act contrary to their recommendation, especially if there be a consensus, unless there be a reason which, in his judgment, is overriding. A bishop who followed this rule also with regard to a consensus of those he was not obliged by law to consult, such as the members of his diocesan synod or his pastoral council, would, even unknowingly, be following the example of Bishop John England, especially if he informed the synod or council that this was his intention.

England's constitution granted to the laity a notable degree of authority in the financial administration of church property, both of the parish and of the diocese. All the property and funds of a parish were to be administered by the vestry, consisting of the clergyman and a number of laymen chosen by the members of the parish. The annual convention had the authority to dispose of the general fund of the diocese, which was vested in a board of trustees, consisting of the bishop, his vicar, five clergymen chosen by the clergy, and twelve laymen, chosen by the lay delegates at the convention. The treasurer of the fund was a layman chosen every year at the convention. While the 1983 Code does not go so far as this, it does require that each diocese have a finance council, composed of at least three members of the Christian faithful truly skilled in financial affairs, and also have a finance officer, whose role it is to administer the goods of the diocese under the authority of the bishop. The bishop must consult his finance council in order to perform the more important acts of administration and needs its consent for acts of extraordinary administration. Each parish must also have a finance council to aid the pastor in the administration of parish goods. So, in different ways, both the constitution and the Code give an important role to lay persons in the administration of the temporal goods of the church.

However, along with the similarities, there remains a major difference between the Code and England's constitution, in that most of the opportunities the Code provides for the participation of the laity in decision-making depend for their effective implementation on decisions that are made by the bishops. It is the bishops conference that decides whether to hold a plenary council and, if so, whether to invite the number of lay people that the law allows the bishops to invite as members with consultative voice. It is the local bishop who decides whether and for what reasons to have a diocesan synod. It is the bishop who decides whether to have a diocesan pastoral council and how their members are to be selected. It is up to the bishop to decide whether each parish of his diocese must have a pastoral council. The bishop is free to decide whether to "give his best consideration" to the advice he receives from his own pastoral council and whether to encourage his parish priests, both by word and example, to do the same with regard to a consensus of their parish councils.

On all of these counts, the strong point in John England's constitution is that it committed the bishop himself to implement its provisions for the participation of the laity in the decision-making process. What a modern Catholic bishop could most profitably learn from Bishop England's example is his wholehearted willingness to "empower the laity to cooperate" in the fulfillment of his own pastoral responsibilities.

Chapter 5

Business Class

Corporate Body and Church Soul in the United States

REV. JOHN P. BEAL

(↭)

Introduction

O N JULY 6, 2004, the Roman Catholic Archdiocese of Portland in Oregon filed for protection under Title 11 of the United States Bankruptcy Code. This action was designed to protect the archdiocese from its creditors while it attempts to come to terms with these creditors and to reorganize itself as a solvent and viable organization. While the bankruptcy proceeding unfolds, the archdiocese is able to continue its everyday operations under the supervision of the court. Since then, two additional American Catholic dioceses, Tucson and Spokane, have filed for bankruptcy protection, and several other dioceses have intimated that they are, or have been rumored to be, considering bankruptcy filings. Even the Archdiocese of Boston, once one of the crown jewels of the American church, has announced that it is closing one-fifth of its 347 parishes and has been rumored to be teetering on the brink of bankruptcy.

These bankruptcy filings have been prompted by the massive amount of compensation, actual and projected, due to victims of clergy sexual abuse as a result of court judgments and out-of-court settlements. Resort to Chapter 11 reorganization is a business tactic for forcing a global settlement of mass tort claim liability suits, a tactic which has been employed in product liability cases by manufacturers of such products as diverse as asbestos-containing building materials, Agent Orange, and the Dalkon Shield birth control device, rather strange partners in the dock for the Catholic Church. Since these church bankruptcy filings occurred, there has been heated discussion both inside and outside the courtrooms about whether the assets of parishes and other church institutions which operate under the diocesan corporate umbrella will be excluded from the "bankruptcy estates" of the dioceses or whether the courts should "pierce the corporate veil" and reject as a sham the canonical argument that the diocese and its parishes and institutions are separate legal entities. There has also been considerable discussion of whether these bankruptcy filings are really warranted by the dioceses' financial predicaments or are "hard ball" legal tactics designed to force plaintiffs to the bargaining table. There has been little if any discussion, however, of the inconsistency between the willingness of Catholic dioceses to place themselves under the guardianship of the federal courts in exchange for protection against their creditors and the proud, and sometimes defiant, claim of the Catholic Church to enjoy the innate right "to acquire, retain, administer and alienate property independently from civil power."[1]

Nor has there been much discussion of the ease with which people, Catholic and non-Catholic, lawyers and lay, have assumed that priests are "employees" of the corporate entity known as "the church" in the same way that accountants and engineers are "employees" of the corporate entity known as "General Motors" and that the legal liability of these corporate entities for the malfeasance of their employees is the same. There has also been almost total silence about the agreements, similar to consent decrees agreed to by corporations accused of patterns of illegal behavior, reached between a few diocesan bishops and local prosecutors, which cede to the latter a considerable share in bishops' canonical authority over the assignment and monitoring of diocesan priests. It is not surprising that, as the public has become aware of the extent to which bishops failed to deal effectively and decisively with abusive priests, there has been no shortage of invidious comparisons between the management failures and malfeasance that led to the clergy sexual abuse scandal in the Catholic Church and the management failures and malfeasance that led to the more or less contemporary corporate scandals at Enron, Tyco, Worldcom, and Adelphia. In fact, for a canon lawyer, one of the most puzzling aspects of the sexual abuse crisis in the Catholic Church in recent years has been the church's own acquiescence to its being defined, and even to defining itself, in terms drawn from the lexicon not of theology or canon law but of business.

The sexual abuse crisis and its consequences have placed in vivid relief the dependence of the Catholic Church on the business culture of the United States and the apparent irrelevance of canon law for defining *ad extra* its place in American society and *ad intra* its own organizational structure. This entanglement of church and business cultures is the product of a long historical evolution. This essay will examine two questions: how the symbiosis of church and business cultures has shaped the development of diocesan structures in the United States in a way that has marginalized the significance of canon law and whether this development suggests a more central role for canon law in maintaining the distinctively ecclesial identity of the institution in a pervasively business-like environment.

The Church as an "Economic Actor"

Since the church is, and recognizes itself to be, in part, a "visible structure ...constituted and organized in the world as a society,"[2] this visible, human dimension can be legitimately examined from the perspective of the human sciences, including economics. Mark Hanna, the Ohio industrialist and Republican Party kingpin, once observed, "Money is the mother's milk of politics." Money is also the mother's milk of the church. Despite Jesus' warning that money is the root of all evil, he and his disciples kept a common purse from which to respond to the needs of the poor. Throughout the history of the church, money has been necessary to build and maintain places of worship, to compensate clergy and other church ministers and employees, and to carry out the enormous range of educational, apostolic, and charitable activities that are part of the church's mission.[3] The church does not simply use money and other temporal goods in the fulfillment of its mission, however. As a visible institution rooted in an economic order, the church is itself "an economic actor." In their pastoral letter *Economic Justice for All,* the Catholic bishops of the United States highlighted the church role as an economic actor to call attention to its institutional responsibility to insure that its own practices were consistent with the demands of social justice. Thus, the bishops insisted:

On the parish and diocesan level, through its agencies and institutions, the church employs many people; it has investments; it has extensive properties for worship and mission. *All the moral principles that govern the just operation of any economic endeavor apply to the church and its agencies and institutions; indeed the church should be exemplary.*[4]

However, the church's activity in the "real" or monetary economy as an employer, investor, and property owner does not begin to exhaust its role as an economic actor. In addition to this "real" or monetary economy, there is also the "economy of symbolic goods," a realm of transactions or exchanges "which do not function according to the law of interest seen as the search for the maximization of (monetary) profit."[5]

From an economic point of view, the church appears as an institution whose "business" is the salvation of souls by providing privileged access to the sacred. Bourdieu has phrased this perspective somewhat more bluntly:

> First, the manifest image: an institution charged with assuring the salvation of souls. Or, at a higher degree of objectivization, with Max Weber: a (sacerdotal) corps holding the monopoly on the legitimate manipulating of the goods of salvation; and, for this reason, invested with a properly spiritual power, exercised *ex officio,* on the foundation of a permanent transaction with the expectations of the laity: the church relies on principles of vision (dispositions which constitute "belief"), which it in part constituted, to orient representations and practices by reinforcing or transforming these principles. It can do this because of its relative autonomy in relation to the demands of the laity.[6]

The economic dimension of religious practices is usually obscured or shrouded in theological language, but it is neither impossible nor entirely inaccurate to discern an economic analogue behind the euphemisms.

> Thus, in order to describe each practice . . . , it would be necessary to use two words, superimposed on each other as if in a musical chord: apostolate/marketing, faithful/clientele, sacred service/paid labor, and so forth. The religious discourse that accompanies practice is an

integral part of the economy of practices as an economy of symbolic goods.[7]

Although such real and symbolic economic activity is not the sole, or even the most important, dimension of the life of the church, an inexorable consequence of being a church that has a very human as well as a divine dimension is its entanglement in the business of the world, an entanglement that has historically been the point of contact between the church and business culture in the United States.

Canon Law and the Institutional Environment of the Church in the United States: An Awkward Fit from the Beginning

When John Carroll became the first bishop of Baltimore in 1789, his flock consisted of perhaps thirty-five thousand souls, mostly settled along the eastern seaboard but already venturing into the "dark and bloody ground" west of the Appalachians. These scattered communities were separated by vast expanses of territory; travel was difficult, and communications slow. This American church had no canonically erected parishes but only small communities of faithful, only twenty-four priests and no seminaries in which to train them, few material possessions to serve as endowments for parochial or diocesan benefices and little likelihood of acquiring them, and none of the traditional canonical structures for diocesan governance or the administration of temporalities. A church infrastructure would have to be created from scratch in a social and legal environment unlike any the church had previously encountered. The canon law Carroll and his successors inherited was and continued to be singularly ill-suited to serve as a blueprint for the ecclesial construction project that faced them.

The instrument evolved in and by the church to regulate its own economic activity, both real and symbolic, and to legitimize the exercise of sacred power has long been canon law. Canon law is the system of norms that defines the structures and procedures by which the Catholic Church is organized and governed. The fundamental problem with the canon law John Carroll and his successors inherited was that it was a system of laws designed to order and maintain a church that was already *in facto esse,* not to guide the birthing of one that was still very much *in fieri*. The received canon law presupposed stable, relatively immobile, ethnically and religiously homogeneous populations organized as a social body into territorial units, most of whose origins went back far beyond the memory of any living person, and governed by office holders whose tenure was, in principle, for life and whose responsibilities were primarily oriented to maintenance and preservation rather than to building and expanding. Since the population encompassed by these territorial divisions was presumed to be religiously homogeneous, little attention was given by the law to the threat of loss of members as the result of the proselytizing activities of other religious bodies or the need to compete with other religious groups to maintain and expand market share. Rather, the primary perceived threat to the order of the church was the encroachment of the state on matters the church considered its prerogative. The contrast between these presumptions underlying traditional canon law and the situation faced by John Carroll and his successors could not have been starker. The Catholic population they had to attempt to order and govern was not stable and immobile, but volatile and mobile. These Catholics were themselves ethnically diverse and immersed in a religiously diverse but militantly Protestant society. As a result, the real threat was not encroachment on church prerogatives by the state but the inroads by Protestant proselytizers.

Not surprisingly, the content of traditional canon law was as ill suited for American conditions as were its presuppositions. Since at least the Gregorian Reform of the eleventh and twelfth centuries, canon law has rested on the fundamental premise that the church is a society, autonomous within its own realm from but parallel to the state. Thus, canon law emerged primarily as what European jurists call "public law," one "concerned with the organization of the state, the relations between the state and the people who compose it, the responsibilities of public officers to the state, to each other, and to private persons, and the relation of states to one another."[8]

As a public law concerned with defining the relation of the church to the secular states within which it operated, canon law carefully mapped out the areas in which the church claimed autonomy from the state intrusions and those in which the church expected the state's cooperation and assistance. These careful efforts to carve out terms for peaceful co-existence between church and state in the church's external public law were useless in the United States, where the First Amendment to the Constitution barred the federal government both from interfering in internal church affairs and from assisting and subsidizing the church's activities and institutions. Since the law recognized the church as a social fact but not as a public law institution, for the Catholic Church to achieve recognition and protection from the law, it would have to be as a private law institution.

Perhaps nowhere was canon law's applicability to the American scene more problematic than in its regulation of the acquisition, administration, and alienation of temporal goods. Canon law emerged in an age where land and its fruits were the basis for wealth and money was simply a convenient medium of exchange with no inherent value. As a result, the canon law elaborated in the *Corpus Iuris Canonici* and developed by the Council of Trent placed the primary emphasis on insuring that real property legitimately acquired by the church was retained and administered fruitfully and not usurped by avaricious nobles or states (usually referred to generically in the law as "laymen") or carelessly alienated from ecclesiastical ownership. By the time of the Council of Trent it was settled canonical doctrine that ownership of church property vested not in the church in general but in the individual juridic entity that had legitimately acquired it. Dioceses, parishes, churches, shrines, and other ecclesiastical institutions through which the actual work of the church was carried out came into possession of their own lands and other properties that became their doweries or endowments and the sources of their operating revenue. Each of these doweries together with the ecclesiastical office it supported was regulated by canon law as a benefice, i.e., a "juridic entity constituted or erected by competent ecclesiastical authority in perpetuity, consisting of a sacred office and the right of receiving the revenue from the dowery attached to the office."[9] Thus, the benefice system radically decentralized the source of funding for church operations, including support of the clergy, made continued funding for church operations dependent on prudent management of existing resources and not on tapping new sources of revenue, and disconnected church income from the community whose spiritual needs were served by the beneficial office holder.

The revenues for the church's everyday operations, including the support of office holders, were presumed to be primarily from customary tithes and other income from church-owned properties and only secondarily from fees for services rendered, especially the administration of the sacraments and sacramentals. Thus, at least in canonical theory, the church had sources of support for the carrying out of its mission which were relatively independent of the faithful it served. These premises of canon law were never adequate to address the situation of the Catholic Church in the United States, where the church was dependent on the free-will offerings of the faithful for its revenue, and their inadequacy required that those responsible for carving out space for the Catholic Church in the public square of the United States turn to extra-canonical resources and models.

The Emergence of Church Organization: Three Critical Periods

It is possible to identify three critical moments in the evolution of the organizational structures and strategies of the Catholic Church in the United States: (1) the period of laying the foundations (1789–1850); (2) the period of expansion and integration (1850–1960); (3) the period of bureaucratization and organizational failure (1960–). Although these periods can be distinguished, they are not consecutive but cumulative, with each subsequent period building on the framework laid in the earlier ones. In each of these periods, the church in the United States found itself in a new and rapidly changing social, economic, and legal environment. The church's institutional survival required that it adapt to this unfamiliar environment, but neither historical precedents nor canon law offered much meaningful guidance on the form or direction that this adoption should take. The organizational strategies pursued and structures developed in these periods often paralleled and even mimicked the adaptations to new environments going on at the same time in the business world. Thus, an examination of the interaction of the church as an economic actor with the economic environment in which it lived and moved and had its being can provide at least partial answers to Oliver Williamson's oft repeated question: "What's going on here?"[10]

Laying the Foundations (1789–1850)

Reviewing the Situation

The Church Environment

Although the core Catholic population of the United States in 1789 consisted largely of middle-class merchants, planters, and businessmen, this middle-class core would soon be submerged in floods of immigrants, most of whom arrived on these shores poorly educated and catechized at best. The American society in which these early Catholics settled was pervasively Protestant with a strong and, at times, vehement anti-Catholic tone and with a zealous proselytizing tendency. In this climate, Catholic leaders would have to carve out their church's place in American society and to maintain its "market share" against its better placed and financed Protestant "competitors." As a result, what church leaders needed above all was a secure vehicle for holding property that would assure their control of the places, materials, processes, and personnel needed to carry out the church's religious "business."

The Business Environment

Shortly before Catholic leaders had begun grasping about for a suitable vehicle for securing their hold on church property, leaders in American business and industry faced a similar quandary. Although the advantages of the factory system for mass production of textiles and other goods had already become apparent, harnessing the potential of this technological advance required considerable capital outlays to bring under unified control all aspects of the production process from acquiring raw materials to shipping finished goods. The risks involved in large-scale manufacturing and transportation operations made it difficult to capitalize them through single proprietorships and partnerships, the most common forms of business organization at the time. Proprietorships and partnerships labored under two additional disadvantages, unlimited personal liability of investors for the debts of the business enterprise and the relative impermanence of the business organization. "Industrial investments required long time horizons, yet partnerships typically lasted only so long as their members and, in fact, only so long as the members wished to remain in business together."[11]

Responses to the Situation

Business

The corporation, a traditional device usually used hitherto by quasi-public services including churches, suggested itself as a way of raising necessary capital by expanding the pool of potential investors. Moreover, since corporations were treated in law as artificial persons responsible for their own debts, the corporate form limited the liability of investors or shareholders for the obligations of the corporation to the amount of their own investments. If the business enterprise failed, investors could lose their own investments, but their personal assets could not be attached in payment for the debts of the insolvent corporation. The corporation form also solved the problem of impermanency of business organizations by creating an artificial legal person with the capacity to hold property and for perpetual existence. In 1813, under a charter granted by the Commonwealth of Massachusetts, the Boston Manufacturing Company, a large textile firm, was the first major industrial firm to be incorporated.[12] As other firms, especially in the fields of banking, transportation, and textile manufacturing, began to opt to organize as corporations, states began to enact general laws simplifying the requirements for businesses to incorporate. Although the corporate form was utilized relatively infrequently by industrial enterprises prior to the Civil War, its success in capitalizing the nascent textile industry and enriching its investors marked the corporation as the form of business organization for the future.

One consequence of the trend for businesses to adopt the corporation as the organizational form of choice was the gradual separation of ownership of productive assets from their control. It was the corporation itself, a person at law, that owned the property, equipment, raw materials, and product. Although stockholders retained an equitable interest in the corporation, the proliferation of stockholders and the dispersion of their holdings inevitably entailed a growing inability on the part of these equitable owners to exercise any meaningful control over the company's policies and practices and the vesting of such control in the hands of the firm's managers. The inexorable trend in American business corporations was to concentrate control of enterprises in fewer and fewer hands and to minimize the role of stockholders in the direction of these corporations. Thus, the concentration of economic power separate from ownership has, in fact, created economic empires, and has delivered these empires into a new form of absolutism, relegating [equitable] "owners" to the position of those who supply the means whereby the new princes may exercise their power.[13]

The Church

A somewhat similar development occurred in the emergence of organizational form in the nascent Catholic Church in the United States where the state acknowledged Catholicism as a social fact but accorded the church no legal recognition. The First Amendment's "wall of separation" meant that neither the Catholic Church nor any other religious organization could look to the government for financial support, privilege, or enforcement of its doctrinal and disciplinary decisions. Catholics, like all citizens of the new republic, were free to organize themselves into congregations and dioceses and to govern these entities according to their traditional polities. However, these ecclesiastical groupings were private, voluntary associations that, per se, enjoyed no recognition in secular law. To obtain the benefits of legal recognition and protection especially of the church's ownership of temporal goods, Catholics had to avail themselves of the same legal devices as other private, voluntary associations. And that is what they did.

When the faithful became sufficiently numerous in a locality, they came together as a "religious society" under the laws of their state or territory, elected their leaders or trustees, purchased land, built a church, and petitioned the bishop for a priest.[14] Since they had contributed the money for the construction and maintenance of the church and held legal title to the property, these trustees assumed responsibility for its financial administration and sometimes asserted the right to nominate and dismiss its rector. In fact, since the bishops were often unable to provide a priest to serve these communities, the trustees sometimes went out on the "free agent" market to hire their own priest from the growing pool of immigrant priests. This trustee system of holding and administering church property was often seen as a republican adaptation of more traditional canonical institutes like the canonical right of patronage, which gave to the nobleman who had contributed the funds for the construction or

renovation of a church the right as its patron to nominate its rector or
pastor.[15]

Perhaps because of this patina of canonical respectability, the trustee
system was not initially seen as essentially incompatible with Catholic
doctrine or discipline. It was tacitly accepted by the first synod of the Diocese of Baltimore in 1791 and the meeting of the bishops of the United
States in 1810. (In fact, the trusteeship model was never condemned out-
right either by the Holy See or by a plenary council.) However, a series of
bitter conflicts with trustees, usually precipitated by the trustees' desire
to hire or fire the rector independently of the bishop, convinced bishops
of their need for greater control of church property. Most bishops were
not content to reform the trustee system as John England had done in
Charleston;[16] they were determined to abolish it or at least render it im-
potent. In 1829, the First Provincial Council of Baltimore decreed that
henceforth no church was to be built or consecrated unless its legal title
was first assigned in writing to the local bishop.[17] Subsequent provincial
and plenary councils expanded episcopal control of church property. By
the mid-1850s the bishops had effectively vanquished the trustees and
"by the Third Plenary Baltimore Council, in 1884, the bishops' authority
in this area was absolute."[18]

Since neither the federal nor the state governments recognized the
claim of the church itself as well as its dioceses and missions to own property as public juridic persons and provided no assistance in enforcing
ecclesiastical discipline, episcopal control of church property appeared
to be the only viable means for making the de jure authority of bishops
de facto power in the American church. Once the bishops owned or held
title to the property of a mission, the civil courts would uphold episcopal control and decisions as proprietary rights against the claims of the
trustees and the rest of the faithful.[19] As they acquired titles to churches,
the bishops used the same devices employed by business to secure their
hold on the property. Like single proprietors, some bishops held title to
the church property in their dioceses in fee simple. Although fee simple
gave bishops almost absolute personal control over church property and
its administration, it complicated the transfer of property to their successors on their death and risked seizure of church property as payment for
the bishop's personal debts. Especially after the debacle caused by the
personal bankruptcy of Archbishop John Baptist Purcell in Cincinnati,

who had held church property in fee simple,[20] most bishops opted for more secure devices for holding property.

Where state law permitted, civil incorporation allowed the church to hold property in perpetuity while allowing the bishop broad freedom to administer it as agent of the corporation, either alone or in concert with a few hand-picked trustees, according as the device chosen was a corporation sole or a corporation aggregate. In the corporation aggregate model pioneered by the State of New York, each "parish" or mission was separately incorporated and governed by trustees who were the diocesan bishop, his vicar general of the diocese, the rector of the church, and two lay parishioners chosen by these three ecclesiastics. The requirement that the business of the corporation be conducted by a vote of the majority of the five statutory trustees could, in theory, serve as a check on the power of the diocesan bishop. Nonetheless, his freedom to appoint and remove the vicar general and the rector made the likelihood of runaway trustees rather remote, as remote as the likelihood of a shareholder revolt in a business corporation in which ownership and control have been thoroughly severed. The corporation sole, which originated in English common law and was incorporated into the statutes of many states, "is one consisting of one person only, and his successors . . . , who are incorporated by law in order to give them some legal capacities and advantages, particularly that of perpetuity, which in their natural persons they could not have had."[21] Although many state statutes allowed for both dioceses and parishes to be organized as corporations sole, almost all bishops opted to hold all church property within the diocese as a single corporation sole over which the bishop himself had absolute civil control. Where provisions for the incorporation of religious associations were inadequate, bishops held title to property as trustees for the parish or diocesan communities. Such trusteeship arrangements "had most of the advantages of the system of absolute ownership by the bishop, without any of its dangers."[22]

The civil devices utilized by bishops to hold church property in the aftermath of the lay trustee controversy gave them greater direct and immediate authority over church property under their jurisdiction than had ever been foreseen or sanctioned by canon law. Unlike the stock corporations favored in the business world, the devices chosen by bishops for holding church property did not separate ownership and control, but their concentration of ownership and control in the hands of the bishops alone had the same effect of disenfranchising those with an equitable interest in the enterprise as did the business corporation. Thus, parishioners who had contributed to the building and support of their church found themselves with as little voice in the institution's affairs as the stockholders who had invested in a business corporation. Although no available civil law device for church organization perfectly mirrored canon law, bishops made little if any effort to adopt the devices that best approximated the canonical model. Instead, they opted for and stubbornly clung to models that maximized their own unfettered discretion in the administration of the church's temporal goods. The lack of congruence between the canonical norm and the American reality did not go unnoticed by the Holy See.

In 1911, just two years after the church in the United States had been removed from the tutelage of the Propaganda Fidei, the Sacred Congregation of the Council, whose competence extended to matters of church property, addressed a letter to the bishops of the United States on the manner of holding church property. The congregation ordered that the holding of property in fee simple was to "be entirely abandoned."[23] The congregation recommended the adoption of the New York parish corporation model where state law made it available and urged that, when this model was not available, bishops "should exert their influence with the civil authorities that it may be made legal as soon as possible."[24] Finally, the congregation reluctantly authorized continued use of the corporation sole model but "only in those places where the civil law does not recognize *Parish Corporations* . . . and until such recognition is obtained."[25] Moreover, continued use of the corporation sole was permissible only "with the understanding that in the administration of ecclesiastical property the Bishop is to act with the advice, and in more important matters with the consent, of those who have an interest in the premises and of the diocesan consultors, this being a conscientious obligation of the Bishop in person."[26] Despite this stern injunction, there is no evidence of concerted efforts by bishops to lobby state legislatures for religious corporation laws more congenial to Catholic polity, to adapt such models where they were available, or even to comply with the letter and spirit of existing norms for consultation with the diocesan consultors and those with an interest in the premises.

In theory, all of the private law devices available to bishops for holding church property entailed a fiduciary relationship between the bishop and the parish or diocesan community, which retained some equitable interest in the property. This fiduciary obligation could have provided the civil law a window of opportunity for bishops to give the voice foreseen in canon law to clergy and others with an interest in property of a church and in its administration. However, the bishops ignored this opportunity and chose instead to leave those who had contributed to building and maintaining churches without a voice in their administration. As we have seen, the inexorable trend in American business corporations throughout the nineteenth century was to concentrate control of enterprises in fewer and fewer hands and to minimize the role of equitable owners in the direction of the corporation.[27] In a similar way, when they succeeded in acquiring legal title to church property, bishops concentrated control over church property in their own hands and resisted encroachments on that control by both clergy and laity. Disenfranchised from participation in the management of the church, the laity were left a role as consumers of the church's services and the lower clergy the role as its employees.

This resistance is vividly illustrated by the adamant opposition of the bishops to pressure both from their own clergy and from the Holy See to erect canonical parishes and to establish cathedral chapters.

1. Since at least the settlement of Maryland as a Catholic colony, there have been stable communities of the Catholic faithful under the pastoral care of designated priests in what is now the United States. Although these stable communities met the popular definition of "parishes," functioned as such, and even were and are called parishes (including by present-day historians), there were virtually no canonically erected parishes in the United States until after the promulgation of the 1917 Code of Canon Law because the bishops resolutely refused to erect them as canonical parishes despite ongoing pressure to do so from both their own clergy and the Holy See. Instead, these stable communities were classified as "missions" and the priests who ministered in them as "rectors" who exercised their functions not in their own right as pastors but as delegates of the bishop. The bishops justified their foot dragging in establishing canonical parishes by citing their need for great flexibility in dealing with rapidly shifting demographic and economic circumstances.

However, as the church became more settled and well established, especially in the urban centers of the East Coast and Midwest, the bishops' claims that local conditions rendered it impossible or inopportune to erect parishes sounded increasingly lame. As a result, at several plenary councils, the Holy See twisted the arms of bishops to exact promises to move toward the canonical erection of parishes. However, no real movement toward the establishment of canonical parishes occurred until 1921 when the Pontifical Commission for the Interpretation of the Code of Canon Law unilaterally declared that all previously existing "missions" had been elevated to the status of parishes by the promulgation of the 1917 Code of Canon Law.[28]

The real reasons for the bishops' resistance to the canonical erection of parishes are not difficult to discern. Erection of a stable community of the faithful as a parish would *ipso iure* make it a moral or juridic person distinct from the juridic person of the diocese. As a result, the property it had already acquired and would subsequently acquire would belong to parish and the diocese would have no claim to it. Pursuant to the canon law governing parishes, the ordinary administration of parish property would rightfully devolve to the pastor in virtue of his office, and the bishop's role in this administration would be limited to supervision. By refusing to establish canonical parishes, the bishops insured that the assets of the "missions" remained firmly under the canonical ownership of the diocese, the sole moral or juridic person in the territory, and retained for themselves the freedom at civil law to involve themselves in the day-to-day financial affairs of local communities.

2. The desire to retain unfettered control of the administration of church property is also evident in the bishops' resistance to the establishment of cathedral chapters even in a modified form in the United States. A cathedral chapter was a traditional canonical structure that consisted of a college of presbyters of the diocese, which served as the bishops' senate. By law, the chapter had a significant voice in the administration of church property within the diocese as well as in the appointment of pastors. Although the bishop had the right to nominate members of the chapter after consulting the chapter itself, he could not easily dismiss capitulars.[29] Having wrested control of church property from the lay trustees, bishops were loath to share responsibility for the administration of property with the clergy. Throughout the nineteenth century, the

bishops beat back attempts by their priests and the Congregation Propaganda Fidei to establish cathedral chapters to be co-responsible with the bishops for the finances of dioceses and their missions. Finally, at the Third Plenary Council of Baltimore in 1884, the bishops again thwarted efforts by the Propaganda to impose chapters but only by succumbing to its pressure to mandate the appointment of diocesan consultors. Nevertheless, they succeeded in "restricting the rights of the consultors as much as possible" and retaining absolute control over their appointment and removal.[30]

Assessment

The bishops' ultimate triumph over the lay trustees and their success in resisting the calls of both their own priests and the Vatican for greater coresponsibility in church governance resulted in the emergence during the nineteenth century of a distinctive organizational structure for the church in the United States, a structure that concentrated unprecedented power over the management of the local church in the hands of diocesan bishops and that had no precedent or parallel in canon law. From a business perspective, the diocese had taken the form of a holding company[31] with the diocese as the primary entity and the parish units as its wholly owned subsidiaries and operating units. This development in the organizational structure of the Catholic Church was not without precedent, however, in the American business world where, as de Tocqueville had observed as early as the 1830s, concentrations of wealth and power were well under way despite the persistence of the republican rhetoric of Jacksonian democracy. These developments in both ecclesiastical and business organization in the nineteenth century were driven by a similar dynamic and followed a similar trajectory as well.

Economic theorists as diverse as Frederick Hayek, Chester Barnard, and Oliver Williamson have noted that "the economic problem of society is mainly one of rapid adaption to changes in particular circumstances of time and place."[32] When the adaptions required by these circumstances demand conscious, deliberate, and purposeful cooperation among several actors, they are most efficiently realized through formal organizations, especially hierarchical organizations where "resort to fiat provides better assurance that adoptions of [this] kind will be performed in a coordinated way."[33] In the business world, reliance on the firm's internal organization rather than on markets for contracting is particularly advantageous in that it permits decision-makers to "deal with uncertainty/complexity in an adaptive, sequential fashion." Instead of having to foresee, specify, and make provision in advance for all possible contingencies, decision-makers can permit events to unfold and devote their attention "to only the actual rather than all possible outcomes."[34] Internal organization is also less vulnerable to the hazards of opportunism, i.e., self-interested behavior involving guile or false and empty promises.[35] Internal organizations reduce the incentives for opportunism by making it more difficult for individuals or subunits within the organization to appropriate gains for themselves rather than to allow them to benefit the overall organization, by providing enhanced capacity for auditing, and by providing for resolution of internal disputes by executive fiat.[36] The inherent advantages of hierarchical internal organizations for adaption to rapidly changing circumstances and markets and for dealing with uncertainty and opportunism almost spontaneously prompted the emergence of early forms of the modern business firm in the United States during the nineteenth century.

One can detect some of the same dynamics at work in the emergence of the hierarchical organizational form of the Catholic Church that emerged in the nineteenth century. It is not surprising, of course, that the Catholic Church in the United States should assume a hierarchical organizational form; what is surprising is that the hierarchical form chosen was drawn not from the world of government but from the world of business. The first challenge facing the church as an actor in the monetary and symbolic economy was to acquire effective control of the places where it conducted its "business," i.e., the churches where the word of God was proclaimed and the sacraments administered. Although the trusteeship system in itself was not an insuperable obstacle to the bishops' conduct of the church's business, recurring disputes with trustees convinced them that the costs in negotiation and sometimes litigation with the board of trustees of each mission over the long haul were disproportionately expensive in time, energy, good will, and money, particularly as the number of "missions" under the diocesan organizational umbrella proliferated. Moreover, the ebbs and flows of immigration as well as the waxing and waning of anti-Catholic sentiment in the larger population made the future highly uncertain. Since many of their disputes with trustees involved the appointment and removal of rectors, bishops easily came to see trustees as potential competitors for control over the church's critical strategic asset, the clergy who controlled the doors to the sacred. Both lay trustees and parish priests could also be expected to engage in opportunistic behavior in dealing with the bishop, "parochialism" in both the literal and most pejorative sense, that could redound to personal or parochial advantage at the expense of the overall good of the church.

While the bishops' education and temperament may have predisposed them to centralize power, this temperament was one they shared with their counterparts in corporate boardrooms. Having chosen to adapt to the American environment by an organizational form more akin to a business than a canonical model, the bishops approached diocesan administration as a form of business administration, of management rather than governance.[37] Nor were they unaware that their choice of organizational forms had resulted in a change in their role and image in the Catholic community. Although he had his share of run-ins with stubborn trustees, John Carroll never disavowed the system, in part because he feared the legal and practical consequences of making bishops owners and managers of ecclesiastical property. Somewhat later, Archbishop Kenrick of St. Louis deplored the "evil results" of making bishops primarily managers of temporal goods. He complained that his "occupation" had become "more secular than episcopal" and that he felt "crushed by the responsibilities I have contracted in my ill judged efforts to promote Religion."[38] Nevertheless, when Archbishop George Conroy reported to the Propaganda on his 1878 apostolic visitation of the church in the United States, he noted:

> In the selection of bishops, priority is given to financial abilities rather than to pastoral.... Whenever there is a deliberation to choose a candidate for the episcopacy, the bishops of a province feel constrained to seek, at all costs, a man skilled in financial administration. Indeed, it has often happened that the most valued gifts in the candidate proposed to the Holy See were properly those of a banker, and not of a Pastor of Souls.[39]

Of course, once the bishops had opted for a business model for church organization, financial acumen was inevitably a critical consideration in the selection of chief executive officer.

Expansion and Integration (1850–1960)

Reviewing the Situation

The Church Environment

By the time Confederate guns began shelling Fort Sumter in Charleston harbor, the American bishops had, except for a few mopping-up operations, effectively vanquished the lay trustees, secured their control on church property, and installed a business model for diocesan governance. However, the face of American Catholicism had already changed markedly since John Carroll and would continue to change rapidly. Wave after wave of immigrants, first from Ireland and Germany and later increasingly from Southern and Eastern Europe, had swelled the Catholic population of the United States until by 1910 it comprised 16 million souls or almost 18 percent of the total population. This burgeoning population had crowded into the cities along the eastern seaboard and had spilled out into the cities and towns of the industrial heartland. The heightened size and visibility of the Catholic population provoked a resurgence of anti-Catholic propaganda and militancy. Protestant proselytizing, both overt and subtle, would challenge Catholic leaders to adopt strategies and build institutions that would retain the loyalty of the often poorly catechized immigrant faithful and thereby maintain the churches' share in a highly competitive religious market. In addition, the Catholic Church itself was changing, not just in the United States but throughout the world. Ultramontane influences were pervasive in every area of church life from the dusty tomes of seminary theology to the sometime saccharine books of popular devotions. The result of the ultramontane movement was what has sometimes been called "the Romanization of the Church,"[40] one of whose consequences was the integration of the American church under the centralized bureaucratic control of the Roman Curia.[41]

The Business Environment

Although American businessmen did not face the widespread popular prejudice and hostility that the Catholic Church did in the period between the middle of the nineteenth century and the middle years of the twentieth, they also confronted a rapidly changing environment which required creative adaptions in their organizational forms. In particular, businesses faced the challenges posed and the opportunities created, on the one hand, by technological progress, especially in transportation and communication, and, on the other, the emergence of a national, mostly urban, market for goods and services. Up to this point, most business organizations had been rather small and oriented toward serving a local market. As a result, businessmen could be content with relatively simple forms of business organization. However, the exploitations of the possibilities of the new technology to capitalize on the potentialities of a mass urban market would require radical changes in business organization.

Responses

Business

In response to this changed environment, the primary form of business enterprise underwent a radical transformation. Until 1850, most business decisions in the United States were still made by entrepreneurs working alone or with a few partners; by 1910, the American economy was dominated by a new and very different type of business organization, the "large, multi-unit enterprise operated by managers rather than owners" which "could not run efficiently without a formal organizational structure."[42] This radical transformation of business organizational models was effected in large part through horizontal integration of the producers or sellers within a particular industry or field and through vertical integration of some or all of the stages of the productive process between raw material and ultimate consumer within individual firms.

"Every economic system requires resources to be allocated; performance of activity cells to be monitored; and the flow of materials, funds, services, and information and the transactions between activity cells to be coordinated."[43] In many sectors of the economy, large, integrated managerial enterprises proved to be the most efficient method for achieving these goals of allocation, monitoring, and coordination. Thus, such enterprises arose not only in industries involved in manufacturing, processing of agricultural products, and extraction of raw materials but in retailing as well. "The first great mass retailer — the department stores — appeared in the 1860's and 1870's to sell to the concentrated urban markets.... Then came the first of the chains in groceries, drugs, and notions that were to become so predominant in the twentieth century."[44] The advantages of this sort of business organization became apparent almost immediately.

> In 1840 annual sales of $500,000 were still exceptional for a merchant specializing in the marketing of manufactured products. In 1873, seven years after Marshall Field established his wholesale house in Chicago, his annual sales reached over $14 million. A decade later, with much the same plant and personnel, they had risen to $23 million. Ten years after it began to compete directly with Montgomery Ward, Sears Roebuck was filling 100,000 orders a day. This was more than most merchants handled in the pre-railroad days in a decade or even a lifetime.[45]

Market share could be expanded by opening new branches to make its goods and services more accessible to consumers and by diversifying product line to serve a greater variety of consumer interests; market share could be maintained in the face of sometimes fierce competition not only by keeping prices low but also by generating brand loyalty through advertising and especially by establishing a product's reputation for distinctiveness and quality through standardization.[46] However, only if the firm had firm control of plant and equipment and a reliable labor force could the benefits of centralized organizational structures for allocation, monitoring, and coordination be achieved.

The Church

This rapidly changing demographic, social, and ecclesial environment also necessitated adaptions in the organizational strategies of the American Catholic Church, strategies that would subtly change its organizational structure. Like business enterprises, the church confronted a mass urban market. Contrary to the conventional wisdom, the urban landscape of late nineteenth- and early twentieth-century America was not an environment hostile to religion. In fact, the open religious environment of cities with easy access to churches and a wide variety of churches from which to choose actually fostered higher rates of church membership and participation than in the countryside and forced "each religious body to appeal successfully to some segment of the religious market, or to slide into oblivion."[47] Comprising about one-third of the urban religious market by the early 1900s, Catholics "added a new competitive intensity to the religious market"[48] and needed to be mobilized to retain their market share in the face of competition.

The divisions of the Catholic Church into distinct, territorially delimited dioceses, which increased in number throughout this period, meant that each diocese was already horizontally integrated within its allotted territory, but these territorial delimitations imposed by the Holy See served as a bar to further horizontal integration. Although these territorial limits also prevented dioceses from exploiting advances in transportation and communication as fully as did business firms, these advances were not without significance for adaptation in church organization. As railroad lines united the nation and urban mass transit systems linked cities, church leaders acquired the ability to visit and monitor the local churches over which they presided. Communications with and, therefore, monitoring and control of local units were also greatly enhanced by the availability of first telegraph and later telephone links. Moreover, the Romanization of the American church would have occurred much more slowly, if indeed it occurred at all, had it not been for steamships which reduced the time for transatlantic voyages from months to weeks and eventually days and the telegraph, which made communications between the Vatican and local churches almost instantaneous.

By the time the bishops had consolidated their hold on church property through vanquishing the lay trustees, the organizational structure of dioceses resembled that of a holding company in which the constituent units (here, the local congregations) retained their operational identities and considerable freedom of action without undue interference from central headquarters (here, the chancery).[49] Nevertheless, the key functions of the central diocesan administration were insuring effective allocation of resources (especially clergy), monitoring the performance (especially the financial performance) of the local units and their leadership, and coordinating the increasingly diverse range of activities in which local units were engaged. Carrying out these functions required adaptions to the rapidly changing environment, adaptions that tended to increase centralized control over the constituent units without eliminating their freedom of initiative altogether. The critical challenge to diocesan leadership was to maintain and, if possible, expand the Catholic share of the religious market.

By its very nature, a Catholic diocese had a local monopoly on the Catholic market, but it had no monopoly on the religious market in urban nineteenth- and twentieth-century America. A crucial strategy for retaining market share in the face of fierce Protestant competition was to make Catholic parishes and institutions or outlets readily accessible. Thus, local congregations with their schools proliferated to meet the needs of the rapidly expanding and mobile Catholic population. Especially in the mid-nineteenth century, the establishment of new local congregations continued to come from local initiative and not from the bishop. As new Catholic groups arrived or existing groups moved to a new location, splintered off from existing groups, or outgrew their original facilities, they continued to build or acquire their own churches and to ask the bishop to assign a priest in return for title to the property. In time, however, the situation on the ground became stable and predictable enough for bishops to become proactive by establishing, dividing, and configuring parishes at their own initiative. Decisions on the part of bishops whether to recognize a new local community or to divide or establish a new one could not be made on the basis of a "field of dreams" belief that "if you build it, they will come." Instead, they required reliable information and shrewd judgment about, among other things, the impact of the new unit on existing ones, the present and future resources available to sustain the new unit, and the long-term stability of its population. In other words, bishops had to make the same sort of decisions about opening new outlets as did their counterparts in the retail chains.

As the Catholic population grew from "a small and relatively homogeneous community in terms of nationality and class to a large, radically diverse population made up of people from at least twenty-eight different nationalities situated at various levels of the social and economic hierarchy"[50] during the nineteenth and early twentieth centuries, so did the possibilities for intra-ecclesial friction, conflict, and even schism. In fact, conflict and schism were not mere theoretical possibilities; diversity in ethnic background and religious sensibilities actually provoked schisms during the nineteenth century. One ingenious institution for defusing ethnic-religious conflicts and averting the danger of defection from the communion of the church was the national or ethnic parish, which allowed Catholics to preserve their native languages, spirituality, and customs under the leadership of "their own" priests while remaining "in the fold."

The multiplication of local communities and their churches brought in its train the proliferation of parochial schools, first elementary schools and later high schools, four thousand of them by time their establishment in every parish was mandated by the Third Plenary Council of Baltimore in 1884.[51] In addition to schools, a wide range of devotional, social, and eleemosynary associations sprang up as outgrowths and adjuncts of the life of local Catholic communities. Although many of these parish-based associations and activities were, in themselves, rather peripheral to the church's core mission of proclaiming the gospel and administering the sacraments, they attracted to and retained in the church many whose piety was a bit tepid. The value of the full-service parish with its wide range of programs and activities for maintaining Catholic market share cannot be underestimated, a lesson that has not been lost on today's evangelical Protestants who pursue the same strategy to build their mega-churches.[52] Like the emerging corporate giants in the field of mass marketing, the church learned that to maintain and expand its market share it needed not only to expand its outlets but also to diversify the range of services and products these outlets offered.

A second strategy pursued by the church during the second half of the nineteenth century and the first half of the twentieth to maintain and expand its share of the religious market was aimed at engendering among the faithful a strong sense of "brand identity" and "brand loyalty." The multiple programs, activities, and associations available under the parish umbrella served this purpose well as did the rapidly emerging institutional apostolates under Catholic auspices. By 1900, there were 827 hospitals, orphanages, old age homes, settlement houses, and other charitable institutions that identified themselves as Catholic.[53] This number continued to grow throughout the first half of the twentieth century. In addition, Catholic colleges and universities were established to provide the opportunity for higher education to young Catholic men and women who could not afford or who were excluded from secular institutions. Although most of these institutional apostolates in the fields of education and charity were founded at the initiative and under the sponsorship of religious institutes, their establishment required the consent of the diocesan bishop of the place where the institution was located, who could not give this consent until he had determined that they were useful and viable.[54] In fact, diocesan bishops often invited religious institutes to establish such institutions and were often forced to establish them under diocesan auspices when religious were not available.

The role of these Catholic institutions in fostering a sense of Catholic identity and loyalty cannot be gainsaid. On the one hand, these institutions created a protective bubble that insulated Catholics from the siren song of the Protestant world outside; on the other hand, by immersing the faithful in a pervasively Catholic environment this network of institutions fostered a sense of the distinctiveness of things Catholic and of their own Catholic identity. In business terms, the net effect of this expansion was to shape a mass market for the "product" the church had to offer. That is, expanding outlets and diversifying their range of services functioned as a kind of marketing strategy.

Brand loyalty was also fostered through mutual fear of the common Protestant enemy without and uniformity enforced by strong central authority in Rome for the universal church and in the chancery office for the local church within. Like the corporate marketers of consumer products, Catholic leaders established the distinctiveness of their product by standardization. The nineteenth and early twentieth centuries saw the emergence of a remarkable uniformity in Catholic life and practice. For example, punctilious rubricism, so often scoffed at nowadays, insured that the celebration of the Mass and other sacraments in Latin was uniform throughout the Catholic world; all children were schooled in the fundamentals of Catholic faith through the same Baltimore Catechism; abstinence from meat on Fridays and distinctive days of fasting set Catholics apart; devotional piety might vary somewhat with ethnicity, but recitation of the rosary, weekly or at least frequent confession, devotion to the Sacred Heart, interest in Marian piety in general and Marian apparitions in particular, and stations of the cross and benediction during Lent were universal.[55] While one can lament the extreme uniformity induced by the "Romanization" of the American church in a rather ultramontane form, from the point of view of marketing and market share, this uniformity probably helped more than it hindered.

By standardizing the "Catholic brand" and making it distinctive, this uniformity fostered brand loyalty among religious consumers.

The key to the bishops' centralized control over a rapidly expanding and highly diverse church institution was maintaining tight control over personnel, especially the deployment and discipline of the clergy. Without control over the priests who actually preached the gospel, administered the sacraments, and managed the day-to-day affairs of local congregations, bishops' names on deeds to property would be meaningless. Priests, on the other hand, sought a meaningful voice in the governance of the local church and in the conditions of their pastoral ministry, a voice that seemed to be granted them in canon law. In particular, sometimes with the support of the Holy See, priests sought a meaningful voice in the selection of their bishops, erection of missions into canonical parishes with the traditional right of pastors to stability in office, and "due process of law" when they were accused of misconduct. The bishops adamantly opposed these desiderata of their lower clergy and regarded the Propaganda's interventions in support of individual priests and of the priests' agenda as unwarranted meddling by those with an inadequate or erroneous understanding of the local situation.[56]

The bishops did not lack legitimate reasons for retaining considerable freedom in dealing with their priests. Rapidly changing demographics required that the bishops have great flexibility in assigning and transferring priests; they also needed the authority to intervene promptly and decisively to deal with ineffective or incorrigible priests. As the Catholic Church became more firmly established, however, episcopal claims that local conditions rendered it impossible or inopportune to accede to priests' demands for participation, stability, and due process became increasingly less credible. In 1878, the Propaganda, wearied by frequent recourses by priests against alleged episcopal arbitrariness, imposed an abbreviated judicial proceeding for criminal trials of clerics. However, the imposed judicial procedure seems to have been honored more in the breech than in the observance, and no real movement toward stability in office for parish priests occurred until the Code Commission declared that all previously existing missions had been elevated to the status of parishes by the 1917 Code.[57]

From a business perspective, the bishops' willingness to ignore and, if necessary, defy canonical norms made perfect sense. As the ones who actually carried out the teaching and sanctifying functions for which the church existed, priests were the key productive factor in the church's "business." If the bishop lost his ability to deploy, discipline, and direct them to meet the needs of the local church as he saw them, the bishop's ability to coordinate the church's mission would quickly evaporate. Throughout the nineteenth and early twentieth centuries, secular employers also jealously guarded their freedom in employment matters and resisted efforts by labor unions and government to restrict their unfettered discretion in dealing with employees. Since secular law viewed priests as employees of the church, it was easy for bishops to carry over prevailing labor-management practices that accorded employers broad discretion and employees few procedural rights into their dealings with their priests. Thus, it is not surprising that bishops viewed efforts by the Propaganda to introduce canonical protections for the rights of priests with the same hostility with which businesses greeted governmental interventions in private employment practices. Despite the Romanization of the American church in general and of its hierarchy in particular, the American bishops remained prepared to defy Rome if it made good business sense. The bishops' willingness to dig in their heels underscored the status of priests as employees of the church.

The period between the end of the First World War and the end of the Second Vatican Council was the longest sustained period of harmonious relations between bishops and their priests in the history of the Catholic Church in the United States. There were numerous causes for this harmony. The removal of the American church's status as a missionary territory under the jurisdiction of the Propaganda Fidei in 1909 and especially the promulgation of the 1917 Code of Canon Law extended to priests most of the rights and procedural protections for which they had been clamoring throughout the nineteenth century. The Code *ipso iure* transformed most former "missions" into full-fledged parishes and their "rectors" into pastors with the full tenure that canon law traditionally has accorded to that office. Moreover, the now thoroughly Romanized bishops were more inclined than their predecessors to follow the law in dealing with priests. The priests themselves, thoroughly imbued with the ultramontane fervor through their long formation in Romanized seminaries, were, on the whole, more docile and less disruptive than many of their nineteenth-century counterparts, in part at least because it was in their long-term best interest to be so. The centralization of authority that had ensconced the bishop as a pope for his diocese had also enhanced the stature of the pastor "so that in the parish he enjoyed a supremacy over the laity not unlike that of the Pope over the entire Church."[58] Pastors who enjoyed the benefits of the system (and priests who were not yet pastors but had well-founded expectations that they would be one day) had limited incentives to "rock the boat."

An often overlooked factor, however, is the qualitative change that occurred in the bishops' way of viewing and dealing with their priests, especially their pastors. As the diocese took on the organizational form of a holding company in which the individual units enjoyed considerable autonomy, pastors, as the ones responsible for these local units, came to be viewed less as parts of the labor pool and more as branch managers. A similar upgrade to professional or managerial status was enjoyed by priests who taught in or administered schools and who worked in the expanding diocesan bureaucracy. During this period, middle-level managers in the corporate sector were also becoming something of cultural icons. In an age that celebrated "the organization man" as the epitome of professional achievement and status, the priest-manager of the local branch of the diocesan enterprise, the revered and sometimes feared "brick and mortar" pastor of legend, could enjoy the same prestige as the president of the local bank or the manager of the local factory of a large corporation. This change in the status of the parish priest did not change his status as an "employee" but was a change in the sort of "employee" he was considered to be, a change from "blue collar" to "white collar" status not unlike the one many of his parishioners were undergoing as Catholics became more upwardly mobile.

Assessment

Throughout the nineteenth and early twentieth centuries, bishops exercised their central control in managing their dioceses, organized in the form of a holding company, with the assistance of a rather spartan administrative staff. Although canon law required the appointment of a vicar general with ordinary executive power roughly equivalent to that of the diocesan bishop, most bishops gave the title "vicar general" as a title of honor to a revered senior priest but did not expect this vicar to exercise any of the powers attached to the office. Instead, the key administrative figure in most dioceses was the chancellor, whose canonical duties were to be the chief notary and archivist of the diocese, but who usually exercised broad powers as delegate of the bishop. This preference for organization of the governance through delegates rather than offices was consistent with the general business orientation of diocesan structures in the United States. As Provost noted:

> Some of the changes are due to the American experience of the separation of church and State, requiring administrators to deal with ecclesiastical organization more in terms of a private business corporation or voluntary association than in European terms of a political state or state-related entity. Another reason for the modified form of administration in this country is the tension which existed in the last century between bishops and priests, and the desire by bishops to hold a much tighter control of church life than the tridentine pattern permitted. In the United States the pattern of administration emerged where the bishop retained personal responsibility for overall supervision and for pastoral care. Instead of vicars in the area of administration, bishops used delegates, especially their chancellors; for pastoral care, instead of pastors with proper authority they appointed delegates as rectors of churches.[59]

In addition to the chancellor, most dioceses had a superintendent of schools, a director of charitable activities, and, if the size of the diocese warranted, episcopal delegates for key areas of church activity. The offices of these three central services were served by skeleton staffs. Most operational decisions for parishes were left to pastors.

The business of the church was funded almost entirely by free-will offerings of the faithful, supplemented by the "stole fee" for the administration of the sacraments and sacramentals and, in some places, by the "door collection" or entrance fee for admission to church services. These free-will offerings were usually given during the offertory collection and other collections taken up in churches on days of precept. As a result, the church's ordinary operating revenue was dependent on local sources and on the means and generosity of the faithful of local communities. Since the diocese itself had no independent benefices or other sources of revenue to defray the expenses of the bishop and his central staff, revenue to support diocesan offices was raised by taxing the incomes of local congregations, often through the traditional canonical tax called the *cathedraticum*. Although the term "tax" suggests a governmental function, it was used primarily to give the patina of canonical respectability to the business practice of allocating the costs of central offices among the other units of the enterprise. The duties of the diocese's central administration were limited primarily to the appointment of priest personnel to the local units, monitoring their performance, and coordinating the activities of these local units. For such limited functions, a central staff of modest size was usually sufficient and the taxes to support them could be rather modest. However, the growth in the number of parish units and the diversification of their activities as well as the assumption of a number of new functions by dioceses themselves had begun to strain the capacity of the now traditional organizational structure by 1950, especially in larger dioceses.

Bureaucratization and Organizational Failure (1960–)

Reviewing the Situation

The Church Environment

Since 1960, the environment in which the church conducted its "business" has been rapidly changing. While the Catholic community has continued to grow until it now encompasses approximately one-fourth of the American population, a decreasing proportion of the Catholics are immigrants, and an even smaller proportion of them are poor and uneducated. However, the majority of the recent and projected growth in the Catholic population is from recent immigrants, especially Hispanics and Asians. Native-born Catholics are increasingly well educated — often better educated than their clergy, middle- to upper-class, and professional.[60] As a result, they have become more discriminating and demanding consumers of the church's services. Increasing numbers of Catholics have moved out of the central cities to the suburbs, and their places in the cities have been taken by a new class of poor who are often not Catholic. This movement of peoples has posed several problems for the church organization. On the one hand, the influx of Catholics to the suburbs has necessitated the creation of new parishes and the related parochial infrastructure to serve their spiritual needs; on the other hand, the emptying of the pews and schools of formerly vibrant inner-city parishes left dioceses with much underutilized infrastructure and few visible means of ongoing financial support.

A final but critical environmental factor that has decisively influenced the evolution of church organizational structures was the Second Vatican Council and the reforms that followed in its wake. One effect of Vatican II, with its ecumenical thrust and its spirit of openness to the modern world, was to usher in a period when the web of parallel structures and associations that had formed the visible and invisible walls of the "Catholic ghetto" and sheltered the immigrant masses from the hostile Protestant culture around them began to evaporate. Catholic hospitals, educational institutions, and other apostolic endeavors have struggled to define and incarnate what it means to be a "Catholic" institution in an environment where they find themselves in often cutthroat competition with secular purveyors of similar services. Especially in the aftermath of Paul VI's encyclical *Humanae Vitae,* Catholics became increasingly selective about which church teachings and disciplines they will observe.[61] Mass attendance declined markedly; enrollment in Catholic schools dropped, and many of these schools were closed; Catholic women of child-bearing age are as likely to practice birth control and Catholics as likely to divorce as their non-Catholic fellow citizens. Of critical importance from an organizational point of view, the number of priests and especially religious women available for service declined drastically, and the numbers show no signs of rebounding in the foreseeable future. This decline in the number of available priests and religious is already making it difficult for the church to continue to provide minimal service to its traditional clientele, much less to expand operations to meet new needs.

The Business Environment

Throughout the twentieth century, large corporations had to do their business in a rapidly changing external environment. Fierce competition, often from domestic upstarts and foreign firms, challenged the traditional market dominance of industry giants. AT&T's dominance in telecommunication was ended not only by intervention of anti-trust enforcers at the United States Department of Justice but especially by the challenge of new domestic service providers, and General Motors continues to lose market share to Japanese and other foreign automakers. Moreover, advances in technology and changing demographics and consumer tastes required rapid innovation and adaption, and the computer revolution permanently altered the way firms acquired, processed, and utilized information. These changes in the external environment posed severe challenges to firms' internal organization. By the 1920s in the largest corporations and somewhat later in others, however, centralized and departmentally compartmentalized firms that had come to dominate their respective markets had begun to experience severe organizational problems that were largely attributable to their success. Growth, often spectacular growth, in the size and scope of their operations and the diversification of their product line overloaded the capacity of the firm's management to be efficient in allocating resources, monitoring performance, and coordinating activities.

> Decision-making by executives in large firms may be strategic or tactical: *Strategic* decisions are concerned with the long-term health of the enterprise. *Tactical* decisions deal more with the day-to-day activities necessary for efficient and smooth operations. But decisions, either strategic or tactical, usually require *implementation* by the allocation or reallocation of resources — funds, equipment, or personnel. Strategic plans can be formulated from below, but normally the implementation of such proposals requires the resources that only the general office can provide. Within the broad policy lines laid down by that office and with the resources it allocates, the executives at the lower level carry out tactical decisions.[62]

Strategic or entrepreneurial decisions determine the basic long-term goals and objectives of the firm and allocate or, if necessary, acquire the resources necessary to translate them into reality. Thus, decisions to expand or diversify activities, to set open new plants or offices or to close old ones, and to add new functions are essentially strategic.[63] When a firm is relatively small and its operations fairly simple, the same persons or group of persons can often make both strategic and tactical decisions effectively. However, as the firm grows both in size and complexity, the centralized firm experiences strains in allocating, coordinating, and monitoring efficiently. The growing inefficiency of a centralized firm can be masked as long as few if any strategic decisions are required. However, when strategic decisions have been required because "technology, markets, and sources of supply were changing rapidly, the defects of such a structure became more obvious."[64]

Despite its historical success in transforming the business landscape of the United States, the centralized unitary form of business has an inherent weakness which

> became critical when the administrative load on the senior executives increased to such an extent that they were unable to handle their entrepreneurial responsibilities efficiently. This situation arose when the operations of the enterprise became too complex and the problems of coordination, appraisal, and policy formation too intricate for a small number of top officers to handle both long-run, entrepreneurial, and short-run, operational and administrative activities.[65]

A common response to the problems in handling the volume and complexity of demands on management is to add new layers of middle-level management. However, the inexorable growth of bureaucracies in hierarchically organized institutions creates new challenges to efficient allocation, monitoring, and coordination. Four of these are worthy of special mention: persistence, communication distortion, bureaucratic insularity, and cooperation limits among lower-level participants.[66]

1. "Persistence" refers, in part, to what in business is known as the "sunk cost phenomena." Once an investment has been made in plant, equipment, personnel, and planning, a project or program is insulated from displacement by alternatives that might otherwise be preferable. Moreover, once administrative authorities have committed their prestige to a project or program, they are loath to second-guess themselves. "If the ... administrative system has committed itself in advance to the correctness and efficacy of its reforms, it cannot tolerate learning of failure."[67] As a result, programs receive much greater critical scrutiny at the proposal and development phase than they do in the execution phase.

2. As additional hierarchical layers are added to the organization, information is distorted at each level of the bureaucracy at which it is

communicated. Some of this distortion is defensive in that subordinates tell their superiors what they think they want to hear; some is assertive in that subordinates report what (but only what) they want their superiors to hear. Whether the distortions are intentional or inadvertent, "almost all organizations tend to produce false images in the decision-maker, and...the more authoritarian the organization, the better the chance that its top decision-makers will be operating in purely imaginary worlds."[68]

3. "Bureaucratic insularity" results from the fact that, since spans of control are finite, "increasing firm size leads to taller hierarchies in which leaders are less subject to control by lower-level participants. The resulting bureaucratic insularity of the leadership permits it, if it is so inclined, to both entrench and engross itself."[69] This inclination of bureaucratically insulated executives to entrench themselves at the expense of the firms they headed was particularly in evidence in the recent corporate scandals at Enron and Adelphia.

4. One of the advantages of integrating functions into an organization is that it promotes among all participants a sense of personal involvement in and responsibility for the whole enterprise and not just their small part in it. However, as the hierarchical organization expands and the individual participant feels dwarfed by the system, his or her sense of moral involvement in the larger enterprise will be impaired. The loss of such a sense of moral involvement tends to promote an erosion of an attitude of voluntary cooperation and group disciplinary pressure and an increase in self-interested behavior.

Responses

Business

The response of business firms to a rapidly changing external environment was to reconfigure themselves by decentralizing operations. This decentralization did not entail spinning off the constituent parts of the enterprise as distinct corporations, but the segregation of strategic and tactical decision-making within the firms, i.e., replacing the unitary structure with a multi-divisional structure. The characteristics and advantages of the multi-divisional form of organization are:

1. The responsibility for operating decisions is assigned to (essentially self-contained) operating divisions or quasi-firms.

2. The elite staff attached to the general office perform both advisory and auditing functions. Both have the effect of securing greater control over the operating divisions.

3. The general office is principally concerned with strategic decisions, involving planning, appraisal, and control, including the allocation of resources among the (competing) operating divisions.

4. The separation of the general office from the (competing) operating divisions provides general office executives with the psychological commitment to be concerned with the overall performance of the organization rather than becoming absorbed in the affairs of the functional parts.

5. The resulting structure displays both rationality and synergy.[70]

First introduced at General Motors and DuPont, this multi-divisional form of organization enjoyed considerable success and was widely emulated. One key to the success of this model is its separation of strategic and tactical decisions; the other key to its success is the willingness and ability of participants to respect this separation of functions both in theory and practice. The advantages and efficiencies of the multi-divisional organization are lost or, at least, compromised when central managers cannot resist the temptation to meddle in the day-to-day affairs of operating units, but "maintaining a separation between these two activities apparently imposes severe strain on some managements."[71] Nor can the multi-divisional form work effectively if those charged with strategic decision-making cannot or will not think strategically.

> In many enterprises the executives responsible for resource allocation may very well concentrate on day-to-day operational affairs, giving little or no attention to changing markets, technology, sources of supply, and other factors affecting the long term health of the company. Their decisions may be made without forward planning or analysis but rather by meeting in an *ad hoc* way every new situation, problem or crisis as it arises. They accept the goals of the enterprise as given or inherited. Clearly wherever entrepreneurs act like managers, whenever they concentrate on short-term activities

to the exclusion or to the detriment of long-range planning, appraisal, and coordination, they have failed to carry out effectively their role in the economy as well as in their enterprise.[72]

Adoption of a multi-divisional organizational form is not a panacea for problems in the business world, as the scandals at Enron, Tyco, and Adelphia make clear. Nevertheless, these scandals and failures in the business world have been due less to problems in organizational structures than to defects in organization cultures.[73]

The Church

Changes in the external environment in which the Catholic Church in the United States has carried out its mission since the close of the Second Vatican Council have certainly called for organizational adaptations. However, the most visible adaptation in diocesan organization during the period has been to increase the size and scope of dioceses' central administration. In essence, the typical diocesan organizational form has shifted, in fact if not always in theory, from that of a holding company to that of centralized unitary firm. Until the early twentieth century, diocesan central administrations were rather lean structures. In the twentieth century and especially in the years following Vatican II, these central administrative apparatuses have expanded greatly. No single reason explains the recent multiplication of agencies in the diocesan central offices. Some were established to advise and assist the bishop in his duties as diocesan chief executive officer, some to coordinate activities going on at several locations (e.g., schools and religious education programs), some to provide direct services that parishes either could not or were not trusted to carry out at their own initiative, and still others to exert episcopal control.

Hierarchical control clearly provided the impetus for the first expansions of diocesan bureaucracies, which were mandated by the Holy See. As part of Pius X's anti-Modernist campaign, dioceses were required to establish commissions to monitor orthodoxy, and in 1935 the Congregation for the Council mandated the establishment of commissions to improve catechetical curricula and the training of catechists. Other additions followed apace until, by 1964, Echeverria could identify thirty-seven organisms typically found in diocesan curiae.[74] The Second

Vatican Council itself called for the establishment of liturgical, missionary, and ecumenical commissions, presbyteral and pastoral councils, vicars for religious, and communications offices. Local needs dictated the establishment of yet additional diocesan offices and commissions.

> The expansion of specialized offices in turn necessitated the creation of other structures that would coordinate the work of the offices and support the personnel needs within them. Diocesan human resource offices were set up to administer and fund the hiring procedures, salary systems and benefit programs that would undergird an enlarged central staff.[75]

While the movement toward expanded diocesan bureaucracies occurred throughout the United States, no nationwide statistics on the size and scope of diocesan central services offices are available. Nevertheless, one study in 1978 of just three dioceses, the Archdioceses of Denver and Detroit and the Diocese of Cleveland, found that

> the number of chancery personnel in the three dioceses combined rose from 42 in 1900, to 214 in 1978; the number of pastoral services (basically agencies and offices beyond those technically required for the curia as described in the Code) increased from 12 in 1900, to 193 in 1978. Viewed from another perspective, pastoral services in these three dioceses combined to grow at the rate of 6 percent per annum, although most of the increase occurred after 1970 with a remarkable 13 percent increase in programs.[76]

Although this study covered only three dioceses, a cursory reading of the *Official Catholic Directory* shows that what was occurring in these three dioceses was not an aberration but the norm.

Since dioceses have few independent sources of revenues for agencies and programs, expansion of diocesan bureaucracy has been funded largely by taxes on parish revenues, sometimes as much as 20 percent of ordinary parish income. However, by 1980, it was becoming apparent that the age of bureaucratic expansion was coming to an end. "Beginning in the mid 1980's, the shortfall of money [raised by taxation of parishes] began to mark the limit of expansion.... Revenues generally began to flatten by 1985."[77]

Assessment

It is somewhat ironic that the dioceses of the United States should address their need for structural change to adapt to a rapidly changing external environment by adopting a centralized unitary organizational form just as businesses were abandoning this form for the more decentralized and flexible multi-divisional form. Although not on a scale with General Motors or Wal-Mart, most diocesan operations are too complex and their problems of coordination, appraisal, and policy formulation too intricate to be handled efficiently by the diocesan bishop alone or even with the assistance of a specialized staff. With sometimes hundreds of parish operating units and a multitude of activities and programs, diocesan strategic and tactical decision-making need to be separated. The results of the failure to separate these functions in the unitary organization of dioceses have often been "crisis" management by central offices, a consequent conspicuous absence of strategizing, and a lack of initiative by pastors, who are the managers of the local units but who have grown wary of acting without directives and approval from above. The growth of diocesan central administration as a response to the growth in the size and complexity of church operations has fostered the problems typical of overly centralized organizations: persistence, communication distortion, bureaucratic insularity, and lowered cooperation levels by lower-level participants.

All four of these predictable consequences of overexpansion of hierarchical systems have been in evidence recently in the organizational behavior of American dioceses.

1. "Persistence" has been exhibited not only in the failure of dioceses to address the longstanding consequences of their underutilized and non-viable parishes (and, more ominously, in their failure to discipline properly clerics guilty of sexual abuse of minors), but also in the resolute refusal of bishops and their advisors to admit mistakes and failures. As Robert Kennedy has observed,

> evaluation has not been a strong point in decision-making within the Catholic Church. Choices once made were set in motion without provision for careful monitoring and evaluation. One reason for such neglect would seem to have been the widely held view that the will of an ecclesiastical superior represents the will of God.

Superiors of the past made choices, and members of the church were instructed to accept such choices as the will of God. Such an approach tended to terminate the decision-making process at the moment of choice, requiring little attention to implementation which was confidently left to the Lord whose will was being implemented, and precluding all concern for evaluation.[78]

It is also evident in the abysmal failure of church agencies at every level to conduct serious performance reviews of programs and personnel.[79]

2. Communication distortions are endemic to the cultures of large centralized organizations. Communications distortions are so commonplace, in part, because acquiring reliable and relevant information is hard work.

The human condition seems to contain a propensity to assert as fact what one desires to be fact rather than what one has ascertained to be fact, to accept half-truths, unsubstantiated rumor, or unquestioned statistics, and to resist probing investigation of asserted facts as insulting lack of confidence in one's truthfulness. As a consequence, the gathering of facts is often careless, incomplete and tainted by error. This can lead to the misperception of the cause or extent of a problem or need and the consequent adoption of an ineffective solution.[80]

This human propensity is exacerbated in an organizational climate, not unusual in the church, where leaders ordained to proclaim the Good News make it clear that they want to hear only good news. The resulting communication distortion allows church leaders to refuse to seek or to ignore data, especially social science data, about the actual state of the church and to prefer Panglossian visions to the growing body of evidence that the church in the United States is, in Peter Steinfels's phrase, "a people adrift" and its leadership is, in Yves Congar's phrase, operating in "a haze of fiction."

3. Bureaucratic insularity is the inevitable result of such communications distortion. As a result of the bureaucratic insularity of ecclesial leaders, the church is looking increasingly like a "lazy monopoly" whose leadership seems unwilling or unable to respond to expressions of dissatisfaction with the quality of the service and product being provided by

the organization.[81] Although there is little evidence to suggest that bishops have exploited their relative immunity from control or even criticism by the lower clergy and the laity to entrench themselves, bureaucratic insulation has allowed them to avoid accountability for their actions and inactions. In recent years, for example, there has been no little wonderment that no bishop has been removed for his mishandling of clergy sexual abuse cases. At a more mundane level, bureaucratic isolation has also allowed church leadership to evade financial accountability. Francis Butler reports:

> One recent advisor to our organization [FADICA] described the state of financial administration in many dioceses as "mom and pop management." Too often mismanagement goes unreported and unpunished.... In a study of the financial reports of thirteen US dioceses, no comparisons could be made among the documents due to lack of uniformity in reporting, and this was in spite of church policies to the contrary. A sad litany of embezzlements, misuse of charitable collections, bad investments, wheeling and dealing, and mismanagement undermine confidence that dioceses are run soundly and accountably.[82]

4. This bureaucratic insularity has also fostered an atmosphere in which cynical knowledge erodes the commitment of clergy and laity alike to sacrifice for the sake of the overall good of the institution.[83] A recent Lilly Foundation study found that lack of accountability for and participation in financial decision-making was "the most influential factor that accounted for a per capita decades-long decline in Catholic giving relative to other faiths."[84]

> One can argue that church problems run much more deeply than those of an administrative and managerial nature. They do. The Church will not be able to get to them, however, if it continues to operate in an atmosphere of declining resources in the form of money and personnel, estrangement, and suspicion among its rank and file, and with a serious demoralization of clergy and church personnel.[85]

Implicit in apologias for the rise and persistence of central service bureaucracies in dioceses is the theological presumption that the diocese itself under the leadership of the bishop is the real and authentic manifestation of the church and that the semi-autonomous juridic status accorded to parishes by canon law is a relic of feudalism. In this view,

> The ecclesiology of Vatican II restored the proper emphasis on the diocese, rather than the parish, as the primary unit of the Church. In keeping with that ecclesiology Vatican II resurrected the pre-feudal tradition of the Church regarding temporal goods, which saw the goods of the Church as a common patrimony meant to serve ecclesial communion as well as the particular ends of certain individuals or groups. In this view there is greater centralization but also more co-responsibility. The diocesan bishop has greater responsibility to see to a more equitable distribution of the resources in the diocese, keeping in mind the needs of the Church outside his diocese.[86]

Whatever the theological merits of this position, it makes little economic sense. In addition to being the source of the bulk of diocesan revenue, the parish is where, for most, the "business" of the church is conducted. It is there that the gospel is proclaimed, there that the sacraments are administered, and there that "people are bonded to the Church, where they 'belong' and so in a very real sense [it] is the local Church for most people."[87] The widespread tendency, especially among church professionals, to equate the diocese with the church and to treat the parish as an anachronism or, at best, an afterthought may be symptomatic of the tendency, epidemic in service organizations including churches, to fail "even to ask the question of what is their business, and this eventually spells trouble."[88]

If parishes or local communities of the faithful akin to them are where the church's primary business is conducted, "trouble" may be too weak a word to describe the condition of the business today. If people do not bond with the church through participation in the liturgy and life of one of these local communities, it is unlikely that they will bond with it at all. It is the function of these local communities to see that the faith is sustained and handed on by the proclamation of the gospel and the celebration of the sacraments. The available evidence suggests that these core functions are indeed being carried out, but that they are not being carried out especially well. The gospel is regularly preached in Catholic parishes, but, as Andrew Greeley's data continue to show, the faithful are not enthusiastic about the preaching they hear.[89] Passing on the faith to the next generation through Catholic schools and religious education programs has also had less than spectacular success. The number of and enrollment in Catholic schools has declined sharply, and about 40 percent of Catholic young people attending public schools are not enrolled even sporadically in parish religious education.[90] Discouragingly, those who do pass through these schools and programs are, in the main, barely literate in the Catholic tradition.[91] The sacraments are administered in Catholic parishes, but the quality of liturgical life in most parishes, even forty years after the reforms initiated by Vatican II, is numbingly mediocre.[92] In short, the parishes where the core business of the church is being conducted now as it has long been have been the victim of benign neglect.

Arguably, the rise of central diocesan bureaucracies during the last fifty years has come at the expense of the life and vitality of local communities of the faithful where the gospel is proclaimed and the sacraments administered. Central services bureaucracies have absorbed a large share of the human and material resources available for the mission of the particular church. Not only are parishes taxed heavily to support these operations, but central bureaucracies often recruit the most talented clergy, religious, and laity away from parish ministry. Although the existence and expense of numerous diocesan offices is justified by their supposed support and assistance to parish units, "the ingrained tendency of experts [is] to create permanent dependence among parish leaders,"[93] to belittle the knowledge and skill of local leaders, and, at times, to bypass benighted pastors and local structures. This somewhat paternalistic attitude toward parish units ignores the fact that permanent dependence of parishes and their leaders on central services is a sign of a critical weakness in the local unit itself. As Peter Drucker has pointed out, healthy organizations "should neither need nor use central staff service to 'advise' the operating managements of the decentralized units. These units should be strong enough to stand on their own feet. If they are not, service staffs will not cure their weakness but compound it."[94]

Reconfiguring diocesan organizations from their present de facto unitary organizational form to a multi-divisional form with parishes as the quasi-autonomous operating units would actually bring diocesan structures into closer conformity with canon law. Such a reorganization would

give parishes considerable autonomy to make tactical operational decisions within the parameters of strategic plans and policies formulated
by the diocesan bishop. The success of such a reorganization would
depend, on the one hand, on the willingness of the bishop and his immediate staff to refrain from meddling in operational matters of the
local units and, on the other hand, on the willingness and ability of
parish priests to move from the largely bureaucratic role of "minding
the store" to the more professional role of building the business. The
great risk of this strategy is, of course, that some of the local units will
fail. Nevertheless, freed from the burden of involvement in day-to-day
decision-making, the bishop could assume the sort of role suggested by
the ancient term *episkopē*. A key element of this *episkopē* would be
monitoring the performance of local units and their leadership and coordinating the activities of these units. However, there is always a danger
that, in exercising this monitoring function, concern for domination will
replace concern for production as the rationale for the bureaucracy itself.
Such a transformation occurred in the bureaucracy of imperial Rome,[95]
and it has occurred in corporate bureaucracies of the United States. It is
not inconceivable that it could also happen in the church.

Conclusion

In their struggles to carve out, maintain, and, at times, expand space in
the public square for the Catholic Church, bishops and their co-workers
have had to make do with the structures and strategies available in the
private sector. For this task, the norms of traditional canon law — and,
to a great extent, even of the recently revised canon law — have proved
less relevant and helpful than structures and strategies of the business
world. Consequently, canonical norms have been frequently adapted,
bent, honored in letter but not in spirit, and not infrequently ignored to
fit the church's actual situation. The result has been the emergence of a
church whose organizational structures and procedures, when stripped
of their theological veneer, look a lot more like designs from the Harvard
Business School than from the Pontifical Commission for the Revision
of the Code of Canon Law.

Decisions to creatively adapt, pay mere lip service to, or simply ignore canonical norms in the structuring of the local church in the United

States were not prompted by ignorance or stubborn defiance of canon law but by a more or less intuitive sense that the underlying presuppositions of these norms were simply inapplicable to the context in which the church found itself in the United States. Nevertheless, canon law was and is the bearer, albeit in a sometimes archaic form, of important ecclesial values that a church organization ignores at its peril. Ever since the corporate form emerged as the device of choice for business organizations, governments, both state and federal, have regulated these entities in the public interest. The corporate forms chosen by the church for its organization in the United States have been largely shielded from these regulatory norms by the First Amendment. If there is a future role for canon law in the church of the United States, perhaps it is to provide the norms to regulate church organizations in the ecclesial interest or to be the ecclesial conscience that prevents a corporation with the soul of a church from becoming a church with the soul of a corporation.

Part Two

INCULTURATION
AND IDENTITY

Chapter 6

Beyond "Liberal" and "Conservative"

The Internal Sectarian Threat to U.S. Catholicism

Mark S. Massa, S.J.

ⓒ❧❦⊰⊱

L IKE MANY in my trade today, I find myself increasingly impatient
with the "liberal" and "conservative" labeling that goes on in identifying the sides in the debates that divide the Catholic academy. One of
many reasons for my own impatience with such labels is that these essentially political monikers actually obscure at least as much as they reveal
in theological debate, and hardly encompass the real levels of complexity
and nuance that inform serious intellectual interchange.[1]

But such conservative/liberal labeling among U.S. Catholics is hardly
new to the twenty-first century: at least since the reception of Pope
Leo XIII's 1899 encyclical *Testem Benevolentiae* — warning Archbishop
Gibbons of Baltimore of the ostensible heresy of "Americanism" — some
version of such labeling has flourished in the American Catholic community. After that 1899 letter, *Americanism* came to be identified as
the creed of those "liberals" who sought a greater accommodation with
the democratic culture of the United States, while "anti-Americanism"
(or, more commonly, *Ultramontanism*) became identified as those "conservatives" who sought a Catholic Church far more closely modeled
on the centralizing impulses then regnant in Rome. This politicizing of
the Americanist Controversy can be witnessed even in the titles of well-
researched scholarly works of the affair — for instance, Robert Cross's
Emergence of Liberal Catholicism in America. We might now allow
that Cross's very smart study (the first scholarly treatment of American
Catholicism by a non-Catholic scholar) was ill-served by its anachro-
nistic title, for there were neither liberals nor conservatives (in the

twentieth- or twenty-first-century sense) in the late nineteenth-century North American church.[2]

These monikers rooting Catholic "liberals" and "conservatives" in Americanist questions of inculturation continued well into the twentieth century, when in mid-century the documents of the Second Vatican Council appeared to offer new canonical texts for positioning conservative and liberal impulses within the church. The document of Vatican II that (at least initially) offered the favored locus for such new positioning was *Sacrosanctum Concilium,* the council's Constitution on the Sacred Liturgy. The "banner and guitar" versus "plainchant and incense" liturgical wars fought in many parishes came to be interpreted by many cultural commentators (as well as by many Catholic theologians) as *really* being simply liturgical shorthand for much larger ideological agenda — agenda as often as not implied as actually identified — in narratives purportedly explaining those (now strangely dated) battles.[3]

But Andrew Greeley is undoubtedly correct in asserting that both *Testem Benevolentiae* and the documents of Vatican II were replaced as the textual loci for defining the "sides" in intra-church debates after 1968 by Paul VI's encyclical on human sexuality and birth control, *Humanae Vitae.* While the ostensible focus of Paul VI's encyclical had been on the "most serious duty of transmitting human life" (as its opening sentence, giving the encyclical its name, announced), the debates it generated — as any theology major at a Catholic college can tell you — quickly focused on section 14 of the document, which declared that "any action which before, at the moment of, or after sexual intercourse specifically intended to prevent procreation" was declared to be not only wrong, but "intrinsically morally disordered."[4]

Thus, the theological debates among North American Catholics about *Humanae Vitae* quickly telescoped from its teaching about human sexuality as a divine gift — hardly a controverted position in any "side" in the Catholic discussion — to its argument about the intrinsic moral disorder of "artificial" birth control. As the U.S. secular press (and large sections of the Catholic academy as well) have come to report the debate over the encyclical even into our new century, theological "liberals" were those who questioned the arguments offered by Paul VI justifying his condemnation of contraception, while theological "conservatives" were those who believed that all faithful Catholics were obliged to give complete assent to the letter's condemnation of contraception.[5]

Elements of all of these previous battles have shaped the internecine debates within the U.S. Catholic community into our new century. But the contemporary debates in the U.S. church between supposed "liberals" and "conservatives" are also now informed by a more insidious — and, potentially, far more destructive — threat: that of sectarianism. The older debates have now been shaped by a deeply disturbing (and profoundly intra-Catholic) impulse that has been growing in the last quarter-century, setting its face against the Catholic tradition of Christianity in North America. And that sectarian threat is the more disturbing — and the more dangerous — because it agitates not from outside the Catholic community, but from within that community's own household.

In making this argument, I am taking as axiomatic a definition of "Roman Catholicism" offered by the great (non-Catholic) philosopher of religion Mircea Eliade. In his entry for Roman Catholicism in the magisterial *Encyclopedia of Religion,* Eliade quite correctly observed:

> As a tradition, Roman Catholicism is marked by several different doctrinal and theological emphases. The very word *Catholic* means "universal...." Therefore, what is most directly opposed to Catholicism is not Protestantism, but sectarianism. Sectarianism is a movement within Christianity that holds that the church is a community of true believers, a precinct of righteousness, set over against an unredeemed world of sin.[6]

According to Eliade's definition, then, "sectarianism" refers to a specific set of impulses within Christianity that understands one of the church's most important duties to be pronouncing judgment on the unredeemed world of sin that surrounds the "community of the saints." That community's duty is to call the unredeemed world around it to repentance while never really entering into dialogue with it — much less entering into collaboration with it on matters of social or political concern. As Eliade — himself borrowing from the work of the seminal German sociologist Ernst Troeltsch — would have it, then, sectarianism considers all dialogue and collaboration with "the world" as simply invitations to compromise.[7]

A survey of the contemporary North American Catholic scene reveals the presence of several small but very well organized networks of groups within the U.S. Catholic Church which press sectarian — and thus from Eliade's (and my own) point of view — profoundly un-Catholic models of Christianity as not only acceptable, but indeed as normative for defining Catholic belief, practice, and identity.[8]

These believers argue that their own (essentially sectarian) understandings of the Catholic tradition of Christianity are the only "orthodox" positions for faithful Catholics to hold, and that those who disagree with their rigid — and oftentimes simplistic — interpretations of a quite complex theological tradition are really just "cafeteria Catholics" or "culture believers" who betray the faith for either cultural comfort or therapeutic ease. Some of these believers press an essentially Reformed Protestant understanding of "church" as a "congregation of gathered believers" set over against the world (an understanding brought with them when they were received into the Catholic communion); other members — being "cradle Catholics" — have adopted what H. Richard Niebuhr once termed the "Christ Against Culture" model of Christianity to stem what they perceive to be the hemorrhage caused by the effects of the Second Vatican Council, the vernacular Mass, or the theological debates set off by *Humanae Vitae*. Still others (to some extent following the lead of Pope John Paul II himself) have sought to disengage the Catholic chariot from the engine of Western, and more specifically North American, "secular culture" — from their point of view a materialistic culture of death headed toward the brick wall of cultural bankruptcy and betrayal of the prophetic "edge" of the gospel.[9]

Several networks of such believers have the support of church figures of considerable influence: ordinaries of certain dioceses who utilize the term "orthodox" to distance their own theological position from other (equally orthodox) Catholics. Others are converts from mainline or evangelical Protestantism who are now editors of journals of opinion or "independent" Catholic institutes who apply the "glories of obedience" to whatever statement issues out of the Vatican. Still others are self-anointed media guardians of what is tiresomely and inappropriately termed "definitive teaching." As Catholic theology over the last millennium has held, "defined teaching" has a quite specific, technical meaning and institutional protocol in the "theological notes" of the *Enchiridion Symbolorum*. Thus, many guardians of such defined teaching, when challenged by critics, have problems pointing to the exact source of such "definitiveness," oftentimes appealing to the rather vast category of "official teaching" — a catchall category that, in their usage, seems to include everything from pronouncements from the Vatican to pastoral letters from local bishops. The irony that I want to emphasize here is that many (most?) of these "watchdogs" might not, ecclesiologically speaking, be Catholic Christians at all, but rather sectarians whose model of the church and tradition — as Eliade so correctly noted — stands at the opposite end of the spectrum from Catholicism.[10]

What makes all of these ostensible "catholic" believers (and the groups in which they press their beliefs) in fact "sectarian" is not a specific ideological stance, nor even any especially distinctive emphasis on the role of papal authority in the governance of the church. Rather, what makes them "sectarian" is an opposition to theological pluralism itself — an opposition to the "several different doctrinal and theological emphases" (in the plural) which Eliade quite correctly recognized as distinctive of the Catholic tradition of Christianity.[11]

Over against precisely the kind of uniformity and theological "cleanness of line" which many of these believers hold as "normative," the Catholic tradition has always sought a fundamental union of belief and practice in the context of "several different doctrinal and theological emphases." Thirteenth-century nominalists and realists; Dominican "rigorists" and Jesuit "laxists" in the seventeenth century; twentieth-century upholders of the *nouvelle théologie* and neo-Thomistic scholastics — all of these fought like theological cats and dogs in their respective eras. But all considered themselves (and their debate partners in often-fierce exchanges) "Catholics" holding a common faith, despite the very different epistemologies, sacramental theologies, and ecclesiologies that informed their common faith.

The tradition of Catholic Christianity has always (wisely) allowed various theological and doctrinal emphases to flourish within its own household. But it is precisely the flourishing of such theological pluralism that makes sectarians within the U.S. Catholic community uneasy: indeed, what unites the congeries of sectarians within the North American church is a determination to replace pluralism — and most especially

ecclesiological pluralism — with one (and only one) "orthodox" model
of Catholicism. That single model of the church is oftentimes elaborated under the rubric of *communio,* that rich Latin word (and concept)
from which we derive the word "communion." But the communion so
presented is always and invariably focused on the institutional church
itself. The "communion" that defines the bonds of this sectarian vision
is, finally, the institutional rubrics, laws, and authority structures of the
Roman Catholic Church, pure and simple. It is, thus, not the rich mystical idea of communion developed in the theology of the *mystici corporis*
(the church as the "mystical body of Christ"); neither is it the "communion" developed in the Catholic theology of the *communio sanctorum*
(the church as the "communion of saints and holy things"); nor is it even
the community as that "People of God" so privileged in the documents
of the Second Vatican Council.[12]

Indeed, for these sectarian believers so preoccupied with safeguarding
Catholicism as *communio,* all other models of church — church as sacrament and servant, church as mystical body and herald, church as People
of God — must bow to rigidly institutional protocols of canon law, liturgical rubrics, and hierarchical arrangements of authority. *Communio*
means primarily (and sometimes even only) being "in communion" with
the bishop of Rome. Any discussion of other models of "communion" as
in any way "normative" (i.e., determinative of "orthodox" Catholicism)
is oftentimes relegated — or even dismissed — as complicit accommodation to "liberal agendas" or "accommodationist impulses" if they are
held in the same authority as the institutional model of the church.

But reducing Catholicism to "institutionally defined protocols" as
the ultimate litmus test of who is — and who is not — a Catholic in
fact represents a significant departure from the theological tradition of
Catholicism, as that tradition has evolved over the past millennium.
The essentially sectarian attempt to eradicate theological (and especially
ecclesiological) pluralism in favor of a model of *communio* that is essentially institutional not only violates the spirit and the letter of the
Second Vatican Council — which utilized different models in different
documents to define the complex reality of the church, most famously the
biblically derived metaphor of church as "People of God." Far more significantly from a historical point of view, the sectarian attempt to replace
a pluralistic ecclesiology which celebrates various kinds of community

with a single, reified understanding of Catholic Christianity as "institution" represents a significant departure from how Catholic Christianity has sought to balance (and preserve) unity and plurality in its God-talk, worship, and governance, in the course of the past millennium.[13]

The most compelling American Catholic theological voice calling for such an ecclesiological balance between pluralism and unity — in the process explaining how an institutional definition of "communion" is defective — is Cardinal Avery Dulles, most famously in his magisterial work *Models of the Church*. In that work Dulles argued that the Catholic tradition *was* catholic and Catholic precisely because it balanced and legitimated various models of the church (in the plural) in defining exactly what Catholic Christians took the church to be. Indeed, Dulles noted that it was this very pluralism in ecclesiology — understanding the church as sacrament and herald, servant and institution — that made Catholic ecclesiology both apostolic and catholic:

> A balanced theology of the Church must find a way of incorporating the major affirmations of each basic ecclesiological type. Each of the models calls attention to certain aspects of the Church that are less clearly brought out by the other models. . . . The most distinctive feature of Catholicism, in my opinion, is not its insistence on the institutional but rather its wholeness or balance. I am of the opinion that the Catholic Church, in the name of its "catholicity," must at all costs avoid falling into a sectarian mentality. Being "catholic," this Church must be open to all God's truth, no matter who utters it.[14]

The model of church privileged after the sixteenth-century Council of Trent had been that posed by Jesuit Cardinal Robert Bellarmine — that of church as "perfect society." In this post-Reformation model, the very structures of the institutional church were elided with the features of the Kingdom of God itself: the hierarchical church, then, sharing in the indefectible qualities of that perfect kingdom, became a "perfect society" on earth, sharing in that guarantee offered by Jesus to Peter that the "gates of hell shall not prevail against it."

> In the popular mind the Catholic Church is identified with what I describe as the institutional model of the Church. Catholics,

therefore, are commonly thought to be committed to the thesis that the Church is most aptly to be conceived as a single, unified "perfect society."[15]

But this popular conception — both outside the church and among Catholics — of the primacy of the institutional model is, according to Dulles, actually untenable; indeed, of all the models presented in his book, "one of the models cannot properly be taken as primary — and this is the institutional model." This is so, he argues, because institutions are, "of their very nature, subordinate to persons." Thus, Dulles observes that in comparison to understanding the church as mystical body, herald, or as sacrament (the model that he personally believes to have "special merit"), church structures in themselves are the least compelling way to define what the church is in its essence because

> structures are subordinate to life. "The sabbath was made for man, not man for the sabbath" (Mk. 2:27). Without calling into question the value and importance of institutions, one may feel that this value does not properly appear unless it can be seen that the structure effectively helps to make the Church a community of grace, a sacrament of Christ, a herald of salvation, and a servant of mankind.[16]

Further, Dulles notes that Catholic theologians should be wary of "routinizing" or freezing any one model of Catholic Christianity as normative, as the church itself — as a living, growing organism in history — always tends toward *pluralizing* its identity in order to be as plastic and flexible as possible to meet new cultural challenges and unforeseen needs. Dulles thus offers "one final caution" at the end of his work about absolutizing any one model in "ranking" the community's self-understanding in its pilgrimage toward a Kingdom that, in fact, is not and cannot be encapsulated in any model of church. Some theologians, he notes,

> tend to assume that the essence of the Church somehow exists, like a dark continent, ready-made and awaiting only to be mapped. The Church, as a sociological entity, may be more correctly viewed as a "social construct." In terms of sociological theory, one may say that the form of the Church *is being constantly modified by the way in which members of the Church externalize their own experience*

and in so doing transform the Church to which they already belong.
Within the myriad possibilities left open by Scripture and tradition,
the Church in every generation has to exercise its options.... The
future forms of the Church lie beyond our power to foresee. The
Church will have to make adjustments in order to survive in the society of the future and to confront the members of that society with
the challenge of the gospel.[17]

Precisely because it is — in every generation — a "social construct,"
then, part of the church's "catholicity" is its rich ecclesiological pluralism. As Dulles himself notes, to privilege any one of the models of the
church (and most especially to privilege the institutional model) as the
normative template for determining Catholic identity represents a sectarian retreat from Catholic ecclesiological identity, as well as a betrayal
of the pluralism that stands at the heart of the Catholic theological
tradition.

The insights of both Mircea Eliade (himself an astute observer "from
the outside" of the Catholic tradition) and Avery Dulles (one of the
most respected intellectual voices within the American Catholic community) offer an intriguing alternative for narrating at least some of the
tiresome — and overused — "conservative/liberal" debates in the North
American Catholic community. Utilizing the insights of both, I would
like to offer four points as a kind of theological prolegomenon as to
why (and how) we should replace those political monikers in at least
some of the theological discussions currently dividing the U.S. Catholic
community.

First: The Catholic tradition of Christianity is marked by "several
different doctrinal and theological emphases" — a foundational insight
about Roman Catholicism elucidated by Mircea Eliade and given theological elaboration by Avery Dulles in one of the most important works
in U.S. Catholic theology. Catholicism, in this understanding, is defined
by an ongoing creative tension between unity and pluralism — between
"oneness" and "manyness." In this creative tension, the pluralism does
(and should) remain as real and decisive as the unity.

But other insights by Eliade in his classic definition of Catholicism
must also be brought into play here in understanding the contemporary
threat of sectarianism in the U.S. Catholic community: the "pluralism"

that Eliade adumbrates at the beginning of his definition of Catholicism is "spelled out" in considerably greater detail in his own definition of the word "Catholic." Constitutive of the "several different doctrinal and theological emphases" marking the Catholic tradition are a "radically positive estimation of the created order" — so that both history and material reality are taken seriously as the locus of God's redemptive purposes. Likewise, the Catholic tradition evinces "a profound respect for rationality as a foundational commitment in understanding God," so that revelation itself must come under the purview of human reason — not to reduce it to human dimensions, but rather to understand that revelation analogically. Further, by its privileging of the "sacramental" as the primary mode of encountering the Holy, and by its "affirmation of the communal dimension of salvation and of every religious relationship with God," the Catholic tradition has always rejected the ahistorical, non-public protocols of sectarianism, with its tendency to distrust the "fallen" world of politics, commerce, and social relations.[18]

In such a read of the Catholic tradition, those who would seek to collapse centuries-long traditions of Catholic theological pluralism into only one privileged model of "church" are *not* "orthodox" (as many style themselves in comparison with fellow Catholics); nor are they "restorationists" in the sense of recovering something from the past lost in the present: on the contrary, that "past" ostensibly being restored was far more diverse, pluralistic, and "messy" than the current ecclesial circumstance putatively being "ordered." Most importantly, they are hardly "conservatives" in the etymological sense of that word — of "conserving" the foundational insights of the Catholic theological tradition. Far from "conserving" the heart of the Catholic tradition, their essentially sectarian efforts represent an assault on the "several different doctrinal and theological emphases" that define Catholicism.

Rather, following the historical development outlined by Jaroslav Pelikan in *The Emergence of the Catholic Tradition,* I think it more appropriate to label them "sectarian catholics." This sectarian impulse, as Mircea Eliade quite correctly noted, stands at the opposite end of the ecclesiological spectrum from what has evolved over the past fifteen hundred years as Catholic Christianity, and represents an inimical impulse to Catholicism itself. While there are historical, sociological, political, and ecclesiological reasons that help explain why this impulse is so attractive to certain Catholics in North America today, it must nonetheless be stoutly resisted by those who seek to guard the Catholic Christian tradition in the United States.

Second: The battleground where these sectarian impulses are most clearly revealed is the theological arena of ecclesiology, in which questions of understanding what the "church" is, and how it should relate to the human cultures around it, are legitimately debated. Catholic (and other) sectarian Christians have tended to adopt what H. Richard Niebuhr once termed the "Christ Against Culture" model of Christianity, a cultural stance that sees the gathered community of believers contending against the "principalities and powers" of what the Epistles of St. John in the New Testament derisively term "the world."[19]

In this "Christ Against Culture" model of church and world, a small community of true believers must defend the faith once delivered to the saints against the sinful compromises of a fallen world, collaboration with which is always (at least potentially) an act that leads to the watering-down of prophetic truth. This ecclesiology informed the stance of the early church limned in the three Epistles of St. John, which reminded its readers that they must not conform themselves to

> this passing world, or anything in this world. The love of the Father cannot be in anyone who loves the world, because *nothing the world has to offer* — the sensual body, the lustful eye, pride in possessions — could ever come from the father, but only from the world. And the world, with all it craves for, is coming to an end.[20]

One of the most famous North American spokespersons for this sectarian ecclesiology was the great nineteenth-century urban revivalist Dwight L. Moody, founder of Chicago's Moody Bible Institute — itself representing something like the "Vatican of U.S. Revivalism." Moody was once asked by a journalist how he conceived his own Bible Institute in relation to the Protestant churches around him, and Moody's (now-famous) answer utilized the metaphor of untrustworthy "barks" on an especially rough sea of human culture heading toward disaster: to Moody, these churches, like "the world" to which they are so conformed, was simply "a sinking vessel, and God has given me a small life-boat, and said to me: 'Moody, save all you can.'"[21]

Catholic ecclesiology has historically resisted this "Christ Against Culture" model, largely in favor of two other Niebuhrian models: those of "Christ Above Culture" and "Christ the Transformer of Culture." As H. Richard Niebuhr argued, the primary exemplar of the "Christ Above Culture" model was Thomas Aquinas, who famously argued that divine grace did not replace or destroy human culture, but rather stated (in one of the most famous lines of medieval theology) that "grace builds on nature." Niebuhr's point, of course, was that Aquinas held that the gospel stood not against culture, nor was its purpose to replace the humanly made world, but rather to complete it — to help it recognize the divine possibilities already latent in human culture. Just one of the many implications of such a model (as Niebuhr is at pains to observe) was that Catholicism has resolutely set its face as a theological tradition against "world-renouncing" models of church.[22]

If the "Christ Above Culture" model largely shaped medieval and Counter-Reformation Catholic theology, the Niebuhrian model that emerged in the twentieth century as the most protean in shaping Catholic theology was that of "Christ the Transformer of Culture" — a model that informs all manner of "political theologies" from feminism and black theology to Latin America–based liberation theologies. This model operates on the assumption that Christian (and Catholic) theology's primary duty is to help liberate people from oppressions of every sort — an assumption undergirding the work of such vastly disparate North American Catholic thinkers as Elizabeth Johnson, Virgilio Elizondo, and Peter Phan.[23]

From the very first, of course, there were sectarian impulses that manifested themselves in the Catholic tradition. But as Ernst Troeltsch and others have observed, Catholicism "siphoned" its sectarian impulses into what was perceived to be the comparatively "safe" channels of monasticism, clerical celibacy, and missionary activity in non-Western ("heathen") cultures. This siphoning off of sectarian impulses into the margins of the tradition helped to insure that the broad mainstream of that tradition remained pluralistic, world-affirming, and multi-textured.[24]

Just part of the success of this "compromise" with the sectarian impulse was the fact that monarchical popes living in Avignon with a very bureaucratic understanding of *ecclesia*, Egyptian monks inhabiting the caves of the desert who sought to flee precisely this monarchical presentation of "church" as represented in Rome and Avignon, scholars living and teaching with their students in the emerging urban centers of Paris, Bologna, and Salamanca, who fought like theological cats and dogs with their local bishops, and illiterate peasants whose understanding of the "mysteries of the faith" was largely untouched by the concerns of any of the foregoing, were *all* nonetheless members of "Holy Mother Church." Those belonging to this messy "manyness" thus defined in this transcultural reality ("messy," at least, from the standpoint of many sectarian believers today) all proudly claimed the title "Catholic" in identifying their faith. From an institutional standpoint, then, the *communio sanctorum* (the "communion of holy ones and holy things") to which they all belonged was not one thing, but rather many levels of practices, authority, spiritualities, and even liturgical rites. Indeed, a succession of supreme pontiffs themselves (after any number of closely fought battles between the "center" and the "margins") stood guarantors that the Roman Rite would be only one among numerous other ways of celebrating the sacraments and — most significantly — the Eucharist, that "center of unity."[25]

Thus, far from being orthodox, traditional, or "conservative," the kind of uniformity being called for by contemporary Catholic sectarians represents an attempt to canonize the kind of papal triumphalism invented in the nineteenth century by ultramontanist bureaucrats who were decisively defeated at the Second Vatican Council — defeated in part because of that council's rejection of precisely that nineteenth century, Eurocentric model of the church in favor of a global vision of Catholicism.[26]

Third: I would agree with University of Chicago theologian David Tracy in his book *The Analogical Imagination* that it is the sacramental impulse (and its theological application as "analogy") that forms the best approach for understanding the distinctively Catholic approach to interpreting the *communio sanctorum* — that "communion of holy ones and things" that contemporary "conservatives" want to institutionalize. This point, of course, has been made by a number of Catholic theologians — Karl Rahner, Hans Urs von Balthasar, David Power — as well as by Tracy. All of these theologians have argued (correctly, I believe) that what unifies and gives identity to the universal "manyness" of the

Catholic tradition is a fundamental devotion to the sacramental worldview, a worldview which privileges the sacramental manner of the Holy
One's coming to us.[27]

As in so much else, one of the balanced statements of this privileged
sacramental understanding of Catholicism was made by Avery Dulles in
discussing the church *as* sacrament:

> In measuring the values in the various models, the sacramental type
> of ecclesiology in my opinion has special merit. It preserves the
> value of the institutional elements because the official structures of
> the Church give it clear and visible outlines, so that it can be a vivid
> sign. It preserves the community value, for if the Church were not
> a communion of love it could not be an authentic sign of Christ.
> It preserves the dimension of proclamation, because only reliance
> on Christ and by bearing witness to him can the Church effectively
> point to Christ as the bearer of God's redemptive grace.[28]

Dulles here offers what I take to be a very balanced Catholic understanding of what Catholic Christians mean when they use the word
"church": it is at base a *communion* sharing in Christ's sacramental
presence through words and actions celebrated in the community, all of
which have some institutional form. But the other models of church —
institution, herald, servant, etc. — are important to the extent that they
support and give concrete form to this deepest level of "being church."

Those who seek to define *communion* in institutional terms without
remainder — or even to define "communion" in primarily institutional
terms — fail to understand one of the most basic dynamics of the Catholic tradition itself. Far from being "orthodox" in their adherence to
that tradition, they have severed the institutional importance of Catholicism from its real roots in that *communion* which legitimates the
institution — not the other way round. The external protocols of the
church as institution are necessary and even basic to such a sacramental
(incarnated) form of Christianity; but "institutional loyalty" and conformity hardly legitimate the "communion" that is the heart of the church's
unity. Indeed, precisely the opposite is the case: the institution is "legitimate" and worthy of adherence to the extent (some Catholic theologians
would say, only to the extent) that it supports and nurtures that deeper,

more fundamental *communion* that is witnessed to and incarnated in the church's sacraments.

Those believers in the U.S. church whom I am identifying as "catholic *sectarians*" share most of the presuppositions enunciated by nineteenth-century evangelist Dwight Moody in his famous metaphor of the "true church" as a small lifeboat on an especially rough sea of "the world": what makes them distinctive as *catholic* sectarians (as opposed to evangelical ones like Moody) is their (very ahistorical) attempt to fashion the institutional church itself into that small lifeboat. Unlike Protestant sectarians like Moody, for whom an individualistic saving encounter with their "personal lord and savior" constituted the normative qualification for redemption, Catholic sectarians see membership in the Roman church — or, more precisely, an almost soldier-like obedience to the protocols, laws, and authority figures of that institution — as the essence of "membership in the Kingdom." For at least some of these believers, the "glories of obedience" to that splendor of truth manifested in the decisions of the Vatican is the phrase (and the idea) that subsumes "communion," "sacramental union," and indeed membership in the Kingdom of God itself in institutional identity. Such an understanding represents a dangerous departure from the Catholic theological tradition.

Fourth and finally: I would argue that these sectarian believers manifest a distinctly Catholic version of that historical fallacy (and theological heresy) known as "primitivism." Primitivism is that belief, so often discussed by scholars of North American Protestant fundamentalism, which posits some primitive "pure" age of belief, practice, and religious identity to which the contemporary Christian community must conform itself. For such believers, the answers to the challenges posed by history to the gospel message can be met by finding the "primitive moment" in Christianity's past when the perfect embodiment of Christianity was achieved, and replicating that moment as a kind of "frozen golden age" in the present. Many evangelical Protestant primitivists posit such a pure moment in the Jerusalem church described in the Acts of the Apostles: for them, that first-century community represents the timeless norm for structuring contemporary faith communities, so that all current offices, liturgical rites, and missionary strategies must conform (as close to a literal copying as possible) to that Jewish-Christian church.

Contemporary Catholic sectarians look not to the primitive church described in the Acts of the Apostles, but rather tend to seek to freeze
the Counter-Reformation church coming out of the Council of Trent, or
the ultramontanist church — centered on the papacy — that emerged in
the nineteenth century from the First Vatican Council, as the normative
"pure" model of how Catholic Christianity should identify itself.[29]

Many of these Catholic adherents of a primitivist vision of "church"
see Cardinal Bellarmine's presentation of church as the *societas perfecta*
(the "perfect society"), limned so clearly in the documents of the Council of Trent, as the form that Catholicism must always, and everywhere,
take. Over against the Protestant Reformers' presentation of the "True
Church" as the "spiritual company of all faithful people" that eluded
historical incarnation, Bellarmine offered an almost one-to-one identity
between the True Church and loyalty to the institution presided over
by the bishop of Rome. In the four centuries after Trent — a period of
Catholic history often labeled "The Post-Tridentine Era" — many Catholic theologians came to close to interpreting the revered fourth-century
phrase *extra ecclesiam nulla salus est* ("outside the church there is no
salvation") in narrowly institutional terms: non-Catholics were, at best,
risky bets in the eschatological lottery. The unraveling of this Tridentine
ecclesiology was evinced as well under way in the United States with the
Leonard Feeney episode in the 1940s and 1950s and was formally laid
to rest at the Second Vatican Council. The Feeney episode — in which
Jesuit Leonard Feeney was excommunicated for disobedience for refusing to stop teaching a "strict constructionist" reading of that phrase
(making all non-Catholics fodder for hellfire) — witnessed to an almost-
universal sense among U.S. Catholic leaders that an institutionally driven
definition of "church" was, by then, *not* the consensus among North
American theologians and bishops. Two decades later, the Second Vatican Council formally redefined *who* belonged to the church, and what
church membership meant vis-à-vis the hierarchical structure in union
with the pope.[30]

From the longer viewpoint of church history, Vatican II was at least
as "conservative" in recovering the Catholic tradition as the Council of
Trent, in that it sought to "conserve" an ancient Catholic insight: the
recognition not only that the church itself — like doctrine — develops
over the course of history, but that there are levels of "belonging to the

church," making any simplistic analogue between "church" and "institution" deeply problematic from the standpoint of Catholic orthodoxy. Further, such a recognition was built on the (sound) Catholic historical awareness that what was necessary in the sixteenth century to counter what was then perceived to be an overly spiritualized understanding of church might not be necessary — or even desirable — in defining the "Mystery of the Church" in the twenty-first century.[31]

Those who would seek to dam the stream of the development of doctrine at that sixteenth-century moment of Trent are hardly "conservatives" in the etymological sense of conserving the best insights and teaching of the past; on the contrary, as Eliade observed, they act on impulses that stand opposed to the living tradition of Catholic theology in their efforts to make that living tradition a closed position, "answered" once and for all by Cardinal Bellarmine. What they are, in fact, advancing is an ahistorical (and intellectually naïve) model of freeze-framing a living tradition of debate, insight, and magisterial pronouncement.

Such primitivist believers fail the test of Catholic orthodoxy precisely because they fail to take to heart the profoundly *orthodox* insight that there is no magically pure moment in the past which "got it all right." Such a primitivist approach to doctrine represents an intellectually analogous position to the (now quaint) creed of those members of Cambridge University's "Ecclesiological Society" in the nineteenth-century Church of England, who pronounced that all true Christian places of worship should be built in the Gothic style — and preferably in the fifteenth-century Perpendicular Gothic style — as that architectural "moment" had forever crystallized true Christian theology and liturgical space. All other styles for church architecture — and most especially those styles of the modern period — were somehow corrupt and "unworthy" of providing a venue for the great mystery of the Eucharist. However interesting (and/or amusing) such a position might be from a purely historiographic point of view as a reaction against nineteenth-century British industrialism and urbanization, it is hardly taken as a serious intellectual position today by either architects, liturgists, or theologians.[32]

Those who oppose such a primitivist understanding of the perfect form of the church (just like those who opposed the Ecclesiological Society's attempt to "freeze" all of church architecture at the Gothic moment) are hardly "liberals" as that term is defined in *Webster's Dictionary:*

"not bound by orthodox tenets or established forms in political philosophy; independent in opinion." On the contrary, those who oppose the primitivist attempt to control the future by freezing the past are, in fact, *precisely* conserving the fluid Catholic understanding of both "church" and theology.[33]

While both Trent's institutionally specific definition of church and Vatican I's location of infallibility in the office of the papacy are normative pronouncements for the further development of Catholic theology, neither can be read as a kind of frozen proposition which siphons the rich pluralism of Catholic theology into one (and only one) ecclesiological stream. On the contrary — as is always the case in such magisterial pronouncements — such official definitions themselves inexorably lead to further, richer theological debate about their application and theological meaning(s).

Those who find this messy task of questioning, debate, and then further questioning of magisterial pronouncements distasteful (or threatening) are neither orthodox, conservative, nor restorationist, but rather sectarian in their understanding of the Catholic tradition of Christianity: true upholders of the Catholic tradition need to be charitable (but firm) in dealing with such unorthodox sectarians.

Chapter 7

A New Way of Being Church in Asia

Lessons for the American Catholic Church

PETER C. PHAN

I F ONE WERE TO SURVEY the rather extensive official documents of the Federation of Asian Bishops' Conferences and the writings of Asian theologians, one would be struck by the dearth of explicit treatments of what is commonly referred to as ecclesiology, or the theology of the church.[1] If anything, there is a conscious shying away from "churchy" themes such as papal primacy and infallibility, apostolic succession, magisterium, episcopal power, the hierarchical structure, canon law, the Roman Curia, and the like. Not that these realities are of no importance for the Asian churches. Of course, they are. But they do not occupy the central position on the theological radar of the Asian churches. Rather, instead of developing an ecclesiocentric or church-centered ecclesiology, Asian bishops and theologians have fostered what may be called a regnocentric or kingdom-of-God-centered way of being church. Their emphasis is not so much on elaborating a theoretical ecclesiology as on implementing ways of being church appropriate to the socio-political, cultural, and religious contexts of Asia. Their ecclesiology, when it comes to be formulated, is born out of the praxis of an authentic way of being church.

In this essay, I first present the central features of this Asian kingdom-centered, praxis-oriented ecclesiology. I next explore how this ecclesiology may inspire a church ministry appropriate to the United States. I conclude with a few suggestions on what further steps the American Catholic Church should take to bring this ecclesiology to greater effectiveness.

An Asian Way of Being Church:
A Local Church Built on Communion and Equality

To be a kingdom-centered church, that is, an efficacious sign of the reign of God anywhere, the church must be a truly local church built on communion and equality everywhere. And to achieve this goal, the church, according to the FABC, must be characterized by the following features.[2]

1. First, the church, both at the local and universal levels, is seen primarily as "a *communion of communities,* where laity, Religious and clergy recognize and accept each other as sisters and brothers."[3] At the heart of the mystery of the church is the bond of communion uniting God with humanity and humans with one another, of which the Eucharist is the sign and instrument par excellence.[4]

2. Moreover, in this ecclesiology there is an explicit and effective recognition of the *fundamental equality* among all the members of the local church as disciples of Jesus and among all the local churches insofar as they are communities of Jesus' disciples whose communion constitutes the universal church. The communion (*koinonia*) which constitutes the church, both at the local and universal levels, and from which flows the fundamental equality of all Christians, is rooted at its deepest level in the life of the Trinity in whom there is a perfect communion of equals.[5] This fundamental equality among all Christians, which is affirmed by Vatican II,[6] annuls neither the existence of the hierarchy in the church nor the papal primacy. Rather, it indicates the modality in which papal primacy and hierarchical authority should be exercised in the church, that is, in collegiality, co-responsibility, and accountability to all the members of the church. Unless this fundamental equality of all Christians with its implications for church governance is acknowledged and put into practice through concrete policies and actions, the church will not become a communion of communities.

This vision of church as communion of communities and its corollary of fundamental equality are the sine qua non for the fulfillment of the church's mission. Without being a communion, the church cannot fulfill its mission, since the church is nothing more than the bond of communion between God and humanity and among humans themselves.

3. This pastoral "discipleship of equals" leads to the third characteristic of the new way of being church in Asia, that is, the participatory and

collaborative nature of all the ministries in the church: "It is a *participatory* church where the gifts that the Holy Spirit gives to all the faithful — lay, Religious, and cleric alike — are recognized and activated, so that the church may be built up and its mission realized."[7] This participatory nature of the church must be lived out not only in the local church but also among all the local churches, including the church of Rome, of course, with due recognition of the papal primacy. This participation must not be conceived of as a one-way street from Rome to the other local churches. Rather, there must be *mutual* learning and teaching, *mutual* encouragement and correction between the church of Rome and the other churches, indeed among all the local churches.

4. The fourth characteristic of the new way of being church in Asia is the *dialogical* spirit: "Built in the hearts of people, it is a Church that faithfully and lovingly witnesses to the Risen Lord and reaches out to people of other faiths and persuasions in a dialogue of life toward the integral liberation of all."[8] Ever since its first plenary assembly in Taipei, Taiwan, 1974, the FABC has repeatedly insisted that the primary task of the Asian churches is the proclamation of the gospel. But it has also maintained no less frequently that the way to fulfill this task in Asia is by way of dialogue, indeed a triple dialogue, with Asian cultures, Asian religions, and the Asians themselves, especially the poor.[9]

5. The fifth and last feature of the new way of being church in Asia is *prophecy:* The church is "a leaven of transformation in this world and serves as a *prophetic sign* daring to point beyond this world to the ineffable Kingdom that is yet fully to come."[10] As far as Asia is concerned, in being "a leaven of transformation in this world," the church must now understand its mission of "making disciples of all nations" not in terms of converting large numbers of Asians to the church (which is a very unlikely possibility) and in the process increasing its influence as a social institution (*plantatio ecclesiae*). Rather, being a "small remnant" and likely to remain so for the foreseeable future, Christians must journey with the followers of other Asian religions and together with them — not instead of, or worse, against them — work for the coming of the kingdom of God.

This necessity to be local churches living in communion with each other was reiterated by the FABC's Seventh Plenary Assembly (Samphran, Thailand, January 3–12, 2000). Coming right after the Asian

Synod[11] and the promulgation of the apostolic exhortation *Ecclesia in Asia,*[12] and celebrating the Great Jubilee, with the general theme of "A Renewed Church in Asia: A Mission of Love and Service," this assembly is of particular significance because it highlights the kind of ecclesiology operative in the Asian churches. In the first place, the FABC takes a retrospective glance over a quarter of a century of its life and activities and summarizes its "Asian vision of a renewed Church." It sees it as composed of eight movements which constitute a sort of Asian ecclesiology. Given its central importance, the text deserves to be quoted in full:

1. A movement toward a Church of the Poor and a Church of the Young. "If we are to place ourselves at the side of the multitudes in our continent, we must in our way of life share something of their poverty," "speak out for the rights of the disadvantaged and powerless, against all forms of injustice." In this continent of the young, we must become "in them and for them, the Church of the young" (Meeting of Asian Bishops, Manila, Philippines, 1970).

2. A movement toward a "truly local Church," toward a church "incarnate in a people, a Church indigenous and inculturated" (2 FABC Plenary Assembly, Calcutta, 1978).

3. A movement toward deep interiority so that the church becomes a "deeply praying community whose contemplation is inserted in the context of our time and the cultures of our peoples today." Integrated into everyday life, "authentic prayer has to engender in Christians a clear witness of service and love" (2 FABC Plenary Assembly, Calcutta, 1978).

4. A movement toward an authentic community of faith. Fully rooted in the life of the Trinity, the Church in Asia has to be a communion of communities of authentic participation and co-responsibility, one with its pastors, and linked "to other communities of faith and to the one and universal communion" of the holy Church of the Lord. The movement in Asia toward Basic Ecclesial Communities express the deep desire to be such a community of faith, love, and service and to be truly a "community of communities" and

open to building up Basic Human Communities (3 FABC Plenary Assembly, Bangkok, 1982).

5. A movement toward active integral evangelization, toward a new sense of mission (5 FABC Plenary Assembly, Bandung, Indonesia, 1990). We evangelize because we believe Jesus is the Lord and Savior, "the goal of human history, . . . the joy of all hearts, and the fulfillment of all aspirations" (*Gaudium et Spes,* no. 45). In this mission, the Church has to be a compassionate companion and partner of all Asians, a servant of the Lord and of all Asian peoples in the journey toward full life in God's Kingdom.

6. A movement toward empowerment of men and women. We must evolve participative church structures in order to use the personal talents and skills of laywomen and laymen. Empowered by the Spirit and through the sacraments, lay men and women should be involved in the life and mission of the Church by bringing the Good News of Jesus to bear upon the fields of business and politics, of education and health, of mass media and the world of work. This requires a spirituality of discipleship enabling both the clergy and laity to work together in their own specific roles in the common mission of the Church (4 FABC Plenary Assembly, Tokyo, 1986). The Church cannot be a sign of the Kingdom and of the eschatological community if the fruits of the Spirit to women are not given due recognition, and if women do not share in the "freedom of the children of God" (4 FABC Plenary Assembly, Tokyo, 1986).

7. A movement toward active involvement in generating and serving life. The Church has to respond to the death-dealing forces in Asia. By authentic discipleship, it has to share its vision of full life as promised by Jesus. It is a vision of life with integrity and dignity, with compassion and sensitive care of the earth; a vision of participation and mutuality, with a reverential sense of the sacred, of peace, harmony, and solidarity (6 FABC Plenary Assembly, Manila, Philippines, 1995).

8. A movement toward the triple dialogue with other faiths, with the poor and with the cultures, a Church "in dialogue with the great religious traditions of our peoples," in fact, a dialogue with all people, especially the poor.[13]

This eightfold movement describes in a nutshell the new way of being church in Asia. Essentially, it aims at transforming the churches *in* Asia into the churches *of* Asia, that is, truly local churches. The requirements for this transformation are manifold: deep interiority, rootedness in the life of the Trinity, authentic participation and co-responsibility, active and integral evangelization, empowerment of laywomen and laymen, and service to life. But the way to achieve this transformation into churches *of* Asia is dialogue, indeed a *triple dialogue:* with the Asian peoples, especially their poor (liberation), with their cultures (inculturation), and with their religions (interreligious dialogue).

This dialogue as a *mode of being church* in Asia does not refer primarily to the intellectual exchange among experts of various religions, as is often done in the West. Rather, it involves, according to the Pontifical Council for Interreligious Dialogue and the Congregation for the Evangelization of Peoples — a position officially adopted by the FABC — a fourfold presence:

a. The *dialogue of life,* where people strive to live in an open and neighborly spirit, sharing their joys and sorrows, their human problems and preoccupations.

b. The *dialogue of action,* in which Christians and others collaborate for the integral development and liberation of people.

c. The *dialogue of theological exchange,* where specialists seek to deepen their understanding of their respective religious heritages, and to appreciate each other's spiritual values.

d. The *dialogue of religious experience,* where persons, rooted in their own religious traditions, share their spiritual riches, for instance, with regard to prayer and contemplation, faith and ways of searching for God or the Absolute.[14]

The Asian Triple Dialogue
and the American Catholic Church

It is this triple dialogue in its fourfold form that is of vital importance for the American Catholic Church. It is here that the experiences and insights of the way of being church in Asia can be of great help to the

American church as its faces the challenges of its new socio-political, cultural, and religious context.[15]

A New Political, Cultural, and Religious Context

Three new features of the American context determine both the modality and the future of the church's ministry in the United States. First, politically and socially, the United States is now the only superpower with overwhelming economic and military might, and if the current Iraq War is any indication, one with imperialistic designs. Embedded in this superpower, how can the Catholic Church credibly preach Jesus' teaching on nonviolence, peace, and justice and act in solidarity with those crushed by the U.S. economic, political, and military power? Second, culturally, new immigrants are bringing to the United States a vast array of diverse patterns of thinking, valuing, and living. In this cultural diversity, how can the church, whose hierarchy is still dominated by whites, relinquish its Eurocentrism and accept other cultures as valid ways of living the gospel? Third, religiously, with immigrants hailing from non-European parts of the world, from Asia in particular, the United States has become religiously pluralistic. In this religious pluralism, how can the church, whose claims to uniqueness and universality are routinely asserted, acknowledge, preserve, and promote the teachings and the ways of worship and life inculcated by other religions? To meet these three sets of challenges effectively, the church must prioritize its tasks, formulate its strategies, and deploy its resources accordingly.

A Church Embedded in the World's Only Superpower: Liberation

For better or for worse, the American Catholic Church is a beneficiary of the United States as the sole superpower. Charles Morris's book *American Catholic* is aptly subtitled: *The Saints and Sinners Who Built America's Most Powerful Church*.[16] Sinners and saints aside, thanks to its numbers, wealth, and political clout, the American Catholic Church is no doubt "America's Most Powerful Church" and wields the greatest power among the world's religious institutions, perhaps Rome included. Theologically and canonically, Rome is said to possess the supreme ecclesiastical power, but in terms of de facto influence on the real world, it may lag far behind the American Catholic Church. It has been quipped, not without a grain of truth, that when the American Catholic Church sneezes, the other churches will catch cold.

But this power carries with it immense costs and responsibilities. The costs flow from the church's "embeddedness" in its host country, a condition vulnerable to the possibility of conniving bedfellows and the risk of muted prophetic voice. Politically, this moral ambivalence was most visible in the American bishops' failure to condemn, forthrightly and publicly, the "preemptive" Iraq War despite its fragrant infringement of the traditional criteria for a "just war" prior to its commencement, and especially after it has become incontrovertible that the reasons for going to war were totally bogus. This episcopal deafening silence will, I submit, be in the long run more detrimental to the church's ministry than the scandal of clergy sexual abuse and its aftermath, given the enormous geopolitical consequences of the Iraq War.

Economically, the United States accumulates its wealth in part on the back of other nations. In the free-market game, which is propagated throughout the world through globalization, and by means of force if necessary, not all players come out as winners. Outsourcing may bring profits to American companies and may even produce jobs in under-developed countries, but extremely low wages, long hours, child labor, unsanitary working conditions, lack of health insurance and other benefits, and ecological devastation are the high costs that the poor of the Third World are paying for the American "pursuit of happiness." Multinational corporations do not always have the interests of the local people at heart. If the bottom line is in the red, they have no qualms in moving the factories to countries with cheaper labor. Indeed, it is a mantra among global economists that in recent years the poor are getting poorer, and the rich, richer. Even if the free-market economy proves to be the most productive of wealth, still it is the Moloch that devours the flesh and blood of the most vulnerable among us.[17]

Willy-nilly, the American Catholic Church benefits from this injustice and exploitation. This collective sin — part of the "original sin" — the church must admit and confess, frankly and honestly, not out of an morbid sense of guilt, much less out of political correctness, but out of the love for truth and for the sake of the church's moral credibility. For only the truth will set us free. If the church's teaching on social sin has any validity, it is here that it has its bite. No Christian can say: "I have nothing to do with this unjust situation." It is not the matter of personally having robbed or cheated. Rather, no hand — yours or mine — is clean, because we would not be able to enjoy all the things we now take for granted in this country unless our sisters and brothers somewhere else were unjustly or unfairly deprived of even the basic necessities of life.

This honest admission must not result in an empty orgy of *mea culpas* and forgiveness-begging. Rather, for the American Catholic Church to discharge its ministry in the economic and socio-political arenas credibly and effectively, this confession must be coupled with nothing less than a public and total commitment to and implementation of policies consistent with the "preferential option for the poor," which in the name of the gospel, liberation theologians, and, in their footsteps, Pope John Paul II have made the mission of the church. The word "poor" here does include the defenseless unborn, but it does not include only them. The church's stand against abortion will be credible and will not be misinterpreted as obsession with sex and a repudiation of women's rights only if it is accompanied by a sincere and effective solidarity with other categories of the "poor" such as the homeless, those without health care, those living in poverty, the unemployed and underemployed, the victims of racism and gender discrimination, the immigrants, and anyone who cannot afford a decent human life, here in the United States as well as elsewhere.

Here *liberation* comes into full play as one of the top priorities of the church's ministry in the immediate future. We American Catholics must be truly persuaded that working for justice — liberation — is a *constitutive* dimension of evangelization, on a par with preaching the Word and liturgical worship. *Denouncing* injustice and *doing* justice, both to succor the victims of injustice and to remove the unjust structures, are a strict demand for the disciple of Christ and not the knee-jerk reaction of liberal Democrats and moderate Republicans. Indeed, it is a massive failure of the leadership of the American Catholic Church in the recent presidential election that they remained mute and did not have the courage to speak truth to power as the country was inflicted with an immoral war, lack of health care for the poorest, massive tax cuts for the wealthy, naked violations of human rights, refusal to establish effective policies to protect the life of the unborn (in spite of fervid anti-abortion rhetoric!), imposition of unconscionable economic burdens on future generations through a colossal federal debt. These are not just economic and political issues. They are quintessentially *moral* challenges — as much as the defense of life in all its stages and the family — that the gospel places on us for the sake of the reign of God. Voting against abortion and gay marriage is not hard; it does not make a big hole in our pockets. But voting in support of the poor and the powerless costs us money and requires personal sacrifices.

In addition to this preferential option for the poor, there is another urgent issue on which the church's ministry must focus in the near future, and that is the current American propensity to use violence and war to settle international problems. With the claim that the terrorist attacks on September 11, 2001, have changed "everything," there is now in the United States a widespread subscription to what Walter Wink calls "the myth of redemptive violence," a willingness to use military might to resolve international conflicts.[18] Worse, this addiction to war, draped in patriotism, invokes God, the Bible, and the symbols of Christianity for self-justification. It is nothing short of idolatry and blasphemy. In this context, the church's most pressing ministry is to proclaim, courageously and unflinchingly, Jesus' teaching on nonviolence as a way of relating not only among individuals but also among nations. Such nonviolent resistance goes beyond pacifism and the theory of just war and points to the church's ministry of reconciliation. To put teeth into its nonviolence policy, church leaders must publicly oppose any candidate for public office — Democrat as well as Republican — who espouse war for political gains.

Liberation in all areas of life, then, must be one fundamental form of Christian ministry of the American Catholic Church in the immediate future if it is to find again its bearings. This is no liberal or conservative agenda. Rather, it is the absolute demand of the God of Abraham, Isaac, and Jacob; the distinctive teaching of the Jewish prophets; the solemn injunction of Jesus; the frequent exhortation of popes and bishops; and the inspiring example of countless Catholic laywomen and laymen. The American Catholic Church has no future if it fails in this ministry of justice, peace, and reconciliation. Without this ministry, the church's teaching is empty rant.[19]

The Church with a Multicolored Cultural Face: Inculturation

Like Joseph's "Amazing Technicolor Dreamcoat," the American Catholic Church is now displaying a dazzling variety of cultural, ethnic, and racial backgrounds. From its very beginning, it has been an "institutional immigrant." Before the massive arrival of European Catholics in the eighteenth and nineteenth centuries, there had already been Catholics among Native Americans, Mexicans, and African Americans on the continent. Even though the Irish and, to a lesser extent, the Germans have dominated the hierarchy, the early presence of Eastern and Southern Europeans as well as of the Chinese, the Filipinos, and the Japanese in the church was not insignificant. However, with laws imposing a severely restrictive quota system of European immigrants in the 1920s and the anti-Asian immigration legislation in 1934, it was predicted that the flow of immigrants would slow down to a trickle. Furthermore, as Catholics moved into the American mainstream, they became less distinctive, and the immigrant character of the church less pronounced. With time, the face of the church as a mosaic of different ethnic groups became blurred, especially after World War II, so much so that some church historians declared that the immigrant era of the church was over.

Recently, however, there has been a huge influx of immigrants, despite an economic slowdown, which tends to discourage immigration, and more stringent restrictions in the wake of September 11, 2001. Currently, more than 34 million immigrants live in the United States, 10 million of them illegally, and a majority of them are Catholic. Immigrants now make up 12 percent of the U.S. household population. The American Catholic Church is becoming an institutional immigrant again. Furthermore, and this is vastly significant for the future of the church's ministry, within a couple of decades these "minorities" will constitute the majority in the church.

What is distinctive about the new arrivals is that they come mostly from non-European countries, especially from Africa, Asia, and Latin America, and bring with them languages, customs, and cultures vastly different from those of their host country. More importantly, unlike their predecessors, these immigrants intend to preserve their native traditions. While working hard to move into the economic and political mainstream, culturally and, as we see below, religiously, these new immigrants refuse to be assimilated into the white, Anglo-Saxon culture. Rather, they want to maintain, for themselves and their descendants, their own languages, customs, and cultures. In addition to various cultures, the new immigrants also bring with them a different brand of Catholicism and a different experience of being church.

The persistence of these non-European traditions and the immigrants' distinctive experiences of being church present the American Catholic Church's ministry with two challenges. First, the church must devise a new style of being immigrant in the midst of the American society. The old immigrant style has been characterized by "group consciousness, defensiveness, willingness to use power to achieve concrete results."[20] While some of these tactics still retain their usefulness, it is clear that the new Catholic immigrants cannot be brought together by means of ecclesiastical centralization, especially around the parish (they do not live in the same neighborhoods), separate education in Catholic schools (which very few can afford), and the use of political power (which they do not as yet possess). Rather, the future challenge for the church is to help immigrants maintain and transmit, especially to their children, their languages, customs, and culture, which are the glue that bind the immigrants together. This cultural task should be carried out at the parish, diocesan, and national levels, with appropriate organizations and activities and with consistent ecclesiastical and financial support.

The second challenge is much more difficult and has barely been begun. It is known by the umbrella term of "inculturation," which is the double process of incarnating the already culture-laden gospel into the various cultures and of bringing the cultures into the gospel whereby *both* the gospel and the cultures are transformed and enriched. Concretely, this inculturation in the American Catholic Church involves the interplay of five components: the message of the gospel itself (divine revelation); the cultures (e.g., Semitic, Hellenistic, Roman, Germanic, etc.) in which the gospel has been transmitted (the Christian Tradition); the American culture (mainly white, Anglo-Saxon, Enlightenment-inspired); the culture — predominantly pre-modern — of a specific ethnic group (e.g., the Vietnamese); and the cultures of other ethnic groups (e.g., black, Mexican, Cuban, etc.). The areas in which inculturation takes place include all aspects of church life: liturgy, catechesis, spirituality, ministerial formation, and theology. Of special importance for inculturation in all of these areas is what is known as popular piety or devotions or popular Catholicism.

It is impossible to foretell what the American Catholic Church would look like if its ministry of inculturation were taken seriously. However, one thing is certain: the church will be very different from what it is now if the resources of other cultures are marshaled to reconceptualize the whole gamut of the church's beliefs, liturgy, moral practices, and prayers. What if the God the church worships is depicted as a multi-ethnic, multiracial, multicolored, gender-inclusive Deity? What if Jesus is presented as the Buddha, the Guru, the Sage, the Ancestor, the Eldest Son par excellence? What if the Holy Spirit is conceived in terms of the Cosmic Breath and Power enlivening the whole creation and all religions and cultures? What if the church is lived as an extended family or a tribe? What if the sacramental celebrations connected with birth, growth, communion, reconciliation, sickness, marriage, and leadership incorporate the cultural traditions and customs that the immigrants celebrate on these occasions? What if Western monasticism adopts the spiritual practices of non-Western monastic traditions?[21]

The Church Journeying with Other Believers: Interreligious Dialogue

The last example brings us to the third feature of the new American context, namely, religious pluralism. Until recently, the religious landscape of America has been occupied almost exclusively by churches (Catholic and Protestant) and synagogues. Now it is dotted, even in its heartlands, by temples, pagodas, mosques, and gurdwaras. Of course, America is still overwhelmingly Christian — a little over 80 percent of the population profess the Christian faith, and its public symbols are overtly Christian. Nevertheless, the subtitle of Diana L. Eck's book, *How a "Christian Country" Has Now Become the World's Most Religiously Diverse Nation,*[22] which attempts to alert Americans to the new phenomenon of religious diversity in their midst, is not far from the truth. Despite their numerical minority, the new non-Christian immigrants strongly and loudly insist that they will continue to practice, publicly and proudly, their religious faiths — particularly Islam, Buddhism, and Hinduism — and refuse to be subsumed into some kind of civic religion or Christianity.

For the Catholic Church, especially after Vatican II and in the light of Pope John Paul II's teaching and activities, religious diversity is not a curse but a blessing. More than the United States, the church has at its disposal vast philosophical and theological resources to deal with not only the mere fact of religious diversity but also the new theologies of religious pluralism. It does not regard religious differences as "a clash of civilizations" and as a threat to its identity, nor does it limit itself to polite tolerance, which is at bottom disguised intolerance. Rather, the church views other religious faiths with respect and admiration and enters into dialogue with them in order to be enriched by them.

This does not mean of course that interreligious dialogue is not an arduous challenge for the American Catholic Church. Because religion and politics are inextricably intertwined, and because, as mentioned above, the American Catholic Church is embedded in the United States, dialogue between the American Catholic Church and the followers of other religions, in particular Muslims, is fraught with suspicion, given the current conflict between the United States and many Islamic countries. Fortunately, with its longstanding tradition of religious freedom and nonestablishment and its considerable religious diversity, the United States can be a fertile laboratory for interfaith dialogue. Hence, notwithstanding significant difficulties, the American Catholic Church enjoys a unique advantage in carrying out such a dialogue. It can demonstrate that religious diversity need not and should not lead to violence, as it has done in many other countries.

It may be urged that given the overwhelmingly Christian majority in the United States, interreligious dialogue is not — or at least not yet — an immediate priority for the church's ministry, as it is in Asia, for example. While this may be true, nevertheless, the increasing frequency of interfaith marriages among Americans poses serious challenges to the church's ministry, which so far has done practically nothing to assist interfaith couples to cope with the difficulties of their marriages and to live out their different faiths in a mutually enriching way. In addition to this pastoral need, the church will also be required through interreligious dialogue to rethink some of its fundamental beliefs, such as the uniqueness and universality of Christ's mediation and the necessity of the church as sacrament of salvation. In the process the church will have to consider whether it is theologically possible to affirm non-Christian religions as ways of salvation in God's eternal plan, the nature of revelation, the modalities of the Holy Spirit's presence in history, the revelatory status of non-Christian sacred scriptures, the spiritual fruitfulness of non-Christian rituals and prayers (in particular, popular religiosity), and so on.[23]

"If the Asian Churches Do Not Discover Their Own Identity, They Will Have No Future"

So declared the participants of the FABC Asian Colloquium on Ministries in the Church held in Hong Kong on March 5, 1977.[24] This prophetic utterance was true of the churches of Asia then as well as now. It is also true of the American Catholic Church. But differently from Asian Christianity, which constitutes barely 3 percent of the Asian population, the American Catholic Church, as mentioned above, is a powerful church, embedded in the only world superpower. It has at its disposal immense resources of various kinds to become a truly local church. Its efforts at inculturation can set a precedent for other churches, and hence it is useful to ask what further steps it can take in order to further the process of becoming a local church.

Perhaps a proposal made by Francis Hadisumarta, O.Carm., bishop of Manokwari, Indonesia, at the Asian Synod may set us on the right path. After speaking on behalf of the Indonesian Bishops' Conference on collegiality and the synodal nature of the church, Hadisumarta urged that the church "move from adaptation to inculturation and create new, indigenous rites." He went on to suggest that "in many crucial pastoral areas we need to adapt church law. We need the authority to interpret church law according to our own cultural ethos, to change, and where necessary, replace it." To achieve this inculturation, the bishop asked pointedly:

Do we have the imagination to envisage the birth of new patriarchates, say the Patriarchate of South Asia, of Southeast Asia, and of East Asia? These new patriarchates, conciliar in nature, would support, strengthen, and broaden the work of individual episcopal conferences. As the episcopal conferences, in communion with neighboring conferences in the same (new) patriarchate, move forward in mission, new Catholic Rites would come into existence. Thus, we envisage a radical decentralization of the Latin Rite — devolving into a host of local Rites in Asia, united collegially in faith and trust, listening to each other through synodal instruments at parish, deanery, vicariate, diocesan, national/regional, continental, and international levels. Then, almost four decades after the Second Vatican Council, we would truly experience a "great synodal epoch."[25]

By using the traditional language of "patriarchate" and "Rite," what Hadisumarta, and with him many Asian bishops, were driving at is a "radical decentralization" of the Roman Catholic Church. As has been remarked by several church historians and ecclesiologists, whereas during its first millennium the ecclesial paradigm was bearing faithful witness to the apostolic tradition with collegiality and communion as the modus operandi, in the second millennium this paradigm shifted to that of actively shaping the church tradition by means of a monarchical papal supremacy.[26] The names of popes such as Gregory VII, Innocent III, and Pius IX immediately come to mind. The affirmation of the papal *plenitudo potestatis* reached its apogee at Vatican I, where papal primacy and infallibility were defined as dogmas over against conciliarism, Gallicanism, control by the state, and the threats of modernity. While reaffirming the two papal dogmas, Vatican II made collegiality and communion its central ecclesial vision. However, during the post-conciliar years, church leaders bent on centralizing power in the papacy and the Roman Curia gained the upper hand and have successfully prevented the implementation of collegial structures.

What is needed urgently now is a radical decentralization as urged by the Asian bishops, and ironically, it is the American Catholic Church that has the resources (though not necessarily the will) to initiate this process by becoming what Hadisumarta calls a new "patriarchate." This church structure, as pointed out by Pottmeyer, is rooted in three theological principles — catholicity, collegiality, and subsidiarity — and implements the triadic church organization of the first millennium: the particular church with its bishop; the regional ecclesiastical units, especially the patriarchal churches with their patriarchs; and the universal church with the pope as its head.[27]

Unfortunately, when in the West there was only the Latin patriarchate of the bishop of Rome, this triadic structure was lost, resulting in the dual structure of the local church/bishop and the universal church/pope and the eclipse of the character of the church as a communion of churches. As a result, the roles of the pope as the patriarch of the Latin West and the pope as the head of the universal church were fused together. In spite of this development, the importance of the "ancient patriarchal Churches" was recognized by Vatican II when it said:

> It has come about through divine providence that, in the course of time, different Churches set up in various places by the apostles and their successors joined together in a multiplicity of organically united groups which, whilst safeguarding the unity of faith and the unique divine structure of the universal Church, have their own discipline, enjoy their own liturgical usage and inherit a theological and spiritual patrimony.[28]

Given the fusion of the two roles of the bishop of Rome and the current excessive centralization of power in the papacy and the Roman Curia, it is high time to separate clearly the competencies of the bishop of Rome as the patriarch of the Latin West and the universal pastor and to create new patriarchates separate from the Latin church. This is exactly what Joseph Ratzinger, now Pope Benedict XVI, strongly suggested shortly after the council as the "task for the future," namely, "to separate more clearly the office proper to the successor of Peter from the patriarchal office and, where necessary, to create new patriarchates and separate them from the Latin church." The reason for creating new patriarchates is that "a uniform canon law, a uniform liturgy, a uniform filling of episcopal sees by the Roman central administration — all of these are things that do not necessarily accompany the primacy as such, but result only from this close union of two offices."[29]

It is therefore no ecclesiastical innovation for the American Catholic Church to form itself (perhaps together with the Canadian church) into a new patriarchate — along and in communion with many other new patriarchates — and develop its own "canon law," "liturgy," "filling of episcopal sees," and "theological and spiritual patrimony," areas in which it has ample resources. In so doing it will complete its old project of developing a truly American church, wrongly condemned as "Americanism," and pave the way for other churches to become truly local churches. What an exciting prospect of being *both* Catholic *and* American!

Chapter 8

An Inculturated Mariology

Mary in the Latino/a Context

NATALIA M. IMPERATORI-LEE

THE TWENTY-FIRST CENTURY has opened with serious challenges for the Catholic Church. Mass attendance and vocations remain in decline; evangelical churches continue to win Catholic converts; young Catholics seem detached from the church. The scandal of sexual abuse bankrupted many dioceses financially, and it likewise impoverished the credibility of the Catholic Church worldwide. The need for ecclesial conversion, accountability, and solidarity with the victims of history is clear. What is not as clear is the manner in which these changes should be carried out. Perhaps one path to a more dynamic church for the twenty-first century can be found by examining the life of the faithful themselves. The Second Vatican Council taught that the faithful, by virtue of their guidance by the Holy Spirit, cannot err in matters of belief.[1] This infallible "sense of the faithful," the *sensus fidelium,* can serve as a starting point on the way to a renewed church, both in the United States and throughout the world.

In order to understand the *sensus fidelium* of the U.S. Catholic Church, it is important to take account of its demographic reality. This reality is increasingly pluralistic, specifically in terms of the ethnic make-up of the church. In particular, the large numbers of Hispanic Americans, together with the steady stream of Latin American immigration, demand that scholars of religion turn their attention to how the religious worldview and insights of this group will shape the future of U.S. Catholicism. According to the 2000 census, while Hispanics account for only 12 percent of the U.S. population, they constitute 39 percent of the U.S. Catholic Church. In all probability, Hispanics will represent the majority of the church by the second decade of the twenty-first century.

These numbers alone demand that we take account of this community's characteristics. But more importantly, given the growing intra-Hispanic diversity of many U.S. cities like Miami, Chicago, and New York, the Hispanic church can provide guideposts for negotiating the intercultural relationships that characterize the church in a context as diverse as the United States. The Latino community is necessarily intercultural, made up of Cubans, Puerto Ricans, Guatemalans, Hondurans, Argentines, among others, as well as interracial, with its long heritage of *mestizaje/mulatez*. The forging of intercultural communities represents a great challenge to the U.S. Catholic Church today, as the model of the national parish has been supplanted, for economic and sociological reasons, by a more multicultural reality. The intercultural insights of the U.S. Latino/a community, along with the demographic facts of this community's presence, demand that theologians attend to the ecclesiological insights often implicit in U.S. Latino/a religiosity. These insights frequently come couched in the multifaceted devotional life of Latino/as.

The Marian devotion of Hispanic Catholics has frequently been cited as one, if not the, major characteristic of this religious contingent.[2] This essay seeks to indicate some ways in which U.S. Hispanic Marian devotion, viewed through the lens of Mexican American devotion to Guadalupe, contains insights about ecclesial conversion, accountability, and solidarity that are relevant to Catholic ecclesiology. Because Hispanics will soon make up the majority of the U.S. Catholic Church, their popular religious practices, including Marian devotion, and the ecclesiological insights implicit in them, are crucial to gauging the *sensus fidelium* of the people of God in the United States.

On the surface, it would seem that to focus on the Marian devotion of this group of Catholics could only fan the flames of traditionalism, encourage nostalgia for baroque Catholicism, and eviscerate the gains that laypeople, especially women, have made in terms of their participation in the church. However, this is not a wistful recalling of long-outdated devotional styles. Scholars have noted[3] that Hispanic popular religiosity differs in important ways from the Euro-American baroque devotionalism that might lead to the aforementioned dangers.[4] Hispanic religiosity tends to be more oral, communal, and lay-based than literate, individualistic, and clerical.[5] Charles Dahm, the pastor of the predominantly Mexican Pius V parish in the Pilsen neighborhood of Chicago, describes the festivities surrounding the feast of Guadalupe in his community:

> Celebration of the feast itself begins at 3:00 am on December 12, with a serenade to the Virgin organized by a radio station. Thirteen hundred people rapidly fill the church beyond capacity, standing in the aisles and sitting around the altar. For two hours, they listen to traditional songs about the Virgin.... The birthday song, *Las mañanitas*, begins the Mass at 5:00 am. In recent years the parish has scheduled an additional Mass at midnight to accommodate the thousands wanting to serenade the Virgin on her feast day.[6]

Rather than private, individual acts of piety, Hispanic devotion to Guadalupe tends to be expressed in large communal festivities, vigils with singing and celebration, and communal prayer.[7] These collective, festive expressions of Hispanic Marian devotion serve as an interesting ecclesiological test case. When a community gathers in a liturgical space to commemorate a shared feast, they express their self-understanding as people of God. It is that self-understanding that this essay seeks to explore.

The sections that follow will trace the contributions of three U.S. Latino theologians to the understanding of the relationship between Marian devotion and ecclesiology. Orlando Espín's seminal work on the category and importance of popular religiosity situates the discussion of devotional practice as a privileged locus of theology. His own ruminations on the Guadalupe event tie this devotion to ecclesiology, though not through the traditional understanding of Guadalupe as Mary of Nazareth. Nevertheless, his understanding of Guadalupe as a phenomenon denoting a popular pneumatology testifies to the ecclesiological importance of this devotion. Next, the work of Virgilio Elizondo, the father of U.S. Latino theology, will focus the essay on the textual basis of Guadalupan devotion, the *Nican mopohua,* and its exegesis. In that exegesis, particular attention will be paid to the ecclesiologically significant aspects of the story of the Guadalupan encounter. The last theologian to be featured is Roberto Goizueta, whose reflections on Guadalupan devotion as revealing a relational anthropology at the heart of U.S. Latino spirituality complement our understanding of the model of church implicit in Mexican American devotion to Guadalupe. These three figures offer a portrait of an ecclesial community that, through its Marian devotion, has come to understand the church's mission as involving conversion, accountability, and solidarity with the poor.

Orlando Espín:
The Church and Popular Religiosity

One of the earliest insights Latino/a theology brought to the mainstream theological community was the academic study of popular religiosity, in its myriad forms. Indeed, to explore the ecclesiological intuitions of the Hispanic church, it is necessary to examine those devotional, liturgical, home-based, and public acts that characterize the faith of these cultures. Spearheaded by Orlando Espín, the study of popular religiosity serves as a cornerstone to any attempt at articulating an ecclesiology from a Hispanic perspective, because popular religiosity intersects with such key ecclesiological insights as Tradition, the sense of the faithful, and the self-understanding of the people of God. By no means does Espín's work claim or even imply that Latinos/as are the only cultural group with popular religious practices that should be studied, but his work focuses on that community. Because the focus on popular religiosity is essentially a spotlight on the religious practices of laypeople, Espín feels he addresses a major lacuna in contemporary ecclesiology, which he claims is "unsuccessful in theologizing on the laity."[8]

Espín has emphasized the importance of popular religiosity as a source for theology, "a conveyor of its own form of Tradition"[9] that complements what ecclesiologists have previously recognized as Tradition, because it represents a manifestation of the *sensus fidelium*. He writes:

> I insist that the people's faith be taken seriously as a true *locus theologicus* and not solely or mainly as a pastoral, catechetical problem.
> ... The vast majority of Catholics in the history of the universal church have always been and still are the lay poor. Consequently, given that Catholic doctrine holds that the church is the infallible witness to revelation, then this *must* mean that the lay poor

(i.e., the immense majority of the church throughout twenty centuries) *are too* infallible witnesses to revelation. However, the way these millions have understood, received, and expressed their faith is undeniably "popular Catholicism...." Popular Catholicism is the real faith of the real Church.[10]

In studying the devotional practices, public acts, and home rituals of Catholics, theologians examine how the Tradition of the church has been received by the people of God, and how this understanding is made manifest outwardly.

Espín notes that a full and proper understanding of Tradition necessitates a richer understanding of the *sensus fidelium,* the sense of the faithful, or "intuitive grasp on the truth of God that is possessed by the church as a whole, as a consensus."[11] He understands one aspect of Tradition to be represented in the decrees of the ecumenical councils, interpreted in the writings of the Fathers of the church, and communicated and witnessed by the magisterium of theologians.[12] This facet of Tradition is what most theologians understand by the term. However, Espín broadens the notion of Tradition to include the living witness of the faithful throughout history, as embodied in the practices, beliefs, and devotions held by the majority of the people of God and reflected in their public prayer, their worship, and their artistic expression.

It is important to note that Espín does not equate popular religion with the *sensus fidelium.* Rather, he avers that popular religion is a manifestation of that faith-full intuition of the people of God. "It is important to remember that what is the infallible bearer of revelation is the discerned, intuitive sense of the faith and not the many symbolic and historical ways employed as its inculturated expressions."[13] As a manifestation, it must be subject to interpretation, much like any attempt to articulate an intuition.

> The main problem with the study of the *sensus fidelium* as a necessary component in any adequate reflection on Tradition is...its being a sense, an intuition. This sense is never discovered in some kind of pure state....It is always expressed through the symbols, language, and culture of the faithful and therefore is in need of... interpretive processes and methods similar to those called for by the written texts of Tradition and scripture.[14]

Thus the symbolic expressions of the *sensus fidelium* that make up popular religion must be subject to criteria of adequacy, in order to judge how faithful these expressions are to the whole of the Christian tradition. "If a sense of the faith is to be discerned as a true or false bearer of the Tradition, it must be capable of promoting the results expected of the Christian message and of Christian living."[15] The insights of popular religiosity do not hold true, then, if their fruits are not borne out in lived commitment to Christian discipleship.

The process of discerning the authenticity of the expression of popular Catholicism involves, according to Espín, three confrontations: with scripture, with the written texts of the Christian tradition, and with "the historical and sociological contexts in which the faithful intuitions and their means of expression occur."[16] Thus, popular religion does not become a *norma non normata;* it too must cohere with and be regulated by the whole of Tradition, even as it enriches that very Tradition.

In looking at Marian devotion, then, Espín's methodology for approaching popular religiosity seems to mesh with that of Paul VI, as explained in his apostolic exhortation *Marialis cultus.*[17] Theologians must attend to popular religious devotions, but these devotions, in turn, must be subject to critical interpretation and evaluation by the scripture and tradition of the church. Insofar as it expresses the infallible intuition of the people of God, we must attend to Hispanic Marian devotion and the insights it offers about the self-understanding of that people. Because it both coheres with and enriches the Tradition of the church, we must look to Marian devotion as a locus of ecclesiological insight.

Since the case has been made for popular religious practice as a locus for theological reflection, and particularly important for ecclesiological reflection, we now turn to two different interpretations of the Guadalupe event. Espín, the proto-ecclesiologist, links Guadalupan devotion to pneumatology, an ecclesiologically significant category. His colleague Virgilio Elizondo links Guadalupan devotion more clearly to Marian devotion, but with deep ecclesiological implications. Interestingly, both theologians approach Guadalupan devotion with ecclesial categories in mind. Thus, both interpretations offer necessary insights in the attempt to articulate a Hispanic ecclesiology.

The Pneumatological Guadalupe:
Espín's Proposal

In the introduction to his *The Faith of the People,* Espín outlines in a brief excursus his thoughts on the relationship between Mary of Nazareth, the Virgin of Guadalupe, and the Holy Spirit. Like his teacher Leonardo Boff, Espín is intrigued by the relationship between Guadalupe, the Mexican virgin, and the Holy Spirit. Because many traditionally pneumatological characteristics (pervasive presence, for example) and functions (accompaniment, enlivening) are attributed to Guadalupe by devotees, and since there lacks an indigenous or popular link between Guadalupe and the historical Mary, Espín suggests that Guadalupe represents a manifestation of the Holy Spirit. Espín does not go as far as Boff, who suggests that the virgin and the Holy Spirit are united hypostatically, rather, his is a different tack. He writes, "I am convinced that it is *not* the Jewish woman Mary of Nazareth, the mother of Jesus, that most Latinos speak of when they refer to the *Virgen de Guadalupe.*"[18] Guadalupe and Mary of Nazareth are two separate beings fused by cultural and religious elites eager to appear to conform to the norms of seventeenth-century Spanish Tridentine Catholicism. This is borne out in his interpretation of the popular understanding of those who invoke Guadalupe's name. Over against a methodology which focuses on the written accounts of Guadalupan devotion, which Espín regards as elitist and exclusive of the majority of the people of God, Espín proposes popular pneumatology as the foundational epistemology for the Guadalupe event. If, instead of the Marian piety so favored by theologians, what occurs in Guadalupan devotion is an expression of orthodox pneumatology, as Espín suggests, then an understanding of this aspect of the popular religiosity of Hispanics has yet to emerge.

Espín proposes an intriguing understanding of Guadalupan devotion, particularly for ecclesiology. The link between the Holy Spirit and the church is at least as old as Pentecost. Moreover, the Holy Spirit has been associated with the feminine or maternal aspect of God in patristic studies and other theological works.[19] The maternity of the Holy Spirit, an attribute which eventually came to apply to the church, soon merged with the motherhood of Mary in an interesting amalgam of femininity, maternity, and sanctity. It is not surprising, then, that Espín would complete the circle, displacing the Marian aspect of Guadalupan devotion in favor of a pneumatological understanding. To identify Guadalupan devotion, which so suffuses the Mexican American community, with a popular pneumatology indicates that Espín understands this contingent of Catholics to be particularly aware of the Holy Spirit's presence in their lives, albeit implicitly, since their devotion is not directed to the Holy Spirit per se. The intimacy with which they call upon Guadalupe and their understanding of her closeness to their lives, her maternal influence, her pervasive accompaniment all recall the role of the Holy Spirit in vivifying and sanctifying the People of God.

Virgilio Elizondo: Guadalupan Theology

It cannot be doubted that Virgilio Elizondo, founder of the Mexican American Cultural Center in San Antonio, Texas, has pioneered the study of Latino Catholicism. Since the 1970s Elizondo's work has explored seminal topics in the now-blossoming field of so-called "contextual" theologies: the import of race, particularly *mestizaje* in religious experience, the role of popular religiosity, the various devotional styles among U.S. Latino/a Catholics, particularly the Mexican American experience in the southwestern United States. Together with Espín, these theologians' focus on popular religiosity as a locus of theology paved the way for scholars to look to religious practices, devotions, and other forms of material culture to discern the theological insight of a community. Inspired by this work, this section seeks to delve into the Guadalupan devotion of Mexican American Catholics. In particular, this section diverges from Espín's strict adherence to lived practice and oral tradition by devoting attention not only to devotional practice but also to the text that spurs Guadalupan devotion, the *Nican mopohua*, in an attempt to discover what ecclesiological awareness lies implicit there. Here I will attempt to interpret, as Espín suggests, three overlooked aspects of the faithful intuition of the People of God which I think are present in Hispanic devotion to Mary in general, and to Guadalupe in particular: its catholicity, its emphasis on dialogue, and its apostolic character.

The first part of the intuition centers on the breadth of Marian devotion. In a nationwide survey of Hispanic Catholics conducted in 1995 by the North Eastern Pastoral Institute, more respondents believed "strongly" that the Virgin Mary is the mother of God than that Jesus died on the cross, rose, and saved us. The survey administrators concluded that this demonstrates the intensity of Marian devotion in the Hispanic community as well as Hispanic Catholics' attachment to the Virgin Mary. Indeed, Marian devotion often serves as the cornerstone of the Hispanic parish. One example would be the December celebrations in many Mexican American parishes, where Guadalupe's feast, celebrated December 12, far overshadows the liturgical festivities surrounding Advent and Christmas.[20]

If we look specifically at the history of Guadalupan devotion of Mexican American Catholics, which has been traced by historians and theologians, it is clear why the devotion spread so quickly at the outset — through blossoming urban networks, migration during the Mexican war of independence, and association with patriotic and social heroes like Zapata, Hidalgo, and Cesar Chavez. In addition, historians like Timothy Matovina have chronicled the popularity and staying power of the Guadalupan devotion, in his case in San Antonio. His research further shows how, in the mid-nineteenth century, this devotion blurred societal gender divisions, since women took an active and visible role in both the planning and the execution of the devotional rituals.[21] In more recent times, Jeannette Rodriguez has argued that for Mexican American women faced with a sense of loss or distance from their cultural heritage, Guadalupe "functions in a restorative manner. She is a central religious and cultural symbolic memory and attachment for many Mexican American women. For these women, she is a tool by which they make meaning of their assumptive world."[22] Guadalupe's availability and accessibility historically to a wide swath of the Mexican American population cannot be doubted.

In practice, this translates into laywomen and laymen, young and old, taking part in the preparations, planning, and activities surrounding Guadalupan devotion. Virgil Elizondo has repeatedly emphasized that Guadalupe is the cornerstone of Mexican American Christianity, and indeed, of Mexican American culture in general. He frequently reminds students that although not every Mexican American can tell you the same version of the Guadalupan apparition narrative, most know at least some version, and for many Mexican American Catholics, Guadalupe serves as their sole contact point with the church — the source of their involvement, the lure that brings them to liturgy, their draw to the institutional church.

What does this mean for the U.S. Catholic Church? What are the popularity and the accessibility of Guadalupan devotion saying about current structures and practices? According to Elizondo, popular religious practices are activities engaged in by the people of God "with, without, or despite the clergy." The fact that so many Hispanic Catholics participate, especially women, indicates not only their desire but in many cases their competency to take active roles in ministry. Initially we might say that laypeople, and especially women, are looking for ways to take an active role in the church. Second, the staying power of the Guadalupan devotion reveals much about how devotions, and how the church itself, can change in order to stay relevant. The present popularity of bilingual services for the Guadalupan festivities testifies to the growing need for multilingual parish ministry. The United States Conference of Catholic Bishops' (USCCB) Secretariat for Hispanic Affairs cites increased intergenerational tensions as one of the main challenges facing Hispanic Catholics in the twenty-first century. Younger Hispanics may feel less comfortable with Spanish, but need not be excluded from participation in Guadalupan devotion because of this. As Elizondo has noted, the meaning of *mestizaje* in the Guadalupan image is that no race, no person is excluded from her message or her welcome. That is certainly a lesson that the Hispanic church, and the Catholic Church generally, try to project, but they could certainly project it more clearly.

Perhaps the appeal of Guadalupan devotion can be traced in part to elements of the apparition itself. The symbolism of the imagery, especially the way in which it marries European and indigenous symbols, the fact that the image itself can be read as a narrative of the melding of two cultures, though important, will not be my focus here. Rather, elements of the story of the *morenita* (little brown one), in particular the importance and effects of listening and being heard in the story, function as the ecclesiologically significant categories for me. In the apparition narrative, the *Nican mopohua*, Juan Diego, to whom the Virgin appears, first becomes aware of a strange happening when he hears a variety of songbirds in and around Tepeyac — the bird in Nahuatl culture is a symbol of mediation between heaven and earth. When he hears this celestial song, his initial question to himself is "Am I worthy of what I am hearing?" Upon focusing on the source of the music, he hears Guadalupe before he sees her, and her first word to him in their encounter is "listen."

When Guadalupe delivers her message to Juan Diego and sends him to the bishop's house, he goes without hesitation. When he arrives, though, the bishop who is "very busy" gives him a standard response, come back later when I can listen to you more closely. Juan Diego's second meeting with the bishop includes a lengthy series of questions by the bishop, just to be certain he has heard Juan Diego correctly, but still the Virgin's message is not received. Still Juan Diego is not heard, because he is not believed. When, before his third encounter with the virgin, Juan Diego tries to elude her by taking a different route, her first words of comfort to him are "Listen and hear well in your heart, . . . that which troubles you is nothing."

So he goes back to the bishop. It is only after the third visit, the third long wait outside the bishop's door, the third time enduring the ridicules of the bishop's staff gathered outside his office, that Juan Diego's message, and Guadalupe's, is truly heard, once the image on his tilma is revealed. Only after this does the bishop offer hospitality, first to Juan Diego and then to his uncle, who had been miraculously healed. It is only then that they are received.

Elizondo notes that while the story of Guadalupe is typically associated with the conversion of the Indians, in truth the converts in the narrative are the bishop and his household — "theologians, catechists, liturgists, canonists and others."[23] They convert "from confident religious ethnocentrism" to something new, exciting, and in many ways beyond their control. "The beginning of this great miracle was that the bishop finally came to listen to the voice and call of the poor, ridiculed, crushed, and often ignored." The narrative demonstrates two kinds of "hearing" — Juan Diego's faithful listening of the heart, filled with trust and belief in the Virgin's message, and the bishop's superficial listening, lacking in trust for many reasons, not least of which was the socio-cultural status of the messenger. Guadalupe's message converts the church to the poor, the colonized, and the ostracized.

At the center of the conversion of the church that takes place in the Guadalupan narrative stands the missionary, the apostle, Juan Diego. He, the neophyte native with little education and no meaningful status in a brutally colonized society, brings the good news of hope to the missionaries who were charged with doing God's work in the New World. Just as Juan Diego was sent by the Virgin, the entire church is sent out, in the narrative, after the conversion of the bishop and his household. Rather than build a church in the center of the city, the typical procedure in the colonies, the institutional church itself must go out, to Tepeyac, a hill outside the city, near various Indian villages. The church is forced to go out to the poor, the center of Catholicism gets pushed to the marginal location in the city, and thus the margin becomes the center. All this is brought about by the message of the insignificant one, Juan Diego. Thus, Juan Diego's own experience of being called and sent transforms the entire Catholic Church and community. Indeed, it changes the religious landscape in a very physical way. Guadalupe sends Juan Diego out, and Juan Diego sends the church itself out, to the margins of the society. This radically active apostolicity models how Guadalupan devotion can and should transform the lives of Hispanic Catholics.

The apostolic thrust of the Guadalupan story reminds us of the apostolic character of the church. More importantly, it reminds us that apostolicity does not reside in the hierarchy alone — the whole people of God is gathered and sent. The whole people of God inherits the legacy of the apostles, the capacity and responsibility to spread the good news and foster conversion intra-ecclesially and extra-ecclesially. Part of this conversion requires a turn toward the margins, a vulnerability and an openness that is willing to risk uncertainty for the sake of the Reign of God.

Roberto Goizueta:
Accompaniment and Relationality

In his *Caminemos con Jesús: Toward a Hispanic/Latino Theology of Accompaniment,* Roberto Goizueta also reflects on devotion to Guadalupe in the Hispanic community. He grounds his reflections in his experience of the community of Mexican Americans that make up the parish at San Fernando Cathedral, in San Antonio, Texas. For all Hispanics, but especially for Mexicans, "no other popular religious devotion is as closely linked to a people's self-identity, or socio-historical context, as is the Mexican devotion to Our Lady of Guadalupe."[24] Goizueta's goal in the book is to outline the contours of this Hispanic self-identity, while elaborating a renewed vision of praxis that takes the aesthetic dimension of reality seriously. In the process, he elaborates a theological anthropology from a U.S. Latino/a standpoint: an anthropology which he describes as relational. This anthropological point is closely tied to his observations about popular religious devotions to Jesus and Mary that he witnessed in San Antonio.

Goizueta's articulation of the Guadalupan narrative, the *Nican mopohúa,* and its central place in the devotional life of the cathedral community, reveals not only the particular practices of one community, but also the implicit self-understanding at work in that community and in the broader Latino community in the United States. "One cannot understand the significance of Guadalupe for popular religion — and for U.S. Hispanic self-understanding — without understanding how this narrative reveals to us who God is, and, simultaneously, who we are."[25] By fleshing out the understanding of the Guadalupan encounter implicit in the narrative and devotion, Goizueta is simultaneously sketching a theological anthropology from a Latino perspective. The characteristics of this anthropology indicate important characteristics of the Hispanic church as well. His ecclesiological contribution can be summed up in three parts: the U.S. Latino church is relational, sacramental, and nurturing of freedom.

To begin, Goizueta notes that the human person, for U.S. Hispanics, is constituted by relationships, is inherently relational. "Each person . . . is defined and constituted by his or her relationships, both personal and impersonal, natural and supernatural, material and spiritual."[26] Over and against what he calls liberal modern individualism,[27] the Latino understanding of humanity rests on this notion of relationality. "I am a particular, concrete, and unique embodiment of all those relationships; when someone encounters me, they also encounter my parents, relatives, friends, community, my people."[28] The human person, for Goizueta, is always already part of an intergenerational, involuntary community. He affirms "the centrality of human relationships as constitutive of our identity as human persons."[29] What Goizueta identifies here, in part, is the Hispanic notion of family, that community which no person chooses but is necessarily constitutive of identity.

Goizueta further claims that Mary, for Hispanics, is never just Mary, but also always the mother of Jesus. Mary symbolizes the "preexistent involuntary community which defines and constitutes the individual person we call Jesus"[30] and this is one reason she is so central to the devotional lives of Hispanic Catholics. Mary is important because she is Jesus' family, but also because she is experienced as part of each person's family. It is not just that Guadalupe or Mary existed, but that she exists today in the lives of the members of the community. This is evident when Goizueta looks to the devotions surrounding the feast of Guadalupe at San Fernando Cathedral. The reenactment of the Guadalupan encounter, which is a fairly common practice, makes the encounter real to those present in the church. Thus it is not merely a memorial, but a reliving of the experience of encounter with Guadalupe each year.[31] As the story is made real again each year, so the encounter with the statue of Guadalupe, with her mantle, are real, tactile experiences, that function as sacramentals, if not sacraments, in that they mediate the supernatural by means of their natural physical presence.[32] For Goizueta, the U.S. Latino understanding of the cosmos as inherently interrelated and interconnected, which bypasses the modern cleavage of form and content, underlies this rich understanding of the Marian symbols and images truly re-creating the experience of encounter in the present. Interestingly, Charles Dahm cites the audible gasp in the community during the reenactment of the Guadalupan encounter on December 12. He notes that the play re-presents the moment when the image of Guadalupe appears on the *tilma,* and it is as if the congregation lives the awe-filled experience anew each year.[33]

Just as Juan Diego comes to an understanding of his humanity through his relationship with Guadalupe, who treats him with dignity, so we come to know ourselves as free individuals through relationships. "A central theme of the narrative is the affirmation of community as the birthplace of authentic human personhood and freedom."[34] Because of this freedom, Juan Diego feels free to disobey the Virgin and go to his sick uncle instead of the bishop, as she had asked. This disobedience, however, is a hallmark of genuine community: true freedom. Authentic community allows for dissent, difference, and criticism. It is the goal of an authentic community to foster the individuality of its members.

Ecclesially, the relational anthropology elaborated by Goizueta is significant. It presents a notion of the people of God that is truly communal and interrelated. Moreover, it speaks to the universal church, which spans space and time, through its network of intergenerational relationships. Most importantly perhaps, Goizueta's understanding of the authentic community as being both constitutive of identity and the nexus of true freedom describes what the church as People of God could truly be.

Conclusion

Hispanic Catholics in no way represent the panacea that will cure the ills of the Catholic Church in the twenty-first century. While we are usually singled out as a vibrant and growing sector of the church in the United States, I sense an undercurrent of unexpressed gratitude for tolerating non-Spanish-speaking clergy, dwindling resources, and tokenistic appointments with little or no protest. The romanticization of U.S. Latinos/as traditional Catholicism, with its strong respect for the family, can obscure the very progressive social agenda of many Hispanic Catholics. There are some ways in which Hispanic Catholics elude the liberal/conservative categories that can so easily be applied to factions in the U.S. church.

Nor has the story of the Hispanic church in the United States been marked only by successes. Witness the problems associated with the demise of the national parish, including the establishment of parallel parishes where one is English-speaking and the other Spanish-speaking or bilingual, the basement communities where the immigrant church prefers to maintain its own space and some measure of autonomy. Or the alternative, the blended parish, which too often includes tokenistic appointments to parish councils. Further, the importing of very conservative clergy from Latin American countries runs the risk of being a hindrance to the church, even if these clergymen do speak Spanish.

However, when we look to the popular religious practices of Hispanic Catholics, hermeneutically as Espín suggests, it is possible to glean insights that point to a way forward for the U.S. church. This essay has shown three ways in which Marian devotion, as a popular religious practice, empowers the faithful and serves as an outlet for the *sensus*

fidelium. Devotion to Guadalupe can be read in a way that reveals positive progressive notions of accountability and responsibility, relevant for
the clergy as well as the laity. These include strategies for warding off
ecclesial monophysitism, like the ecclesial conversion called for in the
Guadalupan narrative and the inclusive sense of apostolicity embodied
by Juan Diego. With the help of the *Nican mopohua* and the communities that have incorporated it into their popular religiosity, we can
imagine a future Catholic Church that is truly accountable, as well as
catholic, apostolic, and holy.

Another key ecclesiological insight of Guadalupan devotion is the
notion of solidarity, particularly with those on the margins of society.
What Mexican American Catholics see in Guadalupe may in fact be a
pneumatological insight as Espín suggests, but the insight has important
ecclesiological meaning. The Mexican American community emphasizes
in its Marian devotion her solidarity with the sufferings of the People of
God. Revered by this community of believers as their mother, Guadalupe truly serves as the mother of the church, a title suggested by Paul VI
after Vatican II. Because Guadalupe is in solidarity with those who suf-
fer, she points the way for the rest of the church: where the poor are the
church should be too. Mexican Americans celebrate the accompaniment
and permanence of Guadalupe's presence with their community. In the
same way, the church is called to be, and remain, in solidarity with those
on the margins.

Chapter 9

Collective Identity and Distinctiveness

The Case of U.S. Conferences of Apostolic Women and Men Religious

MARY JOHNSON, S.N.D.deN.

Q UESTIONS OF IDENTITY always underlie the issue of inculturation, as, simultaneously in societies all over the world, religion meets and shapes culture, and culture meets and shapes religion. Social scientists analyze the intersection of religion and culture through various lenses. One lens focuses on issues of growth and decline in the membership of the religious group. While this is certainly not the only measure of institutional mission effectiveness or spiritual vibrancy, it is a measure that points to generational engagement and future potential for mission, and it raises significant questions about the strength and coherence of the identity of the religious group. Decline in religious group membership is often the impetus for evangelization efforts but, in some groups, it is used as a rationale to decrease the number of services and facilities. So the number of members of a religious group, whether growing or declining, has consequences for those within and outside the group. Those consequences are psychological, programmatic, and structural.

For many years, the sociology of religion has paid attention to issues of growth and decline, especially within mainline Protestantism in the United States. Today, particular attention is being paid to the rise, demographic and political, of American evangelicals. Sociologist Christian Smith, in his *American Evangelicalism: Embattled and Thriving* (1998), has made a significant contribution by formulating a new theory to explain the growth and vibrancy of evangelicals in the United States, critical dimensions of their collective identity. We shall turn to this theory shortly.

179

Attention, of course, is also being paid to the complex collective identity of Catholicism today in the United States. It is paradoxical that while
the church, with 69 million members, continues to grow, its identity is
not considered to be vibrant. The church has been collectively trauma-
tized and weakened by the sexual abuse crisis. While the mission of the
church is made manifest in many places by persons and systems that
work tirelessly on behalf of gospel values, continuing revelations and
ongoing tensions also mark the church as it struggles to go forward.

While critically important internal issues requiring reform consume a
great deal of time and energy in the life of the church, external factors
which have an effect on its growth and vibrancy also demand attention.
We shall focus here on one external factor that is shaping culture and
has the potential to shape religion, for good or ill, and which, along with
other media, has been used successfully by other religious bodies. That
factor is the Internet.

We shall analyze the Internet as a significant medium for the proclamation of the good news, with its particular connection to youth and young
adults, generations critically important to the present and future of the
church, especially in light of their coming of age during the sexual abuse
crisis. Specifically, we shall analyze the case of U.S. conferences of apostolic orders of Catholic men and women religious and how they describe
themselves on the Internet. While the conferences are only one structure
within a large and complex church and while they have distinct members, they do provide grist for the sociological mill in the analysis of the
identity of religious organizations which espouse values that challenge
the dominant culture.

We also chose the conferences as our unit of analysis because, while
they are not representative of religious orders, they do have an influence
on the ethos of religious orders. While, in general, church organizations
need to present themselves in compelling terms so as to gain new members
and supporters from the new generations of the church, the specific mission of religious orders depends on meeting this challenge: how to present
the gospel message to an Internet-savvy generation from the perspective
of decades-old and centuries-old Catholic structures and symbol systems.

While the gospel has been transmitted from generation to generation
and each generation up to this point has been able somehow to build
bridges to the next, we are now confronted with a technology that has

the potential to serve as a bridge but could be transformed, by omission rather than commission, into a barrier. To test whether the use of the Internet is a bridge or barrier, we shall examine the websites of the conferences from three points of view: from the point of view of the self-presentation of the individual conferences; from the point of view of Catholic youth and young adults who, for the most part, do not have a working knowledge of the discourse used by religious orders and conferences; and from the point of view of the broader culture, in order to analyze the reciprocal relationship of the influence of the conferences on the culture and, in turn, the culture on the conferences.

We believe that orders of religious in the Catholic Church have much to share with the church and world, especially with young adults who seek to live lives of meaning and significance. How do they proclaim their mission and its relationship to God, the church, their distinct way of life in the church, their mission in response to the needs of the world, and their hope for the world? These are distinct elements of their identity. There are thousands and thousands of religious orders in the world. Can the self-presentation of the conferences via the Internet shed light on themes that they need to explore? We begin our exploration of that question with a review of the structure and function of the conferences.

Conciliar and Canonical Legitimation of Conferences

The Vatican II decree *Perfectae Caritatis,* on the Renewal of Religious Life, states that conferences of religious are to be "welcomed." The decree continues:

> They can contribute a great deal towards the fuller achievement of the purpose of the individual institutes, towards fostering more effective cooperation for the good of the church, towards a more equitable distribution of ministers of the Gospel in a given territory, and towards treating the problems which are common to all religious.[1]

Conferences of major superiors of religious institutes are described in canons 708 and 709 of the Code of Canon Law (1983):

Major superiors can be associated usefully in conferences or councils so that by common efforts they work to achieve more fully the purpose of the individual institutes, always without prejudice to their autonomy, character, and proper spirit, or to transact common affairs, or to establish appropriate coordination and cooperation with the conferences of bishops and also with individual bishops.[2]

Conferences of major superiors are to have their own statutes approved by the Holy See, by which alone they can be erected even as a juridic person and under whose supreme direction they remain.[3]

From these sources we can see that the church has given its blessing to a structure that can fulfill multiple purposes: a source of help for the internal workings of the institutes, a source of strength for the collective and collaborative external mission of the institutes, and a source of support for the bond between the conferences of religious and the episcopal conferences of individual nations.

Conferences in the United States

There are three conferences of major superiors or leaders of apostolic religious institutes in the United States: the Leadership Conference of Women Religious (LCWR), founded in 1956; the Conference of Major Superiors of Men (CMSM), also founded in 1956; and the Council of Major Superiors of Women Religious (CMSWR), founded in 1992. The United States is the only nation in the world with two conferences for women religious.

There are two other conferences we shall focus on here as well: the National Religious Vocation Conference (NRVC) for those engaged in the work of vocation ministry and the Religious Formation Conference (RFC) for formation ministers.

Genesis of Conferences

LCWR and CMSM came into being in 1956 at the invitation of the Vatican. The challenge from the Vatican Congregation for Religious was for the conferences to respond to "the needs of our time." From the beginning, the foundational charge of LCWR and CMSM was both internal and external to the orders: the spirituality and mission of the sisters, brothers, and priests, and collaboration with other U.S. religious, and with the hierarchy, clergy, and Catholic associations. Collaboration was seen as potentially strengthening the mission of individual orders, while maintaining their autonomy. Today the national headquarters of LCWR and CMSM are located in the same office building in Silver Spring, Maryland.

CMSWR was founded in 1992 and seeks the collaboration of all major superiors who wish to collaborate among themselves and with the conference of bishops. The members envision their conference as a symbol of their unity with the pope and as a channel for the Magisterium's directives regarding religious life. According to their website, the official address for CMSWR is a Post Office Box in Washington, D.C.

NRVC came into being in 1988 as a combination of the National Conference of Religious Vocation Directors and the National Sisters Vocation Conference. The membership of NRVC is made up of vocation ministers of religious congregations. The organization is based in Chicago.

RFC originated in the early 1950s as the Sister Formation Conference, which was concerned with the preparation of young sisters for ministry. RFC was spawned by the National Catholic Education Association. Today RFC is the oldest national conference in the United States serving men and women religious. The membership comprises formation ministers of religious congregations, those in the process of formation, and all who are interested in issues related to formation. RFC is located in Silver Spring, Maryland.

What follows are the theory and methodology used, the presentation of data, the findings, and conclusions.

Theory of Subcultural Identity

The application of sociological theory to data often frames and sharpens analysis. As mentioned earlier, sociologist Christian Smith has formulated a theory of subcultural identity to explain the growth and vibrancy of evangelicals in the United States. This theory contains elements that will be used in our analysis of conference website data as well.

In his book, Smith argues that "contemporary American evangelicalism is thriving. It is more than alive and well. Indeed, ... it appears to be the strongest of the major Christian traditions in the United States today."[4] Smith bases his assertion on survey data measuring the vitality of several Christian traditions using multiple indicators of strength.

Smith critiques several sociological theories of growth and decline of church membership and then presents his own, based on several propositions. Those propositions and the new "subcultural identity" theory follow:

Proposition One: The human drives for meaning and belonging are satisfied primarily by locating human selves within social groups that sustain distinctive, morally orienting collective identities.

Proposition Two: Social groups construct and maintain collective identities by drawing symbolic boundaries that create distinction between themselves and relevant out-groups.

Proposition Three: Religious traditions have *always* strategically renegotiated their collective identities by continually reformulating the ways their constructed orthodoxies engage the changing sociocultural environments they confront.

Proposition Four: Because the socially normative bases of identity-legitimation are historically variable, modern religious believers can establish stronger religious identities and commitments on the basis of individual choice than through ascription.

Proposition Five: Individuals and groups define their values and norms and evaluate their identities and actions in relation to specific, chosen reference groups; dissimilar and antagonistic outgroups may serve as negative reference groups.

Proposition Six: Modern pluralism promotes the formation of strong subcultures and potentially "deviant" identities, including religious subcultures and identities.

Proposition Seven: Intergroup conflict in a pluralistic context typically strengthens in-group identity, solidarity, resource mobilization, and membership retention.

Proposition Eight: Modernity can actually *increase* religion's appeal, by creating social conditions which intensify the kinds of felt needs and desires that religion is especially well positioned to satisfy.

Finally, these propositions undergird Smith's "subcultural identity" theory of religious persistence and strength. The two foci of the theory are these: (1) Religion survives and can thrive in pluralistic, modern society by embedding itself in subcultures that offer satisfying morally orienting collective identities which provide adherents meaning and belonging. (2) In a pluralistic society, those religious groups will be relatively stronger which better possess and employ the cultural tools needed to create both clear distinction from and significant engagement and tension with other relevant outgroups, short of becoming genuinely countercultural.

Methodology

The five conferences present themselves in a variety of ways on the Internet. No two are alike. The presentations vary by length, content, and style. In this chapter, the theory of subcultural identity will be applied specifically to the mission statements of the five conferences, especially seen through the lens of young people and the wider culture. However, on most of the sites, much more information is offered, especially their self-definition, history, and, sometimes, goals. It would be a worthwhile for the reader to peruse the websites in their entirety in order to experience the fullness of the presentations. But for our purposes here, this exercise requires that we hone in on some categories that are widely recognized as providing context to the understanding of organizational life and distinctiveness. Self-definitions will be provided here to serve as context but the analysis will focus on the mission statements because that is the term that is recognized in the wider society as providing insight into an organization's reason for being and its distinct contribution to the society vis-à-vis that of other groups. One final caveat is that the data from the websites that follow were collected and analyzed at the beginning of January 2005. Thus, these are cross-sectional data, representing one point in time. Further longitudinal research is needed on the evolution of websites as organizations respond to new publics and new demands.

Self-Definition of the Conferences

The following excerpts are taken from the websites of the five conferences. These are verbatim accounts of how the organizations define themselves. Again, we present the data as they are, some expansive, some in almost-outline form.

The Leadership Conference of Women Religious

The following portrait of the Leadership Conference of Women Religious is taken verbatim from material presented on its website: *www.lcwr.org*. Presented here are its self-definition and call for 2004–9. Of the three leadership conferences, this one contains the most text.

Self-Definition

The Leadership Conference of Women Religious (LCWR) is the association of the leaders of congregations of Catholic women religious in the United States. The conference has approximately 1,000 members, who represent about 95 percent of the 75,000 women religious in the United States. Founded in 1956, the conference assists its members to collaboratively carry out their service of leadership to further the mission of the Gospel in today's world.

The scope of the conference's concerns is broad and includes collaborating in Catholic Church and societal efforts that influence systemic change, studying significant trends and issues within the church and society, utilizing our corporate voice in solidarity with people who experience any form of violence or oppression, and creating and offering resource materials on religious leadership skills. We serve as a resource to our members, as well as to members of the public seeking information on leadership for religious life.[5]

LCWR Call for 2004–9: Prologue

We, the members of the Leadership Conference of Women Religious, believe that God's call is written in the signs of our time. Our foremothers and founders stepped into the chaos and the unknown of their day, trusting in God's good guidance and great providence. In our time, we are called to do the same. Inspired by the radical call of the Gospel, led by God's Spirit and companioned by one another, we embrace our time as holy, our leadership as gift, and our challenges as blessings.

In this time of God's favor, we live in a world where

- Major social and global changes create fear, anxiety, confusion, and polarization
- Technology, communication, and information shrink time and distances among peoples
- Inaccessibility to basic resources breeds suffering, oppression and violence
- Increasingly, violence, military force and terrorist activity are used to settle disputes
- Multinational corporations exert control over legitimate governments
- Religion is used to justify political and personal aggression
- Environmental degradation threatens all of God's creation

And where people

- Long for justice, peace and communion
- Work to achieve the common good
- Hunger for spirituality and meaning
- Claim personal and communal power for change
- Awaken to the wonder of the universe, and the place of humans within it

In this time of God's favor, we belong to a church whose members

- Struggle to love the Church as both graced and sinful
- Strive to balance traditional teachings with changing realities
- Seek to be a more inclusive, welcoming community
- Hunger for spirituality and the full expression of their baptismal call

And whose leaders

- Experience the pressing impact of a rapidly evolving world and universe
- Struggle with growing diversity in members' views, cultures, and religious practices

- Are confronted with their own humanity and sinfulness
- Bear the call to create structures that free the Church for the ways of God's Spirit
- Carry the responsibility of being welcoming, accountable, and inclusive pastors to all God's People[6]

The Conference of Major Superiors of Men

The following elements are taken verbatim from CMSM's website: *www.cmsm.org.*

Purpose

The Conference of Major Superiors of Men promotes the welfare, community life, ministry and mission of more than 20,000 vowed priests and brothers of 210 Catholic religious communities of men in the United States.[7]

Goals

1. Provide a corporate influence and voice for the male religious in the United States through national and regional structures by: identifying key issues facing the Church and society; educating members on the consequences of the issues; assisting members to respond; and developing and implementing programs to influence the church and society on selected topics.

2. Promote dialogue and collaboration with other major groups in the church and society. This includes dialogues with the U.S. bishops; collaboration with the laity; and outreach to other religious organizations.

3. Support major superiors of men and serve as a resource for them in their role as leaders of their communities. To achieve this goal, CMSM promotes a positive image of religious life, fosters networking and formation among major superiors, and engages in collaborative efforts with other religious institutes.[8]

The Council of Major Superiors of Women Religious

The following information about CMSWR is taken verbatim from its website *www.cmswr.org.*

The Council of Major Superiors of Women Religious is a canonically approved organization founded in 1992, to promote religious life in the United States. Its statutes were definitively approved by the Vatican Congregation for Institutes of Consecrated Life and Societies of Apostolic Life on October 26, 1995.

Composed of major superiors of women religious with communities in the United States, the group is dedicated to Mary, the Mother of the Church and Patroness of the Americas. Members of the Council wish to serve the Church and to foster the progress and welfare of religious life in the United States.

The Council seeks:

- to establish collaboration among major superiors who desire it,

- to serve as a channel of communication among major superiors,

- to provide a forum for participation, dialogue, and education on the patrimony of the Church's teaching on religious life,

- to promote unity among major superiors, thus testifying to their union with the Magisterium and their love for Christ's Vicar on earth, and,

- to coordinate active cooperation with the USCCB [United States Conference of Catholic Bishops].[9]

The Religious Formation Conference

The following is taken verbatim from the Religious Formation Conference website: *www.relforcon.org.*

The Religious Formation Conference, which originated in the 1950's as the Sister Formation Conference, is a national Roman Catholic U.S. organization serving both women's and men's religious institutes, primarily in the U.S. but also in other countries. That service is directed especially toward:

- those in the ministry of incorporation/formation in their congregations

- those presently engaged in the process of incorporation/formation in congregations

- all within member congregations (ongoing formation).[10]

Also, on their website, RFC presents a two-and-a-half-page "Context for Religious Formation at the Dawn of the Twenty-First Century," which critiques U.S. culture and lifts up values that are essential for the formation of men and women religious today. Excerpts are included here:

The RFC wishes to articulate…a world view in which religious formation is taking place at this time in history.

We live in times of extraordinary creativity and extraordinary chaos where traditional expressions of relationship are shifting interiorly, interpersonally, institutionally, socially, universally.

The primary context for anyone seeking to live a vowed, communal life within the Catholic tradition called religious life is God.

In our Catholic tradition, the love of God made manifest through Jesus Christ and through the Holy Spirit is the ground of our being.

…North Americans sometimes live out of myths that are destructive and deceptive: more is better; we are Number One; winning is everything; we are a melting pot where everyone can achieve the American dream.

As its very name implies and as it has done throughout its long history and tradition, the Religious Life also brings a lived wisdom to both society and Church with regard to the struggle for credibility and meaning in our time.…[11]

This document deserves further analysis and to be read in its entirety. Unfortunately for our purposes here, it is distinct from the mission statement as presented on the website.

National Religious Vocation Conference

The following is taken verbatim from the National Religious Vocation Conference website: *www.nrvc.net.*

The National Religious Vocation Conference began in 1988 as a combination of the National Conference of Religious Vocation Directors (NCRVD) and the National Sisters Vocation Conference (NSVC). Today the NRVC has an annual membership of over 1300 women and men, most of whom are vocation ministers for religious congregations. The organization is divided into 14 regions. The National Board consists of eight to twelve representatives, in addition to the NRVC Executive Director.[12]

Conference Mission Statements

The above provide a context for the mission statements of the conferences which follow. They are taken verbatim from the websites.

Leadership Conference of Women Religious

LCWR Mission Statement

The purpose of the conference shall be to promote a developing understanding and living of the religious life by:

- assisting its members personally and communally to carry out more collaboratively their service of leadership in order to accomplish further the mission of Christ in today's world.

- fostering dialogue and collaboration among religious congregations within the church and in the larger society.

- developing models for initiating and strengthening relationships with groups concerned with the needs of society, thereby maximizing the potential of the conference for effecting change.[13]

Conference of Major Superiors of Men Religious

CMSM Mission Statement

The Conference of Major Superiors of Men (CMSM) is an association of the leadership of men in religious and apostolic institutes in the United States. The Conference has a formal tie with the U.S. Conference of Catholic Bishops, the Leadership Conference of Women Religious, the National Assembly of Religious Brothers and other national agencies. CMSM represents U.S. male religious and apostolic communities before a number of national and international bodies, including the Congregation of Religious and Secular Institutes of the Holy See, which officially recognizes CMSM as the national representative body for men in religious and apostolic communities in the United States.

CMSM addresses the life and concerns of religious and communities of apostolic life in the United States, including their evangelizing mission in the context of Church and culture in this country. CMSM is both a voice for major Superiors and a service to them:

a. as a voice, it speaks regionally, nationally and internationally, independently or in concert with other groups; it does so from the perspective of male religious and members of apostolic communities on issues regarding their life, as well as that of the Church and of our society;

b. as a service, it assists major Superiors in their role of leadership in their own communities and in the Conference as a whole, especially in promoting greater fidelity and more effective witness to the Gospel ideal.[14]

This mission statement was approved at the CMSM National Assembly in San Diego in August 1988.

Conference of Major Superiors of Women Religious

CMSWR Purpose

From the statutes of the Council of Major Superiors of Women Religious:

Section 2: It is the Specific Purpose of the Council:
To provide a clear, stable and official channel through which major superiors, assisted by an Episcopal Liaison appointed by the Holy See, can share the vision, principles and directives of the Magisterium with regard to religious life.

James Cardinal Hickey, Archbishop Emeritus of Washington D.C., was the first Episcopal Liaison for the Council. He provided much support and assistance in the early days of the Council.

During the summer of 2001, the Congregation for Institutes of Consecrated Life and Societies of Apostolic Life appointed Most Reverend Justin F. Rigali, then Archbishop of St. Louis, as the Episcopal Liaison for the Council.[15]

Religious Formation Conference

Mission Statement

The Religious Formation Conference, rooted in the Gospel, called by God's prophetic Spirit, and responsive to the signs of our times, supports and serves the ministry of formation in religious congregations of men and women. The Conference does this in a spirit of hope, collaboration and mutuality.[16]

National Religious Vocation Conference

NRVC Mission

The National Religious Vocation Conference is a professional organization of men and women committed to vocation awareness, invitation, and discernment of consecrated life as brothers, sisters and priests.

The NRVC shares in the mission of Jesus in serving its members by providing education, resources, and other supportive services for personal and professional growth. Foundational to this mission is affirming the baptismal call to holiness of all members of the Catholic Church. In an inclusive and collaborative style, we present religious life as a viable option in today's Church.[17]

Findings

A content analysis of the five conference mission statements reveals the following relative to key themes within the data: the Sacred, the church, the life, the mission, and the culture. To reiterate, other material is found elsewhere on the websites, but the focus here is what is contained in the mission statements themselves. Obviously, websites do not reveal the process involved in choosing which text and images are used and where they are located on the site, and in deciding how and why those choices are made.

The Sacred

God is referred to in a variety of ways and contexts in the mission statements. The Leadership Conference of Women Religious (LCWR) refers to "the mission of Christ in today's world." The Conference of Major

Superiors of Men (CMSM) does not make explicit mention of God but refers to "more effective witness to the Gospel ideal." The Council of Major Superiors of Women Religious (CMSWR) also does not make explicit reference to God. The Religious Formation Conference (RFC) refers to "God's prophetic Spirit" and to the Gospel. And the National Religious Vocation Conference (NRVC) speaks of "the mission of Jesus."

The Church

The Catholic Church is referred to in a variety of ways in the mission statements. LCWR refers to part of its mission as fostering dialogue and collaboration among religious congregations "within the church...." CMSM refers to its evangelizing mission "in the context of Church...." CMSWR does not make explicit mention of the Catholic Church but does refer to the Magisterium and to the Episcopal Liaison appointed by the Holy See. RFC does not mention the church in its mission statement. NRVC refers to " ... the baptismal call to holiness of all members of the Catholic Church."

The Life

Religious life is also called by a variety of names across the mission statements. LCWR uses the term "the religious life." CMSM speaks of "male religious and apostolic communities." CMSWR refers to "religious life." RFC refers to "religious congregations of men and women." NRVC speaks of "consecrated life as brothers, sisters and priests." RFC also includes a definition of religious life on its website. It is included verbatim here:

> "Religious life" is a phrase used to designate a way of life that dates back to the early centuries of the Christian church. Today it designates a way of life chosen by a Christian woman or man, based on the values of the Christian Gospel, and formalized by the public profession of certain vows. The men and women who are called to choose this way of life have prayer, community and service as the major pivots of their life, all in the service of mission (i.e., the unfolding of the reign of God in our world.) For the last several decades that mission often takes the form of working for justice in societies all over the world.[18]

The Mission

Some of the conferences describe both internal and external missions; some missions are a combination of the two. Some also describe the mission and the way that it is lived out.

LCWR describes its mission as being "to promote a developing understanding and living of the religious life." CMSM sees itself as "both a voice for major Superiors and a service to them." CMSWR sees its mission as providing "a clear, stable and official channel" through which the major superiors, with the episcopal liaison, can share the "vision, principles and directives of the Magisterium" regarding religious life. RFC "supports and serves the ministry of formation." NRVC provides "education, resources, and other supportive services for personal and professional growth."

Both RFC and NRVC make explicit mention of the spirit or style in which they perform their mission. RFC says they do their work "in a spirit of hope, collaboration and mutuality." NRVC states that they fulfill their mission "in an inclusive and collaborative style."

The Culture

The conferences refer to the wider culture in different ways. LCWR discusses how it makes real its mission by assisting its members to carry out their ministry in order to "accomplish further the mission of Christ in today's world," to foster "dialogue and collaboration among religious congregations within the church and in the larger society," to initiate and strengthen relationships "with groups concerned with the needs of society, thereby maximizing the potential of the conference for effecting change." CMSM locates its mission "in the context of Church and culture in this country." It serves as a voice for male religious and members of apostolic communities "on issues regarding their life, as well as that of the Church and of our society." CMSWR does not make explicit reference to the wider culture. RFC speaks of being "responsive to the signs of our times." NRVC also does not speak of the wider culture.

Conclusions

A content analysis of the mission statements of the five conferences raises the following issues. First, especially from the point of view of young people who meet and learn of organizations while reading websites on the Internet, language has to be clarified. While images now make up a large percentage of the design of web pages, words also matter, especially for newer generations which are not as conversant in this rhetoric as older generations. The choice of words used to describe God, the church, and the religious life has to be deliberate and has to be used knowing that other sites can and will be surfed in order to provide context.

Second, while many of the websites displayed a great deal of text, some requiring much navigation, the actual mission statements, which are considered to be a key descriptor of the interior and exterior workings of an organization were, for the most part, found wanting. Language was often non-specific and unfocused. Certain dimensions of religious life that are constitutive of its identity, such as vows of poverty, chastity, and obedience, community living, prayer, and how those facets of the life relate to mission, were rarely mentioned, if at all.

Third, the internal and external missions of the conferences were difficult to ascertain from the mission statements. What of the mission is directed to the internal work of the organizations and what is directed to the external? And how is the external defined? And, from the point of view of mission, how diffuse is too diffuse?

Finally, the stance toward the wider culture is ambiguous. While reference is made to working for change and working with others, those references beg the questions: What kind of change? What kind of work? With whom? For whose sake? Toward what end? Why?

Christian Smith's provocative theory regarding the growth of evangelicals in the United States has once again brought issues of subcultural identity, and engagement and tension with the wider culture, to the fore in the particular case of religious bodies in pluralistic societies. While the mission statements of the conferences provide much evidence of significance and meaning, there is a need for more deliberate attention to be paid to the articulation of distinct markers that describe the identity of the conferences and to the development of a rhetoric that more aptly describes the conferences' relation to the culture. While we can intuit that the conferences hope, in the end, to shape the culture, they do not communicate powerfully enough how that is to be done or how it will look when it happens. In this case, the culture may have shaped the conferences in the sense that their presentations are quite diffuse.

While Catholics are not evangelicals, and conferences of religious are not representative of the whole church, and mission statements do not capture the whole spirit of the conferences, this content analysis does lift up issues that will not go away until addressed adequately. They also point to questions of organizational effectiveness, a topic that would require other methods of data collection and analysis.

To conclude, the Internet is now a significant medium for the proclamation of the good news. Many, especially young people, are desperate to hear it. How shall it be proclaimed and, more importantly, what will be proclaimed?

Chapter 10

Religious Commitments of
Young Adult Catholics

DEAN R. HOGE

C ARETAKERS OF CATHOLIC INSTITUTIONS today need to understand
young adult Catholics. This is important for more reasons and
deeper reasons than are commonly thought. Let me explain by making two points. First, young adults today are different from their elders.
This fact gives rise to the question of whether they will change with age,
so that they will come to resemble their elders a little later. If this is
the prospect, young versus old differences today do not predict social
change, but are merely different phases of the life cycle. Is it true that
today's liberals are tomorrow's conservatives? Usually, no. According to
the best research, it is not true in most central life values.

Students of American value change have distinguished two patterns,
which for simplicity we will call "all shift" and "generational succession." In "all shift," everyone in the adult society shifts attitudes or
behavior over a period of time, perhaps one or two decades, resulting in
a comprehensive change in the society. An example is the rise in popularity of sport utility vehicles in the 1990s. Americans of all ages seemed
to like the new vehicles, resulting in an across-the-board market shift.[1]
The second type of change, "generational succession," is different, in
that nobody *changed* their mind. Rather, older people died and were
replaced by younger adults who held different values and attitudes from
their early years and who continued holding those values and attitudes
unchanged throughout the life cycle. In this model, older people are more
conservative than young adults not because people become conservative
with age but because the new generations *entered* at a different point.
A good example is the present-day generational gap in attitudes toward

premarital sex. Old and young Americans today are much different on this topic, but the best evidence is that older Americans did not change their attitudes as they aged, and younger Americans are not changing theirs either as they age. Rather, young Americans entered adulthood with different attitudes from early in their lives.

This second model, "generational succession," best matches current research on basic values, social commitments, and worldviews, and it should guide our thinking about young adult Catholics. It raises the question of why the young adults were different in the first place. Why is there not continuity across generations? Here I need to explain the concept "impressionable years." In the typical life cycle in modern society, individuals acquire their most basic worldviews and values at an early age. The exact years are impossible to specify, but estimates range from ten to twenty years of age at the young end to fifteen to twenty-five years of age at the old end.[2] I cannot be more precise, but I believe that ten to twenty is nearer the truth, since youth in present-day society develop more quickly than did their parents and grandparents. They gain more information during their early teens, so the "impressionable years" are surely shifting downward. As a rough guess, let us adopt twelve to twenty-two. Values formed during this decade will be largely determinative for the entire life cycle. There will be exceptions, as when certain individuals have radical conversions of one type or other, or when vivid life experiences of certain persons bring a metanoia.

The "generation succession" model fits most values, but it does not fit the data on Mass attendance. Mass attendance is greatly influenced by social influences and family life, and that complicates the situation. Mass attendance is low for persons in their twenties, but it increases after marriage, parenthood, and settling into a community, as evidenced by buying a house. This is not to say that generational succession is not present—it still is, but it is eclipsed in the data by changes in attendance as adults get older.

The second point I need to make is that young adults today are the carriers of social and cultural change. This has its trivial side, as we watch young adults go headlong for one musical style for a decade, then discard it for another, and continue in this on and on. But it also has a profound side, as we remember that political revolutions in the last century have been initiated and borne mostly by educated young adults. This has been clear in the Russian and Chinese revolutions, in the fall of Communism, and in the unrest of the Middle East. The prototypical agent of social change has been the college student, best exemplified in the novel and Broadway show *Les Misérables,* in which the cadre of young student revolutionaries is pitted in street warfare against the mercenaries of the old regime. Another pertinent example is the Tiananmen Square uprising in Beijing in 1989, in which university students urging more democracy in China held a massive takeover of Tiananmen Square in the middle of the city, even erecting a papier-mâché version of a statue of liberty. Where did the students get their revolutionary ideas? It was from their university educations at home and abroad.

The influence of liberal university education today is not a secret. This raises the conundrum of why the Chinese authorities today are encouraging their brightest and best young people to study in universities in America and Europe. Thousands of Chinese are studying in our universities. Certainly the Chinese leaders know that the students will come back changed, and some of those graduates will form the vanguard of reform movements in the decades ahead. Apparently the leaders see this eventuality as acceptable, or perhaps as inevitable. Maybe they see it as a price they are willing to pay in order to get the best education for their youth.

A rough analogue to China is American Catholicism. Why do American Catholics today encourage their brightest and best young people to study in leading American universities, the majority of which are non-Catholic? Why do they send their children to the Ivy League and the best state universities? Of all American Catholics attending colleges and universities today, an estimated 91 percent are in non-Catholic institutions. Certainly the parents must realize that the students will come back changed. The change will be in the direction of desiring more lay input in formulation of Catholic moral teachings, more participation in institutional decision-making, and more accountability of church leaders to laity. Let me hasten to be clear on one point: the analogy to the Chinese is inexact in that many Catholic young people studying in *Catholic* colleges and universities — not just the non-Catholic ones — will come back changed.

Catholic colleges and universities vary. Some of them will produce graduates who are individualistic and restless with current church rules. It is interesting that in a recent survey of members of the reform movement Voice of the Faithful, 57 percent were found to have studied in Catholic colleges and universities.[3] My point is this: liberal college education influences American youth in the direction of individualistic, democratic values. Apparently Catholic parents and leaders see this influence as a good thing, or at least as acceptable. In institutional planning in American Catholicism we should prepare for this, by expecting that educated young adults will increasingly want more lay input in church governance and more accountability of church leaders to the laity.

Research on Young Adult Catholics Compared with Other Young Adults

Catholic young adults in America today are not much different from other young adults. The best data comparing Catholics eighteen to thirty-nine with all other Americans eighteen to thirty-nine comes from the high-quality annual General Social Survey. It found in 2000 that 24 percent of the Catholics had earned bachelor's degrees, compared with 22 percent of non-Catholics. The percentage who have computers in their home in 2002 was 84, compared with 81 percent among non-Catholics. Average hours per day watching television was 2.64, compared with 2.76 for non-Catholics. Average age of first marriage was about two-thirds of a year higher for Catholics than for non-Catholics (for all Americans the median age of first marriage was twenty-six). Of all the young adult Catholics who are married, an estimated 41 percent had married non-Catholics. Church attendance weekly or oftener in 2000–2002 was about 1 percent higher than for non-Catholics, and the proportion who expressed a great deal of confidence in organized religion was 2 percent higher than for non-Catholics. The proportion of Catholics who said that women should stay in the home and let men run the country, in surveys in the late 1990s, was 10 percent, compared with 12 percent of non-Catholics. The proportion of young adult Catholics who said they had seen an X-rated movie in the last year was 38 percent, compared with 37 percent of all others.[4]

Young adult Catholics today are slightly more liberal than non-Catholics on attitudes about personal behavior. The proportion of Catholics saying that homosexuality is always or almost always wrong in 2000 was 42 percent, compared with 57 percent of non-Catholics. The proportion of Catholics saying that premarital sex is always or almost always wrong in 2000 was 19 percent, compared with 33 percent of all others. Ninety-five percent of the Catholics are in favor of sex education in the schools, compared with 92 percent of all others.

We can also trace trends in survey data. Mass attendance (weekly or oftener) of young adult Catholics dropped from 37 percent in 1972–74 to 19 percent in 2002. (For non-Catholics there was little change over this time, with figures hovering around 20 percent.) Confidence of young adult Catholics in the leaders of organized religion dropped from 39 percent in 1972–74 to 25 percent in 2002. The belief that homosexuality is always or almost always wrong dropped from 68 percent in 1972–74 to 42 percent in 2002. Belief that premarital sex is wrong dropped from 29 percent in 1972–74 to 19 percent in 2002. The belief that women should stay in the home and let men run the country dropped from 20 percent in 1972–74 to 10 percent in the late 1990s. The belief that in general most people today can be trusted dropped from 45 percent in 1972–74 to 29 percent in 2002. In general Catholic young adults resembled others in these trends.

How Are Young Adult Catholics
Different from Their Elders?

As I said above, young adult Catholics are different from their elders since their impressionable years were lived in different circumstances. The best data available on how young adult Catholics differ from their elders comes from the 2003 Notre Dame Catholic survey. It was a good random sample of Catholics eighteen or older.[5] The researchers divided the sample into three age groups. First was age eighteen to thirty-nine, which is our current interest. Second was forty to sixty-two, which represents "Vatican II Catholics," that is, Catholics whose impressionable years included the Second Vatican Council or its aftermath. Third was sixty-three or older, "pre–Vatican II Catholics," whose impressionable years were clearly prior to the council. The second group (born 1941 to

1963) is similar to the Baby Boomers, and the first group (born 1964 or later) are Post-Boomers.

An important fact is that the youngest group, which we will call "young adult Catholics," represents 42 percent of the total, and the pre–Vatican II Catholics represent only 17 percent. The influence of the pre–Vatican II Catholics will disappear in the next two decades, and the two younger groups will become the lay leaders. The uniqueness of these young adult Catholics can be described in the following three statements.

1. Young adult Catholics uphold greater individual authority in religious and moral decisions.

Table 1 on the following page includes five measures of feelings that individuals should rightfully be the locus of authority in religious decision-making. The first item asks if Catholics need to obey church teachings even if they disagree with them. Twenty-six percent of the young adults said yes. But the older pre–Vatican II Catholics held a different view; 42 percent said yes. The young adults were a few points higher than the Vatican II adults (26 percent compared with 20 percent), and the reason is unclear.

In the middle of Table 1 are two statements about making individual religious decisions. The first says that individuals should make religious decisions on their own, and on it the young adults are different from the pre-Vatican Catholics. The Vatican II Catholics (middle group) agree with the young adults. The second item says that if you believe in God, it does not really matter to which religion you belong. Again the young adults and middle-age adults agree with each other, and they agree with the statement more than the older pre-Vatican adults.

The bottom of Table 1 contains four questions about sexual behavior. The possible responses were "always morally wrong," "depends on circumstances," and "depends on the individual." The percentages saying "always morally wrong" are shown. As in the rest of Table 1, the most important gap is between the first two groups and the third. The gap between the youngest and oldest groups is 32 points on homosexual acts, 18 points on abortion, 42 points on premarital sex, and 15 points on birth control. (As a rule of thumb, any difference of 25 percentage points or more is enough to introduce tension between groups.)

Table 1
Individual Authority

	Total	Young Adults (18–39)	Vatican II (40–62)	Pre–Vatican II (63+)
Please tell me which *one* of these statements comes *closer* to the way you think (in percents):				
Catholics must obey church teachings even when they disagree with them	26	26	20	42
Catholics must do what they think is right even when it doesn't agree with church teachings	69	70	76	49
Do not know or refused	5	4	4	9
Individuals should seek out religious truth for themselves and not automatically conform to the doctrines of any church (percent who agree)	76	80	81	54
If you believe in God, it does not really matter which religion you belong to (percent who agree)	86	88	88	76
In your opinion, is this behavior always morally wrong, wrong except under certain circumstances, or is it entirely up to the individual? (percent "always morally wrong")				
Engage in homosexual acts	44	37	40	69
Choose to terminate a pregnancy by having an abortion	39	37	34	55
Engage in premarital sex	30	22	25	64
Use condoms or birth control pills to prevent pregnancy	11	10	8	25

2. Young adult Catholics want more influence of laity in institutional decision-making.

Table 2 shows three questions on which young adults are different from their elders. They want lay people to have more say in choosing parish priests, they want better financial reporting at all levels, and they are more than their elders in favor of withholding donations to the church until lay people have more voice in financial decisions.

Table 2
Decision-Making in the Church
(percent saying "strongly agree" or "somewhat agree")

	Total	Young Adults (18–39)	Vatican II (40–62)	Pre–Vatican II (63+)
Parish Decision-Making				
Lay people should have some say in who their parish priest will be.	73	78	75	53
Financial Decisions and Reporting				
The Catholic Church needs better financial reporting at all levels.	77	80	77	67
Catholic lay people should withhold donations to the church until they have more voice in financial decisions.	40	48	36	30

The gaps between young adults and pre-Vatican Catholics (the first and third age groups in the table) are moderately great; the greatest is on whether lay people should have a say in selecting the parish priest — a gap of 25 points.

3. Young adult Catholics are less invested in the institutional Catholic Church.

Young adult Catholics are less active in the institutional church, and they are less emotionally invested in it (see Table 3). Young adults attend Mass, receive Communion, and go to private confession with a priest much less than older Catholics. (The absolute percentages attending Mass and receiving Communion are unduly high in this survey; other surveys indicate that the percentage of all Catholics attending Mass weekly is closer to 42 percent, not 49 percent. The percentage receiving Communion weekly is also too high, based on other research.)

The percentage of young adults currently registered in a parish is lower than average (49 percent of young adults, versus 60 percent overall). Also the number of friendship ties in the parish is lower. When we asked how many of one's five closest friends go to the respondent's parish, the figure for three or more friends was 22 percent for young adults but 46 percent for the oldest group.

Table 3
Parish Involvement

	Total	Young Adults (18–39)	Vatican II (40–62)	Pre–Vatican II (63+)
How often, if ever, do you do each of the following? (percent "once a week or more")				
Attend Mass	49	38	50	78
Receive Communion	40	28	40	69
About how often, if ever, do you go to private confession with a priest? (percent "several times a year or more")	19	16	17	32
Are you currently registered as a member of a Catholic parish near where you live? (percent yes)	60	49	64	80
How many of your five *closest* friends also go to your parish? (percent 3 or more)	28	22	23	46
(Two questions asked to persons who are registered:) Are the following statements true of you? (percent yes)				
My parish is an important part of my life	74	67	74	84
I regularly attend programs and activities at the parish.	46	41	49	50

The bottom of Table 3 reports two questions asked only of respondents who are registered in a parish. In both of them, young adults are less involved in their parish. They see it as less important in their lives, and they attend fewer programs and activities.

Table 4 includes three statements about the respondent's commitment to the Catholic Church. On all three, young adults and Vatican II adults are similar, but the pre–Vatican II adults have stronger commitment.[6] That is, young adults feel that the church is less important to them personally, they are disproportionately open to the idea of leaving the Catholic Church, and they feel more than others that they could be happy in some other church — it would not have to be Catholic.

Other research confirms that young adult Catholics are not as involved in church life as older Catholics are. A large 1999 study of

Table 4
Catholic Identity and Religious Relativism
(percent "strongly agree" or "somewhat agree")

	Total	Young Adults (18–39)	Vatican II (40–62)	Pre–Vatican II (63+)
The Catholic Church is very important to me personally.	82	79	82	92
I would never leave the Catholic Church.	71	67	69	85
I could be just as happy in some other church — it would not have to be Catholic.	52	56	54	37

participation in Catholic small faith groups found that between five hundred thousand and eight hundred thousand adults and youth participate in such small groups, mainly in parishes, but only 19 percent of the participants were eighteen to thirty-nine years old.[7] Today, reform movements such as Call to Action and Voice of the Faithful find few young adults in their membership. For whatever reason, Catholic young adults are detached from the institutional church.

This raises a basic question. Earlier I said that young adult Catholics want more lay input in church governance and more accountability of leaders to the laity. Will today's young adults be committed enough to the institutional church in the future to give their energies to reform movements? Or will they be only indifferently involved in the church, taking the attitude that "my faith is in God, not in the church, and what the church leaders do does not matter to me"? I would guess: it will be some of each. All we can say for certain is that the current young adult generation will be less involved in the church than their parents.

A book by Colleen Carroll, *The New Faithful: Why Young Adults Are Embracing Christian Orthodoxy,* published in 2002, reports that in the last decade, Catholic young adults have become more traditional and more church-committed.[8] Carroll has no reliable trend data on which to make statements about how things have changed; her book is based only on her travels and interviews. My own review of the research finds that while *some* young adult Catholics are certainly traditional and committed, there is no evidence of a ten-year or twenty-year trend. On the

contrary, young adult Catholics are similar to other adult Catholics ten
or twenty years older. There is not a trend toward orthodoxy large
enough to be visible in nationwide polls.

Are Age Differences on Core Issues
or Peripheral Issues?

The differences we have seen between young adult Catholics and their
elders are on some issues, but not all. It becomes crucial whether they
are on issues core to the faith or peripheral to the faith. For example,
sacramental theology is core to the faith, but the question of female
altar servers is not. How do American Catholics identify what is core?
The core of Catholicism can be defined in theological documents, but
it is more important, if we want to understand actual Catholic behavior, to see how Catholic laity define it. Three studies, as far as I know,
have asked American Catholic lay persons how essential or nonessential various teachings and rules are. One of them was included in the
2003 Notre Dame study. The interviewer said, "Some people say certain
Catholic teachings are an essential part of being Catholic and that other
ones are less important or optional. Please tell me how important the
following nine teachings are to *your vision* of what the Catholic faith
is." The results are shown in Table 5.

Table 5 lists the nine items in the order of the percentage saying "essential" (not in the order in which they were presented in the interview).
Catholic young adults and their elders agreed that "Charitable efforts
toward helping the poor," "Belief that Jesus is really present in the Eucharist," and "Devotion to Mary the Mother of God" are essential. The
most nonessential were "Belief that only men can be priests," "Teachings
which oppose the death penalty," and "Private confession to a priest."
The opinions of the three age groups are similar. Older Catholics rated
most topics as more essential than did young Catholics, yet the rank
ordering by all age groups is nearly the same.

As Table 5 shows, specific institutional rules and specific moral teachings are rated as the least essential — shown at the bottom. This was
the finding in the other research studies also. For example, in a 1997
random survey of Catholics twenty to thirty-nine years old in which
nineteen aspects of Catholicism were assessed, the least essential were

Table 5
How Essential to the Catholic Faith?

Some people say certain church teachings are an essential part of being Catholic and that other ones are less important or optional. How important are the following teachings to *your vision* of what the Catholic faith is about? Would you say essential; may or may not be essential; or not essential? (percent saying "essential")

	Total	Young Adults (18–39)	Vatican II (40–62)	Pre–Vatican II (63+)
Charitable efforts toward helping the poor	82	78	86	85
Belief that Jesus is really present in the Eucharist	81	77	80	92
Devotion to Mary the Mother of God	72	71	69	85
Belief that God is present in a special way in the poor	71	68	71	77
Attending Mass once a week	55	49	53	76
Teachings that oppose abortion	51	48	49	66
Private confession to a priest	38	40	31	54
Teachings that oppose the death penalty	35	37	34	35
Belief that only men can be priests	29	23	26	49

(1) the church's traditional support of the right of workers to unionize, (2) belief that only men can be priests, (3) teachings which oppose the death penalty, and (4) belief that priests must be celibate.[9] By contrast, in all the studies the elements rated as most essential are the sacraments and efforts by Catholics to help the poor and oppressed.

These findings about how the Catholic faithful identify core and periphery help clarify discussions of possible reforms that might strengthen the commitment of young adults to the institutional church. The core of the faith is eternal, but the periphery may be open to reevaluation. The only reforms anyone should countenance are those relating to nonessentials, exemplified by the items at the bottom of the table. That is, the core is true and immutable, but the periphery changes over time and should be subject to reevaluation. The meaning of the most nonessential elements is largely that they are instrumental in serving the core. If they are not serving, they should be adjusted.

Strengthening Catholic Identity of Young Adults

Caretakers of Catholic institutions today are concerned about the Catholic identity of the young adults. We should not be surprised that after the multiple transitions of the twentieth century, American Catholics are faced with new questions of identity. They ask, "What does it mean to be a Catholic?" "Who are we?" "What is distinctive about being a Catholic, and is it important?" "Should we try to keep ourselves apart from other Christian groups?" Young adult Catholics ask these questions most insistently.

We need to recall a transition in American Catholic social life. Catholics were latecomers to America and for decades had feelings of being unwelcome and different from the Protestant majority. Their identity as Catholics was imposed from outside, and they were induced to internalize what others said about them. There was no escaping it. Catholics were clearly identified as different and, in some circles, even as suspicious. Only in the 1950s and 1960s did this abate, due to the much-discussed impact of John F. Kennedy, Pope John XXIII, the Vatican Council, and the cultural revolution. In addition to these events, we should remember that whereas earlier Catholic immigrants often lived in their own neighborhoods, even in "Catholic ghettoes," this was less and less the case beginning in the 1950s, as Catholics moved into the new suburbs.

Whereas a ghetto has boundaries and a clear identity, a new suburb does not. In the suburb the earlier imposed Catholic identity was gone, and for some people it brought a feeling of liberation. Today the situation is different. Catholic identity is chosen, not imposed. This brings new personal freedom and autonomy, but it also brings new spiritual needs. Identity must now be chosen through experience and study, and traditional communities need to teach identity to the next generation intentionally. We should not be surprised that young adult Catholics are uncertain about their Catholic identity, and that denominational identity is a preoccupation of Catholic institutional leaders today. (The American Jewish community has a similar but even more worrisome concern about the Jewish identity of its youth).[10]

"Identity" is a complex concept, similar in meaning to "self-concept."[11] Two types need to be distinguished — objective identity and subjective identity. Young adults may be identified objectively as Catholic because of their family upbringing, but they may not *feel* Catholic and may not think it is at all important. They may say, "Well, I was raised and baptized Catholic and so I guess I'm a Catholic, but now I don't practice and I don't even feel Catholic." Another name for this distinction is "imposed identity" versus "chosen identity." Our concern here, and the concern of Catholic institutional leaders, is subjective identity.

The Psychology of Identity

I need to explain here that the identity of an individual person is a structure of separate elements, arranged more or less hierarchically. Research on identity shows that any element of personal identity, for example, being an engineer, being Republican, being Irish American, or being Catholic, will become strong or weak depending on how it serves the person's overall life goals. As Morris Schwartz advises his young friend in *Tuesdays with Morrie*, "If the culture doesn't work, don't use it."[12] Accepting or rejecting portions of one's identity is not done easily or quickly, but research shows that to strengthen any element of one's identity — for example, being Catholic — that element must genuinely serve the person's basic values.[13] For example, the importance of attending Mass to any person will depend, over time, on how doing so serves that person's most basic needs. The same is true of self-identification as a Catholic. If describing oneself as a Catholic fails to serve one's basic needs, or if there are blockages, the person will slowly withdraw emotional investment from Catholic self-identification, and it will sink to a lower level in personal identity, where it will then have less influence on his or her life decisions. Shifts such as this in the importance of identity elements take time. The process of building Catholic identity should be seen as akin to making a friend or falling in love — it requires time and it depends on a succession of experiences.

Core, Inspiration, and Boundary

We can now see that the question of Catholic identity is a matter of specific aspects of Catholicism, not "being Catholic" *in toto.* We need to pay attention to these aspects. Three topics are foremost — which aspects are core, which are inspiring, and what the boundaries are. First, regarding the core of the faith, Table 5 (page 209) above and other studies show that for young adult Catholics sacraments and service are felt to be at the core of faith.

Second, what aspects of being Catholic are the most inspiring? If we knew that, we could encourage expressions and portrayals of the faith that would be personally energizing for young adults. I have never seen research on this question, but in doing personal interviews with young adults and an informal survey among college students, I can tentatively say that the sacraments, the Real Presence in Eucharist, devotion to Mary the Mother of God, and the lives of exemplary Catholics (including saints) are foremost. In a recent informal survey I asked young adult Catholics which persons in all of church history are the most inspiring to them. The top two were St. Francis of Assisi and Mother Teresa.[14] Nobody should put much stock in an informal survey like this, but it indicates the type of research we need to do in the future.

Third is the analysis of boundaries. All communities and organizations need boundaries. They strengthen collective identity by showing clearly who are members and who are not. Maintenance of boundaries requires clear rules and markers. As examples of boundaries, in Catholicism a person must be baptized or confirmed Catholic to be a communicant; clergy must take a vow of obedience to bishops or religious superiors; clergy status is not transferable from other churches; non-ordained Catholics may not give homilies in the Mass; and so on. Catholicism without boundaries would have a problem of "everything goes" and an enervating vagueness about what being a Catholic means.[15]

The task of building up Catholic identity requires identifying the core, strengthening the inspirational parts, and tending to the boundaries. Strengthening the inspirational memories requires that we recall and celebrate the narratives of our faith and tradition, and tending the boundaries requires that we keep the markers clear and enforce them. Both serve to strengthen Catholic identity, and both must be done. The latter, however, is different in that it is inherently defensive, and when taken alone, is not life-giving. Attention, rather, should be on strengthening the elements of Catholicism which are inspiring. This calls for encouraging young adult Catholics to immerse themselves in the total tradition and reformulate a Catholic faith which is filled with spiritual power.[16] Older adults can help, but in the end they cannot do this for the young adults. Young people must do it for their own generation. Church leadership should recognize that young adults lived their impressionable years in a world with a different spiritual space than the world of their parents, and young people's spiritual choices, while often needing critical reflection, should be heeded.

Conclusions

We have seen that Catholic young adults differ from the prior generation, and they will tend to maintain their basic values as they age. They will continue to be different in that they will uphold greater individual authority in religious and moral decisions and will desire more lay influence in institutional decision-making. Today they are less personally invested in the institutional church, and this tendency will continue. They tend to distinguish faith in God from obeying the rules of the institutional church, clinging more to the former than to the latter, as suggested in the often-heard formula "I'm spiritual but not religious."

Caretakers of Catholic institutions should encourage the young adults to search the richness of the Catholic tradition for themselves and to construct a Catholic identity on the resources which they feel are genuinely inspiring. They need to identify and live out the inspirational core of the faith. The question "What is distinctive about being Catholic?" needs to be answered affirmatively, stressing who we *are* rather than who we *are not*.

On the level of institution, a high priority needs to be regaining trust in church leadership. The 2003 Notre Dame study showed that the sexual abuse crisis is the number-one problem facing the American Catholic Church. In a word, the laity do not have total trust that the American bishops are telling the truth and guiding the church in a way serving the People of God. Lay groups have set forth numerous proposals for reforms. The most viable proposals recommend changes at the periphery of the Catholic faith, not the core. The reform movement Voice of the Faithful, in my opinion, gets it right in its slogan: "Keep the faith, change the Church." I would be even more specific: reevaluate the nonessential and non-dogmatic components of church life today and make innovations where there are problems. Take small steps. For example, the American bishops need to be more transparent and accountable in their actions, and they need to reach out more to laity, including young adults.

In closing, let me note an interesting suggestion made by Rev. Howard Bleichner, a Sulpician priest and former rector of the Theological College of the Catholic University of America. Bleichner believes that a dramatic gesture is needed to restore confidence in Catholic leadership at the national level. Without some symbolic gesture proving that the leadership is listening, the credibility crisis will continue. In his words, "We need a large public gesture of a positive nature to pull us into the future."[17] He recommends calling another plenary council at Baltimore. But this time there should be a difference: representatives of deacons, religious, and laity need to be involved and to have voting power. If such a plenary council were held, it would be of historic proportions and would help restore credibility for the American leadership. Some will say that a plenary council would be too risky, but Bleichner thinks the value outweighs the risk. I agree.

Notes

❦

Chapter 1 / Catholicism and American Political Culture, David Hollenbach, S.J.

This essay presents and adapts arguments that I have previously discussed in my "The Gospel of Life and the Culture of Death: A Response to John Conley," in *Choosing Life: A Dialogue on Evangelium Vitae*, ed. Kevin W. Wildes and Alan C. Mitchell (Washington, D.C.: Georgetown University Press, 1997), 37–45; in *The Global Face of Public Faith: Politics, Human Rights, and Christian Ethics* (Washington, D.C.: Georgetown University Press, 2003), especially chapter 1, "Faith in Public"; and in *The Common Good and Christian Ethics* (Cambridge: Cambridge University Press, 2002), especially chapter 5, "Christianity in a Community of Freedom," and chapter 6, "Intellectual Solidarity."

1. Samuel P. Huntington, "The Clash of Civilizations," *Foreign Affairs* 72 (Summer 1993): 22, 25. This is developed at book length in Samuel P. Huntington, *The Clash of Civilizations and the Remaking of World Order* (New York: Simon and Schuster, 1996).

2. See Christopher Muste, "Hidden in Plain Sight: Polling Data Show Moral Values Aren't a New Factor," *Washington Post*, sec. B4, December 12, 2004.

3. See, for example, the website called "Catholic Answers," which presents these five issues as non-negotiables in its "Voter's Guide for Serious Catholics." It may be viewed online at Catholic Answers, "Voter's Guide for Serious Catholics," *www.catholic.com/library/voters_guide_print_now.pdf*.

4. Congregation for the Doctrine of the Faith, "Doctrinal Note on Some Questions Regarding the Participation of Catholics in Political Life," November 24, 2002, no. 4, *www.vatican.va/roman_curia/congregations/cfaith/documents/rc_con_cfaith _doc_20021124_politica_en.html*.

5. Bishop Michael J. Sheridan, "A Pastoral Letter to the Catholic Faithful of the Diocese of Colorado Springs on the Duties of Catholic Politicians and Voters," *www.diocesecs.org/CPC/Corner/pastoralletters/2004/May.pdf*. Emphasis in the original.

6. Sheridan, "A Pastoral Letter."

7. David D. Kirkpatrick and Laurie Goodstein, "Group of Bishops Using Influence to Oppose Kerry," *New York Times*, sec. A, October 12, 2004.

8. Administrative Committee of the United States Conference of Catholic Bishops, *Faithful Citizenship: Catholic Call to Political Responsibility*, September 2003, *www.nccbuscc.org/faithfulcitizenship*.

9. Task Force on Catholic Bishops and Catholic Politicians in collaboration with Francis Cardinal George, O.M.I., Archbishop Charles J. Chaput, O.F.M.Cap., and

Bishop Donald W. Wuerl, approved by the Bishops Conference as a whole, "Catholics in Political Life," June 2004, *www.usccb.org/bishops/catholicsinpoliticallife.htm.*

10. See the letter to Cardinal Theodore McCarrick, who chaired the bishops committee that developed the June 2004 statement, from a group of Catholic politicians in the U.S. Congress, some pro-choice and some pro-life, at *National Catholic Reporter,* letter to Theodore McCarrick, see *www.ncronline.org/mainpage/specialdocuments/ catholic_congress.pdf.*

11. For a fuller treatment of the developments surrounding the 2004 presidential election, see Thomas Massaro, "Catholic Bishops and Politicians: Concerns about Recent Developments," *Josephinum Journal of Theology* (forthcoming).

12. See H. Richard Niebuhr, *Christ and Culture* (New York: Harper and Row, 1951), chapter 2.

13. See Meghan Dorney, "Archbishop Stresses Importance of Preaching in Chrism Mass Homily," *The Pilot,* April 9, 2004, *www.rcab.org/Pilot/2004/ps040416/Chrism _Mass.html.* See also Archbishop Sean O'Malley, "Homily at the Red Mass at St. Matthew the Apostle Cathedral, Washington, D.C.," October 3, 2004, *www.rcab.org/ News/releases/homily041003.html.*

14. See the conclusion and especially no. 104 in John Paul II, *Evangelium Vitae,* March 15, 1995, *www.vatican.va/edocs/eng0141/_index.htm.*

15. *Evangelium Vitae,* no. 18. Emphasis in the original.

16. See Francis George, "How Liberalism Fails the Church," *Commonweal* (November 19, 1999): 24–29.

17. See Pope John Paul II's address to the U.N. General Assembly, October 10, 1995, no. 2. The text can be found in *Origins* 25 (October 19, 1995).

18. *Evangelium Vitae,* nos. 68–70.

19. *Evangelium Vitae,* no. 20. Here the pope, perhaps without knowing it, echoes John Courtney Murray's critique of theories of democracy that eschewed all truth claims. See, for example, Murray, "The Church and Totalitarian Democracy," *Theological Studies* 13 (1952): 525–63. Murray borrowed the phrase from J. L. Talmon, *The Rise of Totalitarian Democracy* (Boston: Beacon Press, 1952). Murray, however, was at pains to distinguish this form of democracy from that stemming from the American founding, though some of his later work expressed serious doubts whether American public philosophy in the 1950s remained true to its own best insights. To the degree that Murray's fears have been realized in the United States today, the pope's critique hits home in this country. I think, therefore, that the question of whether the encyclical's description of the "culture of death" applies to the United States depends on how democracy is in fact understood in the political culture of this country today. Recent discussions of this question are not encouraging.

20. John Courtney Murray, *We Hold These Truths: Catholic Reflections on the American Proposition* (New York: Sheed and Ward, 1960), viii–ix.

21. See chapter 3 in Murray, *We Hold These Truths.*

22. I have outlined an interpretation of this alternative view of democracy and human rights in *Catholicism and Liberalism: Contributions to American Public Philosophy,* ed. R. Bruce Douglass and David Hollenbach (Cambridge and New York: Cambridge University Press, 1994), chapter 5 and afterword.

23. *Evangelium Vitae,* no. 19. I have discussed the way the relation of freedom and truth is understood by John Paul II and Vatican II more fully in "Freedom and Truth: Religious Liberty as Immunity and Empowerment," in *John Courtney Murray*

and the Growth of Tradition, ed. J. Leon Hooper and Todd Whitmore (Kansas City, Mo.: Sheed and Ward, 1996), 129–48.

24. See Cardinal Joseph Bernardin et al., *Consistent Ethic of Life,* ed. Thomas G. Fuechtmann (Kansas City, Mo.: Sheed and Ward, 1988).

25. *Evangelium Vitae,* no. 20.

26. See Alan Wolfe, *Moral Freedom: The Search for Virtue in a World of Choice* (New York: W. W. Norton, 2001). Wolfe seems at times to suggest that Americans view "moral freedom" as not being coerced or directed by some authority such as the state. At other times he seems to imply that "moral freedom" means there are no preexisting moral standards whether coercively enforced or not. It is not entirely clear to me which meaning of moral freedom Wolfe finds present in American culture, though on p. 224 he states it is the former rather than the latter. The difference between these meanings of freedom is very important, as I hope will become clear below. See also Wolfe's expression of relief that the high value placed on free choice makes serious cultural or religious conflicts unlikely in the United States, in Alan Wolfe, *One Nation After All: What Middle-Class Americans Really Think about God, Country, Family, Racism, Welfare, Immigration, Homosexuality, Work, the Right, the Left, and Each Other* (New York: Viking, 1998), especially chapter 2.

27. See *Evangelium Vitae,* the whole of chapter IV, which is subtitled "For a New Culture of Life."

28. Niebuhr, *Christ and Culture,* chapter 6.

29. *Evangelium Vitae,* no. 73.

30. Vatican Council II, *Dignitatis Humanae,* in *The Documents of Vatican II,* ed. Walter M. Abbott (New York: Crossroad, 1989), no. 4.

31. *Dignitatis Humanae,* no. 7.

32. *Dignitatis Humanae,* no. 7.

33. *Dignitatis Humanae,* no. 7. See John Courtney Murray's comments on this passage in n. 20 to the Declaration in the Abbott edition of *The Documents of Vatican II* being cited here.

34. For careful development of the suggestions made in this paragraph, see Margaret A. Farley, "Stem Cell Research: Religious Considerations," in *Handbook of Stem Cells,* vol. 1, ed. Robert P. Lanza (Boston: Elsevier Academic, 2004), 765–73, esp. 770–72.

35. *Evangelium Vitae,* no. 60.

36. For a suggestive though not fully developed argument on the economic context of abortion decisions, see Glen Harold Stassen, "Pro-life? Look at the Fruits," *Louisville Courier-Journal,* Op-Ed page, October 11, 2004, *www.courier-journal .com/cjextra/editorials/2004/10/11/oped-stassen1011-5709.html.*

Chapter 2 / Resilient Citizens, Nancy A. Dallavalle

1. Luke Timothy Johnson, "Abortion, Sexuality, and Catholicism's Public Presence," in *American Catholics in the Public Square,* vol. 2: *American Catholics, American Culture: Tradition and Resistance,* ed. Margaret O'Brien Steinfels (Lanham, Md.: Rowan & Littlefield, 2004), 33.

2. Archbishop William J. Levada, "Reflections on Catholics in Public Life and the Reception of Holy Communion," June 13, 2004, *www.usccb.org/bishops/reflections .shtml.*

3. U.S. Conference of Catholic Bishops, *Catholics in Public Life*, June 21, 2004, *www.usccb.org/comm/archives/2004/04-116.htm*.

4. Dennis O'Brien, "No to Abortion: Posture, Not Policy," *America* 192 (May 30, 2005).

5. Christine E. Gudorf, "Renewal or Repatriachalization? Responses of the Roman Catholic Church to the Feminization of Religion," *Horizons* 10 (1983): 236, emphasis added.

6. Gudorf, "Renewal or Repatriachalization?" 238.

7. Pius XII, address to Italian women, October 21, 1945, cited in Gudorf, "Renewal or Repatriachalization?" 239.

8. Karl Rahner, "The Position of Woman in the New Situation in Which the Church Finds Herself," *Theological Investigations* 8 (New York: Herder & Herder, 1964), 89.

9. The "Letter to Women" was written in advance of the Fourth International United Nations Conference on Women (1995). See John Paul II, "Letter to Women," *www.vatican.va/holy_father/john_paulii/letters/documents/hf_jp-ii_let_29061995_women_en.html*.

10. Whether such an anthropological claim is "new" is too complex to treat in this essay.

11. See no. 3 in Congregation for the Doctrine of the Faith, "Letter to the Bishops of the Catholic Church on the Collaboration of Men and Women in the Church and in the World," May 31, 2004, *www.vatican.va/roman_curia/congregations/cfaith/documents/rc_con_cfaith_doc_20040731_collaboration_en.html*.

12. See Pope John Paul II, *Ordinatio Sacerdotalis* (Apostolic Letter on Reserving Priestly Ordination to Men Alone), May 22, 1994, *www.ewtn.com/library/papaldoc/jp2ordin.htm*.

13. See, for example, Angelo Scola, "The Nuptial Mystery: A Perspective for Systematic Theology?" *Communio* 30 (2003): 209–34.

14. See Stephen E. Flynn, "The Neglected Home Front," in *Foreign Affairs* (September–October 2004), online *www.foreignaffairs.org/20040901faessay83504/stephen-e-flynn/the-neglected-home-front.html*.

15. Flynn, "The Neglected Home Front."

16. I borrow this image from Peter Steinfels, *A People Adrift: The Crisis of the Roman Catholic Church in America* (New York: Simon and Schuster, 2003).

17. David Hollenbach, S.J., *The Global Face of Public Faith: Politics, Human Rights, and Christian Ethics* (Washington, D.C.: Georgetown University Press, 2003), 163.

18. Meeting in Chicago on June 17, 2005, the U.S. bishops voted to retain the "zero-tolerance" policy for the next five years.

19. Avery Dulles, "Rights of Accused Priests: Toward a Revision of the Dallas Charter and the 'Essential Norms,'" *America* 190, no. 20 (June 21, 2004).

20. Michael J. Himes and Kenneth R. Himes, *The Fullness of Faith: The Public Significance of Theology* (New York: Paulist, 1993).

21. Michael J. Baxter, "Review Essay: The Non-Catholic Character of the 'Public Church,'" *Modern Theology* 11 (1995): 257.

22. National Pastoral Life Center, "Called to Be Catholic: Church in a Time of Peril," in *Catholic Common Ground Initiative: Foundational Documents* (Eugene, Ore.: Wipf and Stock, 2002), 41.

Chapter 3 / Women Theologians as Gift of an Inculturated U.S. American Church, Mary Ann Hinsdale, I.H.M.

1. See Paul's speech on the Areopagus (Acts 17:22–31) and 1 Corinthians 9:16–23. Acts 15, the so-called Council of Jerusalem, recognized the need of inculturating the gospel in its settlement of the question of whether conformity to Mosaic law was required of Gentile converts. The history of the formation of the New Testament canon itself witnesses to the church's conviction that the gospel must be inculturated in many cultures.

2. *Ad Gentes,* no. 22. I am indebted to the following authors for much of the history surrounding the use of the term "inculturation": Thomas G. Grenham, "Interculturation: Exploring Changing Religious, Cultural and Faith Identities in an African Context," *Pacifica* 14 (June 2001): 191–206; Carl F. Starkloff, "Inculturation and Cultural Systems, Part I," *Theological Studies* 55 (1994): 66–81; Carl F. Starkloff, "Inculturation and Cultural Systems, Part II," *Theological Studies* 55 (1994): 274–94; Peter C. Phan, "Contemporary Theology and Inculturation in the United States," in *The Multicultural Church: A New Landscape in U.S. Theologies,* ed. William Cenkner (New York: Paulist Press, 1996), 109–30; Robert Schreiter, *The New Catholicity: Theology between the Global and the Local* (Maryknoll, N.Y.: Orbis Books, 1998).

3. See, for example, Kwok Pui-lan, "Jesus / The Native: Biblical Studies from a Postcolonial Perspective," in *Teaching the Bible: The Discourses and Politics of Biblical Pedagogy,* ed. Fernando F. Segovia and Mary Ann Tolbert (Maryknoll, N.Y.: Orbis Books, 1998), 75–80. Kwok recounts how the curricula of girls' schools established by missionaries in China were meant to instill the cult of "true womanhood" and to reinforce the domesticity of women. See her *Postcolonial Imagination and Feminist Theology* (Louisville: Westminster John Knox Press, 2005), 62.

4. See the foreword to *Studies in the International Apostolate of Jesuits* (Washington, D.C.: Jesuit Missions, 1978), 1–9. See also Starkloff, "Inculturation and Cultural Systems, Part I," 66, n. 1. Aylward Shorter, however, while acknowledging the Jesuit origin for the term, attributes its first mention not to Arrupe, but to Joseph Masson, S.J., a professor at the Gregorian University. See Aylward Shorter, *Toward a Theology of Inculturation* (Maryknoll, N.Y.: Orbis Books, 1988), 10. See also J. Masson, "L'Église ouverte sur le monde," *Nouvelle Revue Théologigue* 84 (1962): 1038. For an even more extensive history of this term, see Arij Roest Vrollous, "What Is So New about Inculturation?" *Gregorianum* 59 (1978): 721–38.

5. Pedro Arrupe, S.J., "Letter to the Whole Society on Inculturation," 2. Cited in Grenham, "Inculturation," 192.

6. Aylward Shorter, *Evangelization and Culture* (London: Geoffrey Chapman, 1994), 35. Shorter credits the work of theologians such as Johann Baptist Metz and Jean-Yves Calvez and others with illuminating the "paschal mystery" interpretation.

7. Shorter, *Evangelization and Culture,* 32. Shorter discusses the history and usage of "inculturation" and the development of the term "interculturation" in his *Toward a Theology of Inculturation,* 10–16. Peter Phan sees inculturation as involving three stages: translation, acculturation, and inculturation; steps that are essential to the theological method of all contextual and local theologies. See Phan, "Contemporary Theology and Inculturation in the United States," 109–10. Robert Schreiter discusses inculturation and the distinction between it and other terms in

his important works: *Constructing Local Theologies* (Maryknoll, N.Y.: Orbis Books, 1986) and *The New Catholicity.*

8. Shorter, *Toward a Theology of Inculturation,* 13.

9. "A Message to the People of God," *Origins* 15 (December 19, 1985): 450.

10. John Paul II, *Redemptoris Missio* (July 12, 1990), no. 52, document available online at *www.vatican.va/holy_father/john_paul_ii/encyclicals/documents/hf_jpii_enc_07121990_redemptoris-missio_en.html.*

11. In addition to *Redemptoris Missio,* see *Evangelium Vitae* (1995), where he denounces "the culture of death," *Fides et Ratio* (1998), and most recently, the Apostolic Letter *Novo Milennio Ineunte* (2001).

12. See no. 64 in John Paul II, *Evangelium Vitae, www.vatican.va/holy_father/john_paul_ii/encyclicals/documents/hf_jp-ii_enc_25031995_evangelium-vitae_en.html.*

13. *Redemptoris Missio,* no. 59.

14. See William Portier's introduction to *The Inculturation of American Catholicism 1920–1900* (New York: Garland Publishing, 1988) and the essays by David P. Killen and Margaret Mary Reher in this same volume, 405–57.

15. It is beyond my scope to discuss Murray's contribution here. See Donald E. Pelotte, *John Courtney Murray: Theologian in Conflict* (New York: Paulist Press, 1975), and Charles E. Curran, *Catholic Social Teaching, 1891–Present: A Historical, Theological and Ethical Analysis* (Washington, D.C.: Georgetown University Press, 2002), 224–33. See also Curran's *American Catholic Social Ethics* (Notre Dame, Ind.: University of Notre Dame Press, 1982), 172–232.

16. The concept of "dangerous memory" is derived from the work of Johann Baptist Metz. Bradford E. Hinze shows how "failed" U.S. ecclesial experiments, such as the U.S. Bishops "Call to Action Conference" (1977) and the failed "Women's Pastoral," can hold out hope for the future transformation of the church. See Bradford E. Hinze, *Practices of Dialogue in the Roman Catholic Church: Aims and Obstacles, Lessons and Laments* (New York: Continuum, 2006).

17. It could be said that theologians in general have become an "underutilized ecclesial resource" over the last twenty-five years (particularly those who creatively engage questions at the new frontiers of theology: religious pluralism, feminism, ecological concerns, etc.); nevertheless, I believe the large number of professional women theologians that currently distinguishes U.S. theologians as a body warrants such a consideration.

18. Portions of the following material have appeared in Mary Ann Hinsdale, *Women Shaping Theology* (Mahwah, N.J.: Paulist Press, 2006).

19. In concentrating mainly on *professional* women theologians in the academy, I would be remiss if I did not acknowledge that a truly thoroughgoing treatment of the theological gifts that U.S. women have brought to the church ought to include the many "organic intellectuals," or "local theologians," who lead grassroots theological reflection in Christian base communities; who give spiritual direction and staff renewal centers; who engage in contemplative prayer in monastic communities; who run homeless shelters, parish discussion groups, and liturgy committees; who organize church reform movements and community development initiatives; who produce the music, art, and architecture that enhances our worship; who serve as directors of religious education, campus ministers, prison and hospital chaplains,

missionaries, catechists, and schoolteachers; and who have dedicated their lives to witness for justice and peace.

20. Rosemary Ruether, for example, credits both the civil rights and anti-war movements as having deeply shaped her theological reflections. See her "The Emergence of Christian Feminist Theology," in *The Cambridge Companion to Feminist Theology*, ed. Susan Frank Parsons (Cambridge: Cambridge University Press, 2002), 9; Rosemary Ruether, "The Development of My Theology," *Religious Studies Review* 15 (1989): 1–4; and "Autobiographical Roots of Dialogue," in Rita M. Gross and Rosemary Radford Ruether, *Religious Feminism and the Future of the Planet: A Christian Buddhist Conversation* (New York: Continuum, 2001), 48–62. Susan Ross assesses the impact of the women's movement on theology in "The Women's Movement and Theology in the Twentieth Century," *The Twentieth Century: A Theological Overview*, ed. Gregory Baum (Maryknoll, N.Y.: Orbis Books, 1999), 186–203. See also her essay "Catholic Women Theologians of the Left," in *What's Left? Liberal American Catholics*, ed. Mary Jo Weaver (Bloomington: Indiana University Press, 1999), 19–45.

21. Gail Porter Mandell, *One Woman's Life*, the 1994 Madeleva Lecture in Spirituality (New York: Paulist Press, 1994), 42–43, and Sandra M. Schneiders, *With Oil in Their Lamps: Faith, Feminism and the Future*, the 2000 Madeleva Lecture in Spirituality (New York: Paulist Press, 2000), 74–76.

22. For a history of the Sister Formation Movement, see Marjorie Noterman Beane, *From Framework to Freedom: A History of the Sister Formation Conference* (Lanham, Md.: University Press of America, 1993). See also Judith Ann Eby, R.S.M., " 'A Little Squabble among Nuns'? The Sister Formation Crisis and the Patterns of Authority and Obedience among American Women Religious, 1954–1971" (Ph.D. dissertation, St. Louis University, 2000). Eby's study examines the organizational struggles the movement had in relationship to the Conference of Major Superiors of Women.

23. Lora Ann Quiñonez, C.D.P., and Mary Daniel Turner, S.N.D.deN., *The Transformation of American Catholic Sisters* (Philadelphia: Temple University Press, 1992), 6.

24. Bertrande Meyers, D.C., *The Education of Sisters: A Plan for Integrating the Religious, Cultural, Social and Professional Training of Sisters* (New York: Sheed and Ward, 1941). See also Judith Ann Eby's discussion of this period in " 'A Little Squabble among Nuns'?" 47–60.

25. Sister M. Madeleva, C.S.C., *My First Seventy Years* (New York: Macmillan, Macmillan Paperbacks Edition, 1962), 132. See also Gail Porter Mandell, *Madeleva: A Biography* (Albany, N.Y.: SUNY Press, 1997), 188–90. In 1975 the Sister Formation Conference was renamed "The Religious Formation Conference." The proceedings from the jubilee celebration, held in November 2003, can be found at Religious Formation Conference, *www.relforcon.org*.

26. "Instruction of the Congregation de Propaganda Fide concerning Catholic Children Attending American Public Schools, November 24, 1875," in *Public Voices: Catholics in the American Context*, ed. Steven M. Avella and Elizabeth McKeown (Maryknoll, N.Y.: Orbis Books, 1999), 74–77.

27. Anita M. Caspary, *Witness to Integrity: The Crisis of the Immaculate Heart Community of California* (Collegeville, Minn.: Liturgical Press, 2003). See also Mark

Massa's account of this controversy in *Catholics and American Culture* (New York: Crossroad, 1999), 172–94.

28. For sociological assessments of this phenomenon, see Helen Rose Ebaugh, *Women in the Vanishing Cloister: Organizational Decline in Catholic Religious Orders in the United States* (New Brunswick, N.J.: Rutgers University Press, 1993), and Patricia A. Wittberg, *Creating a Future for Religious Life: A Sociological Perspective* (Mahwah, N.J.: Paulist Press, 1991). Sandra M. Schneiders, however, considers women religious a "perennial life form" in the church. See *Finding the Treasure: Locating Catholic Religious Life in a New Ecclesial and Cultural Context* (New York: Paulist Press, 2000).

29. See the discussion below on page 52.

30. Mary McDevitt, I.H.M., "Foreword," *Light Burdens, Heavy Blessings: Challenges of Church and Culture in the Post–Vatican II Era*, ed. Mary Heather MacKinnon, S.S.N.D., Moni McIntyre, and Mary Ellen Sheehan, I.H.M. (Quincy, Ill.: Franciscan Press, 2000), xii. Brennan's courageous and imaginative leadership extended to the International House of Prayer movement and encouraging U.S. contemplative women religious to found their own association. After serving as president of her order and the Leadership Conference of Women Religious (LCWR), she taught pastoral theology to hundreds of students in the Toronto School of Theology for twenty-five years.

31. Statistics on the actual number of Catholic women theologians, let alone the number who are women religious, are hard to obtain. However, in 2004, the online membership directory of the Catholic Theological Society of America lists 490 women members. It should be pointed out, however, that Catholic women theologians may belong to other professional societies, such as the Catholic Biblical Association, the American Society of Church History, or the Society of Christian Ethics (for which I do not have data); thus, the number of Catholic women theologians is probably even larger than this. During the 1970s 56 percent of women CTSA members belonged to religious communities, and 44 percent were lay; in the 1980s the number of women religious dropped to 52 percent, with 48 percent laywomen. In the 1990s, the number dramatically diminished to 33 percent women religious and 67 percent laywomen. By 2005, 85 percent of the women members of CTSA were laywomen.

32. I am indebted for the information that follows to Mary J. Oates, "Sisterhoods and Catholic Higher Education, 1890–1960," in *Catholic Women's Colleges in America*, ed. Tracy Schier and Cynthia Russett (Baltimore: Johns Hopkins University Press, 2002), 161–94; Karen M. Kenelly, "Faculties and What They Taught," in Schier and Russett, *Catholic Women's Colleges*, 98–122; and *Gender Identities in American Catholicism*, ed. Paula Kane, James Kenneally, and Karen Kenelly (Maryknoll, N.Y.: Orbis Books, 2001), 119–33.

33. Jane C. Redmont, "Live Minds, Yearning Spirits: The Alumnae of Colleges and Universities Founded by Women Religious," in Schier and Russett, *Catholic Women's Colleges*, 195–234.

34. The appendix to Schier and Russett's *Catholic Women's Colleges in America*, compiled by Thomas M. Landy, lists all the American colleges and universities founded by women religious for lay students.

35. Jill Ker Conway, "Faith, Knowledge and Gender," in Schier and Russett, *Catholic Women's Colleges in America*, 13. See also the testimony of Linda McMillen,

"Telling Old Tales about Something New: The Vocation of a Catholic and Feminist Historian," in *Reconciling Catholicism and Feminism: Personal Reflections on Tradition and Change,* ed. Sally Barr Ebest and Ron Ebest (Notre Dame, Ind.: University of Notre Dame Press, 2003), 82–95.

36. Mandell, *Madeleva: One Woman's Life,* 41. See also Madeleva, *My First Seventy Years,* 134.

37. Mandell, *Madeleva: One Women's Life,* 41. Sandra Yocum Mize presents an extended discussion of the role the Graduate School of Sacred Theology played in developing women's contributions to a vital Catholic intellectual life in the mid-twentieth century. See her " 'A Catholic Way of Doing Every Important Thing': U.S. Catholic Women in the Mid-Twentieth Century," *U.S. Catholic Historian* 13 (1995): 49–69.

38. The women were Cathleen M. Going and Elizabeth Farians, both laywomen who received their doctorates in 1956 and 1958, respectively.

39. See Mary Daly, *Outercourse: The Be-Dazzling Voyage Containing Recollections from My Logbook of a Radical Feminist Philosopher (Be-Ing on Account of My Time/Space)* (San Francisco: HarperSanFrancisco reprint edition, 1994).

40. Examples for Catholic girls include the Young Christian Students (YCS), the Sodality of Our Lady, the Grail, the Catholic Worker, and, on the local level, diocesan-sponsored organizations such as the Chicago Area Lay Movement (CALM).

41. Murphy Davis, "The Seminary Quarter for Women at Grailville: Toward a Feminist Approach to Theological Education," *Theological Education* 11 (1975): 67–74.

42. Janet Kalven, *Women Breaking Boundaries: A Grail Journey, 1940–1995* (Albany, N.Y.: SUNY Press, 1999), 49.

43. See also Janet Kalven, "Feminism and Catholicism," in Barr Ebest and Ebest, *Reconciling Catholicism and Feminism* 32–46.

44. Professor Margie Pfeil, a theologian at the University of Notre Dame, is one of the founders of the St. Peter Claver Catholic Worker house in South Bend, Indiana. On the history of the Catholic Worker and its influence on American Catholicism, see Mel Piehl, *Breaking Bread: The Catholic Worker and the Origin of Catholic Radicalism in America* (Philadelphia: Temple University Press, 1982); Nancy Roberts, *Dorothy Day and the Catholic Worker* (Albany, N.Y.: SUNY Press, 1984); Patrick G. Coy, *A Revolution of the Heart* (Philadelphia: Temple University Press, 1988); James T. Fisher, *The Catholic Counter Culture* (Chapel Hill: University of North Carolina Press, 1989); *Voices from the Catholic Worker,* ed. Rosalie Riegle Troester (Philadelphia: Temple University Press, 1993).

45. See Catherine LaCugna's insightful account of the impact Vatican II had on women becoming ministers and theologians: "Catholic Women as Ministers and Theologians," *America* 167 (1992): 238–48. Vatican II's influence on theologians Monika Hellwig, Lisa Sowle Cahill, Joan Chittister, O.S.B., and Elizabeth Johnson, C.S.J., are recorded in *Vatican II: Forty Personal Stories,* ed. William Madges and Michael A. Daley (Mystic, Conn.: Twenty-third Publications, 2003). See also the testimonies of Rosemary Radford Ruether, "Beginnings: An Intellectual Autobiography," in *Journeys: The Impact of Personal Experience on Religious Thought,* ed. Gregory Baum (New York: Paulist Press, 1975), 34–56; and Monika Hellwig, "The Mandalas Do Not Break: A Theological Autobiographical Essay," in Baum, *Journeys,* 117–46.

46. On October 22, 1963, at the conclusion of the second council, Cardinal Suenens declared that since "half of humanity" was not present, this situation should be rectified. As a result, twenty-three women were invited to participate as auditors. This little-known episode and the remarkable influence that women had behind the scenes at Vatican II is recorded by M. Carmel McEnroy in *Guests in Their Own House: The Women of Vatican II* (New York: Crossroad, 1996). See also Helen Marie Ciernick, "Cracking the Door: Women at the Second Vatican Council," in *Women and Theology*, ed. Mary Ann Hinsdale and Phyllis Kaminski (Maryknoll, N.Y.: Orbis Books, 1994), 62–80.

47. For a discussion of the impact that women's entrance into theological schools had on the subject matter of theology, see Mary Ann Hinsdale, *Women Shaping Theology* (Mahwah, N.J.: Paulist Press, 2006).

48. Robert J. Schreiter, *The New Catholicity: Theology between the Global and the Local* (Maryknoll, N.Y.: Orbis Books, 1997), 15.

49. Schreiter, *The New Catholicity*, 16.

50. The four global theological flows singled out by Schreiter include: liberation, feminism, ecology, and human rights.

51. Schreiter, *The New Catholicity*, 18

52. Schreiter, *The New Catholicity*, 18.

53. Schreiter, *The New Catholicity*, 18.

54. Susan Frank Parsons, "Preface," *The Cambridge Companion to Feminist Theology*, ed. Susan Frank Parsons (Cambridge: Cambridge University Press, 2002), xiii–xiv. Similar evaluations have been made by David Tracy, William Burrows, and Julia Ching in "*Concilium* Round Table: The Impact of Feminist Theologies on Roman Catholic Theology" in *Concilium (1996/1), Feminist Theology in Different Contexts,* ed. Elisabeth Schüssler Fiorenza and M. Shawn Copeland (Maryknoll, N.Y.: Orbis Books, 1996), 90–97.

55. For historical accounts of the development of feminist theologies, see Anne Clifford, *Introducing Feminist Theology* (Maryknoll, N.Y.: Orbis Books, 2001); Sarah Coakley, "Feminist Theology," in *Modern Christian Thought*, vol. 2, *The Twentieth Century*, 2nd ed., ed. James C. Livingston and Francis Schüssler Fiorenza, with Sarah Coakley and James H. Evans Jr. (Upper Saddle River, N.J.: Prentice Hall, 2000), 417–42; Susan A. Ross, "The Women's Movement and Theology in the Twentieth Century," in *The Twentieth Century: A Theological Overview*, ed. Gregory Baum (Maryknoll, N.Y.: Orbis Books, 1999), 186–203; Susan A. Ross, "Catholic Women Theologians of the Left," in *What's Left? Liberal American Catholics,* ed. Mary Jo Weaver (Bloomington: Indiana University Press, 1999), 19–45; Rosemary Radford Ruether, "The Emergence of Christian Feminist Theology," in *The Cambridge Companion to Feminist Theology*, 3–22; and her chapters in *Women and Redemption: A Theological History* (Minneapolis: Fortress Press, 1998), which deal with both Protestant and Catholic feminist theologians from a global perspective.

56. Kwok Pui-lan, "Feminist Theology as Intercultural Discourse," in *The Cambridge Companion to Feminist Theology*, ed. Susan Frank Parsons (Cambridge University Press, 2002), 24.

57. Technically, the first feminist theological writing in the United States has been attributed to Valerie Saiving, "The Human Situation: A Feminine Viewpoint," *Journal of Religion* 40 (1960): 100–112. However, Daly's book represents the first

feminist writing by a U.S. Catholic woman. See *The Church and the Second Sex* (Boston: Beacon Press, 1965, 1985).

58. Rosemary Radford Ruether, *New Woman, New Earth: Sexist Ideologies and Human Liberation* (New York: Seabury Press, 1975; with a new preface, Boston: Beacon Press, 1995).

59. Rosemary Radford Ruether, *Sexism and God-Talk: Towards a Feminist Theology* (Boston: Beacon Press, 1983, 1993).

60. Elisabeth Schüssler Fiorenza, "Feminist Theology as a Critical Theology of Liberation," *Theological Studies* 36 (1975): 605–26.

61. Indian-born Susan Abraham and Van Pham (Vietnam) and Rachel Bundang are three recent Asian Catholic voices, soon to be joined by doctoral students Tracy Tiemeier, Patricia Panganiban, and Karen Enriquez. Beginning in the mid-1970s Filipina Catholics, such as Virginia Fabella, Mary John Mananzan, and Cristina Astorga were active in EATWOT, the Ecumenical Association of Third World Theologians. In 1988 Asian Christian women theologians founded the Asian Women's Resource Centre for Culture and Theology, which publishes the ecumenical journal *In God's Image*. Finally, the collection *We Dare to Dream: Doing Theology as Asian Women*, ed. Virginia Fabella and Sun Ai Lee Park (Maryknoll, N.Y.: Orbis Books, 1989) brings together a number of essays by women theologians from the Philippines, India, Taiwan, Hong Kong, Malaysia, and Korea.

62. An example given by Sandra Schneiders is the incident described by Lora Ann Quiñonez and Mary Daniel Turner in *The Transformation of American Catholic Sisters* (Mahwah, N.J.: Paulist Press), 107, in which they interview Archbishop Thomas C. Kelly, O.P., and ask him "what he believed was the major objection of the Congregation for Religious to LCWR. Without a pause he answered, 'Feminism.' " Cited in Sandra M. Schneiders, *Finding the Treasure: Locating Catholic Religious Life in a New Ecclesial and Cultural Context* (New York: Paulist Press, 2000), 422, n. 33.

63. The major documents include *Mulieris Dignitatem* ("On the Dignity of Women") in 1988, the "Letter to Women" in 1995, and *Evangelium Vitae* ("The Gospel of Life") in 1995. For an understanding of von Balthasar's anthropology, see Corinne Crammer, "One Sex or Two? Balthasar's Theology of the Sexes," in *The Cambridge Companion to Hans Urs von Balthasar*, ed. Edward T. Oakes and David Moss (Cambridge: Cambridge University Press, 2004), 93–112. For a critique of John Paul's use of this anthropology, see Tina Beattie, "Feminism, Vatican-Style," *The Tablet* (August 17, 2004), *www.thetablet.co.uk*.

64. *Evangelium Vitae*, no. 99; electronic version at *www.vatican.va/holy_father/ john_paul_ii/encyclicals/hf_jp-ii_ency_25031995_evangelium-vitae_en.htm*.

65. Congregation for the Doctrine of the Faith, "Letter to the Bishops of the Catholic Church on the Collaboration of Men and Women in the Church and the World," May 31, 2004; online: *www.vatican.va/roman_curia/congregations/cfaith/ documents/rc_con_cfaith_doc_20040731_collaboration_en.htm*.

66. Beattie, "Feminism Vatican-style."

67. Sidney Callahan, "Ratzinger, Feminist?" *Commonweal* 132 (April 22, 2005), *www.commonwealmagazine.org*.

68. "Confidential Memorandum" of Monsignor William P. Fay, general secretary of the USCCB to "All Bishops" regarding "New Document from the Congregation for the Doctrine of the Faith," July 22, 2004.

69. *Women in Christ: Toward a New Feminism,* ed. Michelle M. Schumacher (Grand Rapids, Mich.: William B. Eerdmans, 2004). This volume includes essays by Prudence Allen, R. Francis Martin, Jean Bethke Elshtain, Elizabeth Fox-Genovese, and others. It was originally published in French as *Femmes dans le Christ: Vers un nouveau feminisme* (Toulouse: Editions du Carmel, 2003). Most of the contributors are philosophers. Schumacher, Elshtain, and Martin are the only theologians included in the book.

70. Mary Shivanandan, *Crossing the Threshold of Love: A New Vision of Marriage in Light of John Paul II's Anthropology* (Washington, D.C.: Catholic University of America Press, 1999).

71. *Why Humanae Vitae Was Right: A Reader,* ed. Janet Smith (San Francisco: Ignatius Press, 1993).

72. Hallensleben's German commentary on the "Collaboration" document can be found online at Barbara Hallensleben, commentary on the CDF, *www.kath.ch/sbk-ces-cvs/text_detail.php?id=8219.* Although I can find nothing in print by her on the "Collaboration" document, the other woman appointed to the International Theological Commission is Sara Butler, M.S.B.T., an American theologian who teaches at St. Joseph's Seminary, Dunwoodie, New York. Both Butler and Hallensleben are on record for supporting the papal arguments prohibiting women's ordination.

73. Schreiter, *The New Catholicity,* 33–45.

Chapter 4 / The Participation of the Laity in Decision-Making in the Church, Francis A. Sullivan, S.J.

1. Ignatius Reynolds, *The Works of the Rt. Rev. John England* (Baltimore: John Murphy & Co., 1840), 5:91–108.

2. As quoted by Peter Guilday, *The Life and Times of John England, 1786–1842* (New York: America Press, 1927), 1:349.

3. Quoted by Guilday, *The Life and Times of John England,* 1:524–25.

4. Guilday, *The Life and Times of John England,* 1:525.

5. With regard to the restriction of membership to men, one has to remember that it would be another century before the nineteenth amendment to the U.S. Constitution granted to women the right to vote.

6. I have emphasized this clause, because it is a distinctive element in England's Constitution that it does not give to bishops the *exclusive* power of legislation in the church.

7. Reynolds, *The Works of the Rt. Rev. John England,* 5:92.

8. Reynolds, *The Works of the Rt. Rev. John England,* 5:95.

9. Reynolds, *The Works of the Rt. Rev. John England,* 5:97.

10. Reynolds, *The Works of the Rt. Rev. John England,* 5:97. The term "members of that district" means those in the district who are members of the corporation.

11. Reynolds, *The Works of the Rt. Rev. John England,* 5:99.

12. Reynolds, *The Works of the Rt. Rev. John England,* 5:103.

13. Reynolds, *The Works of the Rt. Rev. John England,* 5:104–5.

14. Reynolds, *The Works of the Rt. Rev. John England,* 5:100–101.

15. Guilday, *The Life and Times of John England,* 1:349–50.

16. Reynolds, *The Works of the Rt. Rev. John England,* 5:93.

17. Guilday, *The Life and Times of John England,* 1:350.

18. Guilday, *The Life and Times of John England,* 1:362.
19. *Lumen Gentium,* no. 32.
20. *Lumen Gentium,* no. 37.
21. *Christus Dominus,* no. 16.
22. *Christus Dominus,* no. 27.
23. Sacred Congregation for Bishops, *Directory on the Pastoral Ministry of Bishops* (Ottawa: Canadian Catholic Conference, 1974), 105.
24. *Christifideles Laici,* no. 25.
25. *Christifideles Laici,* no. 27.
26. *Pastores Gregis,* no. 44.
27. John Paul II, "Address of John Paul II to the Bishops of the Ecclesiastical Region of Pennsylvania and New Jersey (U.S.A.) on the 'Ad Limina' Visit," *Origins* 34, no. 16 (September 30, 2004): 253–54.
28. *Codex Iuris Canonici* (Vatican City: Libreria Editrice Vaticana, 1983), c. 439, 441, 443.
29. *Codex Iuris Canonici,* c. 440–45.
30. *Codex Iuris Canonici,* c. 443.5.
31. *Codex Iuris Canonici,* c. 460–66.
32. *Codex Iuris Canonici,* c. 511–14.
33. *Codex Iuris Canonici,* c. 492–93, 1277.
34. *Codex Iuris Canonici,* c. 536.
35. *Codex Iuris Canonici,* c. 537.

Chapter 5 / Business Class, Rev. John P. Beal

1. *Codex Iuris Canonici* (Vatican City: Libreria Editrice Vaticana, 1983), c. 1254, no. 1. Hereafter the *Codex* will be referred to as *CIC,* together with its date, as 1983 *CIC.*
2. *Lumen Gentium,* no. 8.
3. 1983 *CIC,* c. 1254, no. 2. The enumeration of the purposes for which the church owns temporal goods in this canon goes back to Gratian and beyond. See Garrett J. Roche, "The Poor and Temporal Goods in Book V of the Code," *The Jurist* 55 (1995): 299–348.
4. National Conference of Catholic Bishops, *Economic Justice for All: Pastoral Letter on Catholic Social Teaching and the U.S. Economy* (Washington, D.C.: NCCB, 1986), no. 347.
5. See Pierre Bourdieu, *Practical Reason: On the Theory of Action* (Stanford, Calif.: Stanford University Press, 1998), 93; more generally, see 92–126.
6. Bourdieu, *Practical Reason,* 124.
7. Bourdieu, *Practical Reason,* 114.
8. See "public law" in Henry Campbell Black, *Black's Law Dictionary: Definitions of the Terms and Phrases of American and English Jurisprudence, Ancient and Modern,* 6th ed. (St. Paul, Minn.: West Publishing Co., 1990).
9. 1917 *CIC,* c. 1409.
10. See Oliver E. Williamson, *The Mechanisms of Governance* (New York: Oxford University Press, 1996), 149 et passim.
11. Naomi R. Lamoreaux, "Entrepreneurship, Business Organization, and Economic Concentration," in *The Cambridge Economic History of the United States,*

ed. Stanley Engerman and Robert Gallman (New York: Cambridge University Press, 1996), 2:410.

12. Adolf A. Berle and Gardner C. Means, *The Modern Corporation and Private Property* (New York: Simon and Schuster, 1937), 10.

13. Berle and Means, *The Modern Corporation and Private Property*, 124.

14. Jay P. Dolan, *The American Catholic Experience* (New York: Doubleday, 1985), 110.

15. Patrick J. Carey, *People, Priests, and Prelates: Ecclesiastical Democracy and the Tensions of Trusteeism* (Notre Dame, Ind.: University of Notre Dame Press, 1987), 27–31.

16. For a discussion of John England's attempt to accommodate the legitimate interests of the lay trustees, see the contribution to this volume by Francis Sullivan.

17. *Concilia Provincialia Baltimori habitata ab anno 1829 usque ad annum 1849* (Baltimore: J. Murphy, 1851), 65.

18. Dolan, *The American Catholic Experience*, 172.

19. Carey, *People, Priests, and Prelates*, 281.

20. See *Mannix v. Purcell et al.*, 46 Ohio St. 102, 19 N.E. 572 (1888).

21. See "corporation, aggregate and sole," *Black's Law Dictionary*.

22. Chester J. Bartlett, *The Tenure of Parochial Property in the United States* (Washington, D.C.: Catholic University Press, 1926), 68–69.

23. Sacred Congregation of the Council, letter of July 29, 1911, *Canon Law Digest*, 2:445.

24. Sacred Congregation of the Council, letter of July 29, 1911.

25. Sacred Congregation of the Council, letter of July 29, 1911.

26. Sacred Congregation of the Council, letter of July 29, 1911.

27. Berle and Means, *The Modern Corporation and Private Property*, 69–125.

28. Letter of the Apostolic Delegate to the United States, November 10, 1922, *Canon Law Digest*, 1:149–51.

29. For a discussion of the cathedral chapter and its functions, see Franz Xaver Wernz, *Ius Decretalium* (Prati: Libreria Giachetti, 1915), II-2: 583–632.

30. Robert F. Trisco, "Bishops and Their Priests in the United States," in *The Catholic Priest in the United States*, ed. John Tracy Ellis (Collegeville, Minn.: Liturgical Press, 1971), 229.

31. *Black's Law Dictionary*, "holding company": "a company that usually confines its activities to owning stock in, and supervising the management of, other companies.

32. Frederick Hayek, "The Use of Knowledge in Society," *American Economic Review* 35 (1945): 524. See also Chester Barnard, *The Functions of the Executive* (Cambridge, Mass.: Harvard University, Press, 1938), 6, and Oliver Williamson, *The Mechanisms of Governance*, 149–51.

33. Williamson, *The Mechanisms of Governance*, 149.

34. Oliver E. Williamson, *Markets and Hierarchies: Analysis and Antitrust Implications* (New York: Free Press, 1975), 25.

35. Williamson, *Markets and Hierarchies*, 26.

36. Williamson, *Markets and Hierarchies*, 29.

37. James H. Provost, "Canonical Reflection on Select Issues in Diocesan Governance," in *The Ministry of Governance*, ed. James Mallett (Washington, D.C.: CLSA, 1986), 212.

38. Carey, *People, Priests, and Prelates*, 73.

39. Cited in Gerald P. Fogarty, *The Vatican and the Americanist Crisis: Denis J. O'Connell, the American Agent in Rome, 1885–1903* (Rome: Gregorian University Press, 1974), 27.

40. See Jay P. Dolan, *In Search of American Catholicism* (New York: Oxford University Press, 2002), 47. See also Gerald P. Fogarty, *The Vatican and the American Hierarchy from 1870 to 1965* (Wilmington, Del.: Michael Glazier, 1985), 195–213, and John T. McGreevy, *Catholicism and American Freedom: A History* (New York: W. W. Norton, 2003), 19–42.

41. See Joseph A. Komonchak, "Modernity and the Construction of Roman Catholicism," *Christianesimo nella Storia* 18 (1997): 353–85.

42. Alfred E. Chandler, "Decision Making and Modern Institutional Change," in *The Essential Alfred Chandler: Essays Toward a Historical Theory of Big Business*, ed. Thomas K. McGraw (Boston: Harvard Business School Press, 1988), 345–46.

43. Alfred E. Chandler, "Administrative Coordination, Allocation and Monitoring: Concepts and Comparison," in *The Essential Alfred Chandler*, 398.

44. Chandler, "Decision Making," 347.

45. Chandler, "Decision Making," 348.

46. Chandler, "The Beginnings of 'Big Business' in American Industry," in *The Essential Alfred Chandler*, 71.

47. Roger Finke and Rodney Stark, "Religious Economies and Sacred Canopies: Religious Mobilization in American Cities, 1906," *American Sociological Review* 53 (1988): 47. See also Roger Finke and Rodney Stark, *The Churching of America, 1776–1990: Winners and Losers in Our Religious Economy* (New Brunswick, N.J.: Rutgers University Press, 1992).

48. Finke and Stark, "Religious Economies," 44.

49. See Williamson, *Markets and Hierarchies*, 143–44, and Chandler, "The Beginnings of 'Big Business,'" 58.

50. Dolan, *The American Catholic Experience*, 191.

51. John Tracy Ellis, *American Catholicism* (Chicago: University of Chicago Press, 1969), 104.

52. See Jonathan A. Miller, "The Soul of the New Exurb," *New York Times Magazine*, March 27, 2005.

53. Ellis, *American Catholicism*, 105.

54. See 1917 *CIC*, c. 497, no. 3; c. 1489, no. 1.

55. See James M. O'Toole, ed., *Habits of Devotion: Catholic Religious Practice in Twentieth-Century America* (Ithaca, N.Y.: Cornell University Press, 2004); Robert Orsi, *The Madonna of 115th Street: Faith and Community in Italian Harlem, 1890–1950* (New Haven, Conn.: Yale University Press, 2002); and Robert Orsi, *Between Heaven and Earth: The Religious Worlds People Make and the Scholars Who Study Them* (Princeton, N.J.: Princeton University Press, 2005).

56. On the long nineteenth-century battle between priests and bishops, see Trisco, "Bishops and Their Priests in the United States," 111–292.

57. Letter of the Apostolic Delegate, U.S., November 10, 1922, in *Canon Law Digest*, 1:149–51.

58. Dolan, *The American Catholic Experience*, 190.

59. James H. Provost, "Diocesan Administration: Reflections on Recent Developments," *The Jurist* 41 (1981): 83.

60. For an overview of the demographic data on the Catholic population, see James Davidson et al., *The Search for Common Ground: What Unites and Divides Catholic Americans* (Huntington, Ind.: Our Sunday Visitor, 1997); Andrew Greeley, *The American Catholic: A Social Portrait* (New York: Basic Books, 1977); and George Gallup and Jim Castelli, *The American Catholic People: Their Beliefs, Practices and Values* (New York: Doubleday, 1987).

61. See, for example, Leslie Woodcock Tentler, *Catholics and Contraception: An American History* (Ithaca, N.Y.: Cornell University Press, 2004).

62. Alfred D. Chandler, *Strategy and Structure: Chapters in the History of the American Industrial Enterprise* (Cambridge, Mass.: MIT Press, 1962), 11.

63. Chandler, *Strategy and Structure*, 13.

64. Chandler, *Strategy and Structure*, 41.

65. Chandler, *Strategy and Structure*, 383–84.

66. These issues are discussed with greater technical precision in Williamson, *Markets and Hierarchies*, 117–31.

67. Donald Campbell, "Reforms and Experiments," *American Psychologist* 24 (1969): 410.

68. Kenneth E. Boulding, "The Economics of Knowledge and the Knowledge of Economics," *American Economic Review* 58 (1966): 8.

69. Williamson, *Markets and Hierarchies*, 127.

70. Williamson, *Markets and Hierarchies*, 137.

71. Williamson, *Markets and Hierarchies*, 149.

72. Chandler, *Strategy and Structure*, 12.

73. See Sydney Finkelstein, *Why Smart Executives Fail* (New York: Portfolio/Penguin, 2003) and James Surowiecki, *The Wisdom of Crowds* (New York: Doubleday, 2004).

74. Lamberto Echeverria, "La Curia Episcopal Pastoral," in *Aspectos del derecho administrativo canónico* (Salamanca: Instituto Raimundo de Peñafort, 1964), 211–48.

75. Kevin McDonough, "Diocesan Bureaucracy," *America* (October 11, 1997): 10.

76. Provost, "Diocesan Administration," 85. See Francis K. Sheets, "A Sketch of American Diocesan Organization 1900–1978," in *CARA Church Management Program, Proceedings, Diocesan Organization Workshop*, ed. Francis K. Sheets (Washington, D.C.: CARA, 1980), 28–38.

77. McDonough, "Diocesan Bureaucracy," 10–11.

78. Robert T. Kennedy, "Shared Responsibility in Ecclesial Decision-Making," *Studia Canonica* 14 (1980): 19.

79. See Kevin McDonough, "Beyond Bureaucracy: New Strategies for Diocesan Leadership," *CLSA Proceedings* 61 (1999): 264.

80. Kennedy, "Shared Responsibility in Ecclesial Decision-Making,"12.

81. See Albert O. Hirschman, *Exit, Voice and Loyalty: Responses to Decline in Firms, Organizations and States* (Cambridge, Mass.: Harvard University Press, 1970).

82. Francis Butler, "Financial Accountability: Reflections on Giving and Church Leadership," in *Governance, Accountability, and the Future of the Church*, ed. Francis Oakley and Bruce Russett (New York: Continuum, 2004), 156.

83. See Fred H. Goldner, R. Richard Ritti, and Terence Ference, "The Production of Cynical Knowledge in Organizations," *American Sociological Review* 42 (1977): 539–51.

84. Butler, "Financial Accountability," 157.

85. Butler, "Financial Accountability," 160.

86. Robert Kealy, "Methods of Diocesan Incorporation," *CLSA Proceedings* 48 (1986): 176.

87. Provost, "Diocesan Administration," 98.

88. Provost, "Diocesan Administration," 99. See also Peter F. Drucker, *Management: Tasks, Responsibilities, Practices* (New York: Simon and Schuster, 1974), 131–66, esp. 158.

89. See, most recently, Andrew Greeley, *Priests: A Calling in Crisis* (Chicago: University of Chicago Press, 2004), 92–93.

90. Peter Steinfels, *A People Adrift: The Crisis of the Roman Catholic Church in America* (New York: Simon and Schuster, 2003), 228.

91. See Dean Hoge et al., *Young Adult Catholic: Religion in the Culture of Choice* (Notre Dame, Ind.: University of Notre Dame Press, 2002). See also Steinfels, *A People Adrift*, 203–52, and John Cavadini, "Ignorant Catholic: The Alarming Void in Religious Education," *Commonweal* (April 9, 2004): 12–14.

92. See Steinfels, *A People Adrift*, 165–202.

93. McDonough, "Diocesan Bureaucracy," 11.

94. Drucker cited in McDonough, "Diocesan Bureaucracy," 11.

95. See Robert J. Antonio, "The Contradiction of Domination and Production in a Bureaucracy: The Contribution of Organizational Efficiency to the Decline of the Roman Empire," *American Sociological Review* 44 (1979): 895–912.

Chapter 6 / Beyond "Liberal" and "Conservative," Mark S. Massa, S.J.

1. A compelling example of such exasperation with the conservative/liberal labeling can be found in Allan Figueroa Deck, S.J., "A Pox on Both Your Houses: A View of Catholic Liberal-Conservative Polarities from the Hispanic Margin," in *Being Right: Conservative Catholics in America*, ed. Mary Jo Weaver and Scott Appleby (Bloomington: Indiana University Press, 1995), 88–104.

2. Robert Cross, *The Emergence of Liberal Catholicism in America* (Cambridge: Harvard University Press, 1958), 200ff. For similar labeling in discussing the "Americanist" episode, see Thomas Wangler's "Emergence of John J. Keane as a Liberal Catholic and Americanist," *American Ecclesiastical Review* 166 (1972): 457–78.

3. My own attempt to relate an ideologically more neutral story of those battles can be found in "Into Uncertain Life: The First Sunday of Advent, 1964," in *Catholics and American Culture: Fulton Sheen, Dorothy Day, and the Notre Dame Football Team* (New York: Crossroad, 1999), 148–71. A more recent, fine example of the same (post-ideological) strategy to recover the U.S. Catholic past can be found in Margaret McGuinness, "Let Us Go to the Altar: American Catholics and the Eucharist, 1926–1976," in *Habits of Devotion: Catholic Religious Practice in Twentieth-Century America*, ed. James M. O'Toole (Ithaca, N.Y.: Cornell University Press, 2005), 187–235.

4. Andrew Greeley, *The American Catholic: A Social Portrait* (New York: Basic Books, 1977), 37, 149, 156ff; Andrew Greeley, *Humanae Vitae and the Bishops: The Encyclical and the Statements of the National Hierarchies* (Shannon, Ireland: Irish University Press, 1972). Quote from the opening sentence of the encyclical: 33; 41.

5. Richard McCormick, S.J., *Corrective Vision: Explorations in Moral Theology* (Milwaukee: Sheed and Ward, 1994), 10. John Ford, S.J., and Germain Grisez, "Ordinary Magisterium," *Theological Studies* 39 (1978): 259. William H. Shannon, *The Lively Debate: The Response to Humanae Vitae* (New York: Sheed and Ward, 1970). See especially chapters 5 ("The Second Phase of the Debate on the Pill," 41–55) and 6 ("The Widening of the Birth Control Debate," 56–69).

6. Mircea Eliade, "Roman Catholicism," in *The Encyclopedia of Religion,* ed. Mircea Eliade (New York: Macmillan, 1987), 429–30.

7. Ernst Troeltsch, *The Social Teaching of the Christian Churches,* trans. Olive Wyon (New York: Macmillan, 1949), vols. 1 and 2. See especially 1:331–69, in which Troeltsch contrasts what he terms the "church type" of Christianity with the "sect type": "the church is that type of organization which . . . to a certain extent accepts the secular order, and dominates the masses; in principle, therefore, it is universal, i.e., it desires to cover the whole life of humanity. The sects, on the other hand, are comparatively small groups; they aspire after personal inward perfection. Their attitude toward the world, the State, and Society may be indifferent, tolerant, or hostile, since they have no desire to control and incorporate these forms of social life; on the contrary, they tend to avoid them" (331).

8. See "Christ Is My Life: An interview with Fr. Marcial Maciel, L.C.," Legionaries of Christ, *legionariesofchrist.org/eng/articulos/articulo.phtml;* also Josemaría Escrivá, "In Love with the Church; Loyalty to the Church," *www.escrivaworks.org/book/in_love_with_the_church/point/13.*

9. See, for example, the essays of James Sullivan, "Catholics United for the Faith: Dissent and the Laity," 107–37; George Weigel, "The Neo-Conservative Difference: A Proposal for the Renewal of Church and Society," 138–62; and Helen Hull Hitchcock, "Women for Faith and Family: Catholic Women Affirming Catholic Teaching," 163–85, in *Being Right,* ed. Mary Jo Weaver and Scott Appleby (Bloomington: Indiana University Press, 1995). H. Richard Niebuhr, *Christ and Culture* (New York: Harper & Row, 1951), 45–82.

10. "Theological notes" are those numbers attached to papal pronouncements, declarations of episcopal synods, or decrees of ecumenical councils that "weight" them from *de fide definita* (a belief that is essential to the faith, and therefore heretical to deny) to "pious and salutary beliefs" which are not obligatory for belief. Much of what is presented by these watchdogs as "definitive teaching" is not listed, in fact, as *de fide definita* (and therefore obligatory on the consciences of believers) in the *Enchiridion Symbolorum.*

11. Examples of such problematic interpretation of "definitive teaching" include numbers 13, 22, 24, 30, 31, and 47 of Josemaría Escrivá's list of teachings for his followers in Opus Dei, in *In Love with the Church,* Josemaría Escrivá's writings, *www.escrivaworks.org.*

12. See Jaroslav Pelikan, *The Christian Tradition: A History of the Development of Doctrine,* vol. 1: *The Emergence of the Catholic Tradition* (Chicago: University of Chicago Press, 1971). See especially pp. 108–20 ("Criteria of Apostolic Continuity") and 349–57 ("Orthodox Catholicism in the West").

13. My own understanding of the balance between institutional membership in the Roman Catholic Church and other, deeper, meanings of "communion" has been informed by Robert Kaslyn, S.J., *"Communion with the Church" and the Code of Canon Law: An Analysis of the Foundation and Implications of the Canonical Obligation to Maintain Communion with the Church* (Lewiston, Me.: E. Mellen Press, 1994).

14. Avery Dulles, *Models of the Church* (Garden City, N.Y.: Doubleday, 1978), 13–14.

15. Dulles, *Models of the Church*, 14.

16. Dulles, *Models of the Church*, 205.

17. Dulles, *Models of the Church*, 205–6. Italics in the quote are my own.

18. Eliade, "Roman Catholicism," 429–30.

19. Niebuhr, *Christ and Culture*, 45–82. See esp. 47–50.

20. 1 John 2:15–16. *The Jerusalem Bible* (Garden City, N.Y.: Doubleday, 1966), 413. Italics are my own.

21. James F. Findlay, *Dwight L. Moody: American Evangelist, 1837–1899* (Chicago: University of Chicago Press, 1969).

22. Niebuhr, *Christ and Culture*, 128–36. Thomas Aquinas, *Summa Theologiae* I, 1, 8 and 2: "cum enim gratia non tollat naturam sed perficiat."

23. Elizabeth Johnson, *She Who Is: The Mystery of God in Feminist Theological Discourse* (New York: Crossroad, 1992); Virgilio Elizondo, *Galilean Journey: The Mexican-American Promise* (Maryknoll, N.Y.: Orbis Books, 2000); Peter Phan, *Christianity with an Asian Face: Asian-American Theology in the Making* (Maryknoll, N.Y.: Orbis Books, 2003).

24. Troeltsch, *Social Teaching*, 1:100–110; 241–45.

25. The Eucharist as "center of unity" in *Eucharisticum mysterium* ("Instruction on the Worship of the Eucharistic Mystery"), chapter 1, no. 6 in *Vatican Council II: The Conciliar and Post-Conciliar Documents*, ed. Austin Flannery (Northport, N.Y.: Costello Publishing Co., 1980). An excellent "history from below" describing popular belief at the end of the Middle Ages can be found in Eamon Duffy, *The Stripping of the Altars: Traditional Religion in England, 1400–1580* (New Haven: Yale University Press, 1992).

26. My own understanding of the Eurocentric factors informing the discussions of the First Vatican Council has been shaped by James Hennesey, S.J., *The First Council of the Vatican: The American Experience* (New York: Herder and Herder, 1963), 82–129. For an excellent contextualization of Vatican I from the twentieth-century standpoint of Vatican II, see *The Reception of Vatican II*, ed. Guiseppe Alberigo, Jean-Pierre Jossua, and Joseph Komonchak (Washington: Catholic University of America Press, 1987), introduction.

27. David Tracy, *The Analogical Imagination: Christian Theology and the Culture of Pluralism* (New York: Crossroad, 1981), 412–15.

28. Dulles, *Models of the Church*, 204–5.

29. For an excellent description of the primitivism impulse, see Theodore Dwight Bozeman, *To Live Ancient Lives: The Primitivist Dimension in Puritanism* (Chapel Hill: University of North Carolina Press, 1988); and George Marsden, *Fundamentalism and American Culture: The Shaping of Twentieth-Century Evangelicalism, 1870–1925* (New York: Oxford University Press), 223–24.

30. The description of church as the "spiritual company of all faithful people" is from the Anglican/Episcopal *Book of Common Prayer*. In its Decree on Ecumenism (*Unitatis Redintegratio*), the Second Vatican Council declared that "all who have been justified by faith in baptism are incorporated into Christ; they therefore have a right to be called Christians by the children of the Catholic Church" (Flannery, *Vatican II*, 455). On Leonard Feeney and the "Boston Heresy Case," see chapter 1 ("Boundary Maintenance: Leonard Feeney, The Boston Heresy Case, and Postwar Culture") in my *Catholics and American Culture: Fulton Sheen, Dorothy Day, and the Notre Dame Football Team* (New York: Crossroad, 1999), 21–37.

31. The phrase "Mystery of the Church" is the title of the first chapter of the Dogmatic Constitution of the Church (*Lumen Gentium*) promulgated at the Second Vatican Council. See Flannery, *Vatican II*, 350.

32. On the "Camden" (or "Ecclesiological Society") that began at Cambridge University in nineteenth-century England as a Romantic reaction to industrialism, see T. J. Jackson Lears, *No Place of Grace: Antimodernism and the Transformation of American Culture, 1880–1920* (New York: Pantheon Books, 1981), 185ff.

33. *Webster's New Collegiate Dictionary* (Springfield, Mass.: G. & C. Merriam Co., Publishers, 1949), s.v. liberal.

Chapter 7 / A New Way of Being Church in Asia, Peter C. Phan

1. My reflections are based on the documents of the Federation of Asian Bishops' Conferences (FABC) and of its various offices. The FABC was founded in 1970, on the occasion of Pope Paul VI's visit to Manila, the Philippines. Its statutes, approved by the Holy See *ad experimentum* in 1972, were amended several times and were also approved again each time by the Holy See. For the documents of the FABC and its various institutes, see *For All the Peoples of Asia: Federation of Asian Bishops' Conferences, Documents from 1970 to 1991,* ed. Gaudencio Rosales and C. G. Arévalo (Maryknoll, N.Y., and Quezon City, Manila: Orbis Books and Claretian Publications, 1992); *For All the Peoples of Asia: Federation of Asian Bishops' Conferences, Documents from 1992 to 1996,* ed. Franz-Josef Eilers (Quezon City, Manila: Claretian Publications, 1997); and *For All the Peoples of Asia: Federation of Asian Bishops' Conferences, Documents from 1997 to 2002,* ed. Franz-Josef Eilers (Quezon City, Manila: Claretian Publications, 2002). These will be cited as *For All Peoples,* followed by their years of publication in parentheses. By Asian theologians, I refer to those working in South, Southeast, and East Asia (mainly in India, Indonesia, Japan, Korea, Malaysia, the Philippines, Sri Lanka, Hong Kong, Taiwan, Thailand, and Vietnam).

2. What follows has been presented more extensively in my "A New Way of Being Church: Perspectives from Asia" in *Governance, Accountability, and the Future of the Catholic Church,* ed. Francis Oakley and Bruce Russett (New York: Continuum, 2004), 183–88.

3. *For All Peoples* (1992), 287. The FABC's vision of the church as "communion of communities" applies to the church both at the local and universal levels: "It [the Church] is a community not closed in on itself and its particular concerns, but *linked* with many bonds *to other communities of faith* (concretely, the parishes and dioceses around them) and to the one and universal communion, *catholica unitas,* of the holy

Church of the Lord" (*For All Peoples* [1992], 56). In other words, not only the diocese but also the church universal is a communion of communities. The universal church is not a church above the other dioceses of which the local churches are constitutive "parts" with the pope as its universal bishop. Rather, it is a communion in faith, hope, and love of all the local churches (among which there is the Church of Rome, of which the pope is the bishop), a communion in which the pope functions as the instrument of unity in collegiality and co-responsibility with other bishops.

4. For an extended discussion of communion ecclesiology, see J.-M. R. Tillard, *Church of Churches: The Ecclesiology of Communion,* trans. R. C. De Peaux (Collegeville, Minn.: Liturgical Press, 1992), and *Flesh of the Church, Flesh of Christ: At the Source of the Ecclesiology of Communion,* trans. Madeleine Beaumont (Collegeville, Minn.: Liturgical Press, 2001). For a presentation of communion ecclesiologies, see Dennis M. Doyle, *Communion Ecclesiology* (Maryknoll, N.Y.: Orbis Books, 2000).

5. For a theology of the Trinity as a communion and *perichoresis* of persons, see Leonardo Boff, *Trinity and Society,* trans. Paul Burns (Maryknoll, N.Y.: Orbis Books, 1986).

6. See *Lumen Gentium,* no. 32: "All the faithful enjoy a true equality with regard to the dignity and the activity which they share in the building up of the body of Christ."

7. *For All Peoples* (1992), 287. See also *For All Peoples* (1992), 56: "It [the church] is a community of authentic *participation and co-responsibility,* where genuine sharing of gifts and responsibilities obtains, where the talents and charisms of each one are accepted and exercised in diverse ministries, and where all are schooled to the attitudes and practices of mutual listening and dialogue, common discernment of the Spirit, common witness and collaborative action." The FABC is concerned that all people with their varied gifts have the opportunity to participate in the ministry of the church.

8. *For All Peoples* (1992), 287–88.

9. For the intrinsic connection between the proclamation of the gospel and dialogue in its triple form, see *For All Peoples* (1992), 13–16.

10. *For All Peoples* (1992), 288.

11. The Special Assembly of the Synod of Bishops for Asia (the Asian Synod) is one of the five synods convoked by Pope John Paul II to celebrate the third millennium of Christianity. It met in Rome from April 19 to May 14, 1998. For a presentation of the Asian Synod, see *The Asian Synod: Texts and Commentaries,* ed. Peter C. Phan (Maryknoll, N.Y.: Orbis Books, 2002).

12. Pope John Paul II's Post-Synodal Exhortation *Ecclesia in Asia* was promulgated in New Delhi, India, on November 26, 1999. The English text is available in Phan, *The Asian Synod,* 286–340.

13. *A Renewed Church in Asia: A Mission of Love and Service: The Final Statement of the Seventh Plenary Assembly of the Federation of Asian Bishops' Conferences, Samphran, Thailand, January 3–12, 2000,* 3–4. (The document is available from FABC, 16 Caine Road, Hong Kong.) For the Final Statement of the Seventh FABC Plenary Assembly, see *For All Peoples* (2002), 1–16.

14. The Pontifical Council for Interreligious Dialogue and the Congregation for the Evangelization of Peoples, *Dialogue and Proclamation* 42 (May 19, 1991). The

English text of the document is available in *Redemption and Dialogue: Reading* Redemptoris Missio *and* Dialogue and Proclamation, ed. William Burrows (Maryknoll, N.Y.: Orbis Books, 1993), 93–118. See also *For All Peoples* (1992), 21–26.

15. For a detailed elaboration of the ideas that follow, see Peter C. Phan, "Cultures, Religions, and Power: Proclaiming Christ in the United States Today," *Theological Studies* 65 (2004): 714–40, and "Where Are We Going? The Future of Ministry in the United States," *New Theology Review* 18, no. 2 (2005): 5–15.

16. Charles Morris, *American Catholic: The Saints and Sinners Who Built America's Most Powerful Church* (New York: Vintage Books, 1997).

17. In this context it is necessary, though not possible here, to discuss the positive and negative impact of globalization on developing countries. See the articles in *Journal of Catholic Social Thought* 2, no. 1 (2005), which is entirely devoted to the issue of globalization.

18. Walter Wink, *The Powers That Be: Theology for a New Millennium* (New York: Doubleday, 1998), 56.

19. For further reflection on liberation, see Peter C. Phan, *Christianity with an Asian Face: Asian American Theology in the Making* (Maryknoll, N.Y.: Orbis Books, 2003).

20. David O'Brien, *In Search of an American Catholicism: A History of Religion and Culture in Tension* (New York: Oxford University Press, 2002), 55.

21. For further reflections on inculturation, see Peter C. Phan, *In Our Own Tongues: Perspectives from Asia on Mission and Inculturation* (Maryknoll, N.Y.: Orbis Books, 2003).

22. Diana Eck, *A New Religious America: How a "Christian Country" Has Now Become the World's Most Religiously Diverse Nation* (San Francisco: HarperSanFrancisco, 2001).

23. For further reflections on interreligious dialogue, see Peter C. Phan, *Being Religious Interreligiously: Asian Perspectives on Interfaith Dialogue* (Maryknoll, N.Y.: Orbis Books, 2004).

24. *For All Peoples* (1992), 70.

25. Phan, *The Asian Synod*, 120–21.

26. See Hermann Pottmeyer, *Towards a Papacy in Communion: Perspectives from Vatican I and II* (New York: Crossroad, 1998).

27. See Pottmeyer, *Towards a Papacy of Communion*, 132.

28. *Lumen Gentium*, no. 23.

29. Joseph Ratzinger, *Das neue Volk Gottes: Entwürfe zur Ekklesiologie* (Düsseldorf: Patmos, 1969), 142. Cited by Pottmeyer, *Towards a Papacy in Communion*, 134.

Chapter 8 / An Inculturated Mariology, Natalia M. Imperatori-Lee

1. See *Lumen Gentium*, no. 12, in *Vatican Council II: The Conciliar and Postconciliar Documents*, ed. Austin Flannery (Collegeville, Minn.: Liturgical Press, 1992).

2. Orlando Espín writes: "It is difficult to find, besides the crucified Christ, another more powerful religious symbol." "Tradition and Popular Religion: An Understanding of the *Sensus Fidelium*," in *Frontiers of Hispanic Theology in the*

United States, ed. Allen Figueroa Deck (Maryknoll, N.Y.: Orbis Books, 1992), 71–72.

3. Mark R. Francis, "Building Bridges between Liturgy, Devotionalism, and Popular Religion," *Assembly* 20, no. 2 (April 1994): 636; also Roberto Goizueta, *Caminemos con Jesus: Toward a Hispanic/Latino Theology of Accompaniment* (Maryknoll, N.Y.: Orbis Books, 1995), 26–28.

4. Charles W. Dahm, O.P., *Parish Ministry in a Hispanic Community* (New York: Paulist Press, 2004), 156.

5. These categories are elaborated by Francis, "Building Bridges," 636.

6. Dahm, *Parish Ministry,* 164–65.

7. See Virgil Elizondo, "The Treasure of Hispanic Faith," in *Mestizo Worship,* ed. Virgil Elizondo and Timothy Matovina (Collegeville, Minn.: Liturgical Press, 1998), 73–80; also Dahm's description of Guadalupan festivities at Pius V, *Parish Ministry,* 161–67.

8. Orlando Espín, *The Faith of the People: Theological Reflections on Popular Catholicism* (Maryknoll, N.Y.: Orbis Books, 1997), 4.

9. Orlando Espín and Sixto García, "Sources of Hispanic Theology," *CTSA Proceedings* 43 (1988): 123.

10. Espín, *The Faith of the People,* 3.

11. See "Sacrament" and "Sacramentals" in *The HarperCollins Encyclopedia of Catholicism,* ed. Richard P. McBrien (San Francisco: HarperSanFrancisco, 1995).

12. Espín, *The Faith of the People,* 65.

13. Espín, *The Faith of the People,* 71.

14. Espín, *The Faith of the People,* 66.

15. Espín, *The Faith of the People,* 67.

16. Espín, *The Faith of the People,* 66.

17. Pope Paul VI, apostolic exhortation *Marialis Cultus* (Vatican City: Typis Polyglottis, 1974).

18. Espín, *The Faith of the People,* 7.

19. Though some theologians have embraced this turn toward feminine pronouns in reference to the Holy Spirit, many find it problematic. For analysis of this, see Elizabeth Johnson, "Mary and the Female Face of God" *Theological Studies* 50 (1989): 500–526.

20. See Dahm, *Parish Ministry,* 161, 166–67.

21. See Timothy Matovina, "Our Lady of Guadalupe Celebrations in San Antonio, Texas, 1840–1841," in *Mestizo Worship,* 49–67.

22. Jeannette Rodriguez, *Our Lady of Guadalupe: Faith and Empowerment among Mexican-American Women* (Austin: University of Texas Press, 1994), 125.

23. Virgilio P. Elizondo, *Guadalupe, Mother of the New Creation* (Maryknoll, N.Y.: Orbis Books, 1997), 95.

24. Goizueta, *Caminemos con Jesus,* 38.

25. Goizueta, *Caminemos con Jesus,* 39.

26. Goizueta, *Caminemos con Jesus,* 50.

27. In the third chapter of *Caminemos con Jesus,* Goizueta analyzes "modern liberal individualism," which he deems characteristic of U.S. culture. Modern liberal individualism is expressed politically, religiously, and economically. It finds its roots in the Enlightenment notion of the autonomous self. Community is reduced to a "collection of individuals" (55), religious belief is divorced from community, and

the market represents the sole arbiter of value. This individualism leads ultimately to isolation, since any and all relationships are engaged by the individual on a voluntary basis. The cleavage between the individual and community characterizes the anthropology of modern liberal individualism. This is the anthropology in contrast to which Goizueta elaborates Latino (relational) anthropology. See *Caminemos con Jesus*, 53–60.

28. Goizueta, *Caminemos con Jesus*, 50.

29. Goizueta, "Resurrection at Tepeyac: The Guadalupan Encounter," *Theology Today* 56 (October 3, 1999): 344.

30. Goizueta, *Caminemos con Jesus*, 66.

31. Goizueta, *Caminemos con Jesus*, 45.

32. A sacrament can be defined as a "principal liturgical rite of the church through which participants experience the love and power of God (grace) that flows from Christ's Passion, death, and Resurrection." A "sacramental" is a "sacred sign instituted by the Church, similar to the seven major sacraments in that they 'signify effects, particularly of a spiritual kind, that are obtained through the Church's intercession. They dispose people to receive the chief effect of the sacraments and they make holy various occasions in human life'" (*HarperCollins Encyclopedia of Catholicism*, 1148). See also Goizueta's notion of sacrament as relational, *Caminemos con Jesus*, 48–49.

33. Dahm, *Parish Ministry*, 166.

34. Goizueta, "Resurrection," 343.

Chapter 9 / Collective Identity and Distinctiveness, Mary Johnson, S.N.D.deN.

1. See *Perfectae Caritatis*, *The Documents of Vatican II*, ed. Walter M. Abbott (New York: Crossroad, 1989), no. 23.

2. *Codex Iuris Canonici* (Vatican City: Libreria Editrice Vaticana, 1983), c. 708.

3. *Codex Iuris Canonici*, c. 709.

4. Christian Smith, *American Evangelicalism: Embattled and Thriving* (Chicago: University of Chicago Press, 1998), 20.

5. Leadership Conference of Women Religious, homepage, *www.lcwr.org*.

6. Leadership Conference of Women Religious, LCWR Call for 2004–9, *www.lcwr.org/lcwraboutus/lcwrcall.htm*.

7. Conference of Major Superiors of Men, fact sheet, document available online at *www.cmsm.org/about-factsheet.shtml*.

8. Conference of Major Superiors of Men, fact sheet.

9. Council of Major Superiors of Women Religious, about us page, *www.cmswr.org/about/about.htm*.

10. Religious Formation Conference, What Is RFC? *www.cmswr.org/2_about/2_about.htm*.

11. Religious Formation Conference, context statement, document available online at *www.relforcon.org/Context%Statement_files/Context/%20Statement.htm*.

12. National Religious Vocation Conference, about us page, *www.nrvc.net/index.php?option=com_content&task=view&id=12&Itemid=1*.

13. Leadership Conference of Women Religious, mission statement, *www.lcwr.org/lcwraboutus/missionstatement.htm*.

14. Conference of Major Superiors of Men, mission statement, *www.cmsms.org/about.shtml.*

15. Council of Major Superiors of Women Religious, episcopal liaison, *www.cmswr.org/about/cmswr_liaison.htm.*

16. Religious Formation Conference, mission statement, *www.relforcon.org/2_about/2A_rfc_faqs.htm#mission%20statement.*

17. National Religious Vocation Conference, mission statement, *www.nrvc.net/index.php?option=com_content&task=view&id=16&Itemid=1.*

18. Religious Formation Conference, religious life, *www.relforcon.org/3_rel_life/3_rel_life.htm.*

Chapter 10 / Religious Commitments of Young Adult Catholics, Dean R. Hoge

1. This paragraph is adapted from Robert D. Putnam, *Bowling Alone: The Collapse and Revival of American Community* (New York: Simon & Schuster, 2000), 33–35 and chapter 8.

2. Karl Mannheim says that the impressionable years for European youth begin at seventeen, but all later American researchers have argued that they begin earlier. See Karl Mannheim, *Essays on the Sociology of Knowledge* (New York: Oxford University Press, 1952), 276–320.

3. William D'Antonio and Anthony Pogorelc, unpublished survey, Catholic University of America, Washington, D.C., November 2000.

4. These data are from the General Social Survey, 1974 to 2002, provided by National Opinion Research Center, Chicago.

5. James D. Davidson and Dean R. Hoge, "Catholics after the Scandal: A New Study's Major Findings," *Commonweal* (November 19, 2004): 13–19. The 2003 survey had 1,119 interviews.

6. The finding that the largest age gap among Catholic adults occurs between the pre–Vatican Catholics and all others is not unique to the Notre Dame study. It has been demonstrated in three other recent surveys of American Catholics. See William V. D'Antonio, James D. Davidson, Dean R. Hoge, and Katherine Meyer, *American Catholics: Gender, Generation, and Commitment* (Walnut Creek, Calif.: Alta Mira Press, 2001), 44–45, 110, 121–29.

7. Bernard J. Lee, *The Catholic Experience of Small Christian Communities* (New York: Paulist Press, 2000), 50.

8. Colleen Carroll, *The New Faithful: Why Young Adults Are Embracing Christian Orthodoxy* (Chicago: Loyola University Press, 2002).

9. Lee, *Catholic Experience,* 49.

10. Alan M. Dershowitz, *The Vanishing American Jew* (New York: Simon and Schuster, 1997).

11. D'Antonio et al., *American Catholics,* 32.

12. Mitch Albom, *Tuesdays with Morrie* (Garden City, N.Y.: Doubleday, 1997), 34.

13. Michael A. Hogg and Dominic Abrams, *Social Identifications* (London: Routledge, 1988); Morris Rosenberg, *Conceiving the Self* (New York: Basic Books, 1979).

14. In the same interviews and informal survey, I asked if any elements of Catholicism were offputting or alienating. Most young adults can identify some. The most commonly mentioned were Catholic teachings about contraception, homosexuality, and women's status in general, and the ostentatious wealth of the Vatican. These inhibit Catholic identity and commitment.

15. D'Antonio et al., *American Catholics*, 38–45.

16. Two empirical studies of denominational research among American Protestants are pertinent here. Both found that Protestant denominations with liturgical and Pentecostal traditions have stronger identities than the oldline Protestant denominations such as the Methodists, Presbyterians, and United Church of Christ. It seems that liturgical tradition, a priority on non-cognitive bases of religious authority, and ethnic identity from recent immigrant history bolster denominational identity, and from this it would appear that American Catholicism would have a stronger denominational identity, if it were measured, than most Protestant denominations. This supports the expectation that in the future, American Catholicism will not closely recapitulate the twentieth-century history of oldline American Protestant denominations. See David Roozen, "National Denominational Structures' Engagement with Postmodernity," in *Church, Identity, and Change: Theology and Denominational Structures in Unsettled Times*, ed. David Roozen and James Nieman (Grand Rapids, Mich.: Eerdmans, 2005). One of the empirical studies was the Faith Community Today survey of 1999, done at Hartford Seminary. The other was done in 1998 for the Protestant Church-Owned Publishers Association; see Reginald W. Bibby, "The PCPA Congregational Resource Study: Summary Report," unpublished report, 1998.

17. Howard P. Bleichner, *View from the Altar: Reflections on the Rapidly Changing Catholic Priesthood* (New York: Crossroad, 2004), 212.

Contributors

Rev. John P. Beal, School of Canon Law, Catholic University of America

Nancy A. Dallavalle, Department of Religious Studies, Fairfield University

Mary Ann Hinsdale, I.H.M., Department of Theology, Boston College

Dean R. Hoge, Life Cycle Institute, Catholic University of America

David Hollenbach, S.J., Department of Theology, Boston College

Natalia M. Imperatori-Lee, Department of Theology, Notre Dame University

Mary Johnson, S.N.D.deN., Department of Sociology and Religious Studies, Emmanuel College

T. Frank Kennedy, S.J., Jesuit Institute, Boston College

Mark S. Massa, S.J., Department of Theology, Fordham University

Peter C. Phan, Department of Theology, Georgetown University

Francis A. Sullivan, S.J., Department of Theology, Boston College

Index

Of related interest

Howard Bleichner

VIEW FROM THE ALTAR
*Reflections on the Rapidly Changing
Catholic Priesthood*

"*View from the Altar* is a must-read for all who are interested
in understanding the causes of the scandal of sexual abuse by
members of the Catholic clergy.... I am grateful to the author
for handling this sensitive topic with both raw honesty and
brotherly compassion.... *View from the Altar* reminds us that
spirituality must be at the core of seminary formation."

— *America*

0-8245-2141-2, paperback

Check your local bookstore for availability.
To order directly from the publisher,
please call 1-800-707-0670 for Customer Service
or visit our Web site at *www.cpcbooks.com*.
For catalog orders, please send your request to the address below.

THE CROSSROAD PUBLISHING COMPANY
16 Penn Plaza, Suite 1550
New York, NY 10001

All prices subject to change.

crossroad